theorising resistance

theorising resistance

Narratives in History and Politics

Jasbir Jain

Rawat Publications

Jaipur • New Delhi • Bangalore • Hyderabad • Guwahati

ISBN 978-81-316-0540-0

Published by
Prem Rawat for **Rawat Publications**
Satyam Apts, Sector 3, Jawahar Nagar, Jaipur 302 004 (India)
Phone: 0141 265 1748 / 7006 Fax: 0141 265 1748
E-mail: info@rawatbooks.com
Website: www.rawatbooks.com

New Delhi Office
4858/24, Ansari Road, Daryaganj, New Delhi 110 002
Phone: 011 2326 3290

Also at *Bangalore, Hyderabad* and *Guwahati*

Typeset by Rawat Computers, Jaipur
Printed at Chaman Enterprises, New Delhi

For
Abhimanyu, Simranjit and Nidhaanjit

Contents

Acknowledgements

The essays in this collection have all been written in response to invitations for conferences, symposiums, public lectures or inaugural sessions. I acknowledge my debt to all those friends who provided the opportunity for me to challenge my mind.

Some of these have subsequently been published in journals and anthologies: 'A Phoenix Called Resistance' in *Journal of Postcolonial Writing,* Vol. 43, No. 2, August, 2007; 'How Strangeness Takes Possession' in *Indian Literature*, No. 244, March–April, 2008; 'Purdah, Patriarchy and the Tropical Sun' in *The Veil*. Ed. Jennifer Heath, University of California Press, 2008; 'Issues in Historiography' in *The Critical Endeavour*, Vol. XVI, January, 2010; 'From Encounters to Introspection' in *Indian Literature*, No. 260, November–December, 2010; and 'Contrapuntal Narratives', in an abridged version in the ICLA journal *Literary Research/Recherché Litteraire*, Vol. 27, Summer, 2011.

My thanks are due to a large number of people: Nilofer Bharucha, A.J. Thomas, Subodh Sarkar, John Foster, Jennifer Heath, Somdatta Mandal, Angshuman Kar, B.K. Das, Avadhesh Kumar Singh, Prafulla Kar, Parvathi and also to various agencies: Sahitya Akademi, Katha, FOSWAL (SAARC), ICLA and the organisers of the conferences for providing the initial motivation.

Jasbir Jain

Introduction

This collection of essays has shaped itself over the years and unbeknown to me, has built itself a thread of consistency. These essays are concerned with violence, power and aggression; they are concerned with acts of resistance and the counter-discourses which come to constitute a parallel historical discourse. The interaction between reality and its recording does not work merely at a surface level. There is also another factor, that of the human agency: the manner in which men and women react to their immediate surroundings; their perception of them and their working relationship with the immediate. Further the role which tradition and memory play in their views and the conflict which takes place in their minds between reason and emotion – all these questions acquire an importance in the interpretation and recording of history.

Ordinarily, there is a tendency to relate primarily to our world, our immediate environs and draw conclusions based on our interpretations of them. But in order to theorise, there is a need to explore the extensions of this world. The trends are not necessarily oppositional; often, they run parallel to each other and join in a common flow. Else, why is it that similar trends can be perceived the world over. Again, a literary construct locates itself in the midst of time and history, between the past and the present; the act of literary representation concretises this reality and brings in both the individual and the individual psyche. Another aspect which is of significance is the manner in which an individual sets about defining the need for freedom and the ethical stances necessary to validate it. The individual psyche is a product of its environs, of the interaction between politics and history and in turn, contributes to the environ birthing around it all the time. A complex phenomenon in itself.

Several of these essays go back to the eighteenth and nineteenth centuries as the continuities of slave histories, colonial discourses, the fall out of the two world wars, the partition of India, the religious conflicts and the consequential riots and struggles for democratic space are explored. These conflicts with their low intensity warfare and/or a constantly nourished strand of hatred occupy the public imagination. But they do not exist in limbo; they are rooted in the ideas of justice, social equality and ideology. They are indicators of an on-going encroachment into the territory of the other as well as an act of preservation and defense against this encroachment. The separating lines between resistance and terrorism are very slim. Except for the fact that resistance can work at many levels and in different modes, all of which are not available to terrorism. The element of intellectual debate can save resistance from descending into violence. Further, it also has the ability to reach out to the future, no matter how feebly.

The burst of artistic radical creativity and restlessness which was evident in the fifties and sixties, and which perhaps survived into the seventies, was marked by a return to earlier forms and structures. The experimentation and freedom were related to the search for a meaning in the new world which was fluid and elusive, born out of the Second World War, the Holocaust, Hiroshima and Nagasaki, the Partition of India and dislocation of huge chunks of population. The new conservatism which caught up with us by the beginning of the eighties, in thought as well as in art, was an indication of the growing fundamentalism, firming inherited identities, marking separation and division. This has led to multilayered conflicts: the ongoing conflict between East and West and the need to constantly question the western definitions of modern and pre-modern constitutes only one layer. The world has also gone through another phase of the conflict between communism and capitalism, of the wars they have generated outside the territories of both the US and the USSR and the legacy of pain these wars have left behind, plus the long-drawn cold war and the lurking fear of nuclear weapons, all this and the rise of fascist trends in Europe clearly indicates that the struggle for freedom is far from over, that democracy is constantly under threat and renegotiations are going on all the time. The anti-racism and the strict immigration laws, the prejudices against the immigrants and their persecution on grounds of their difference are happening in countries we have long admired for their democratic traditions. Stieg Larsson's *The Expo Files: Articles by a Crusading Journalist* is a revealing book which documents the day-to-day resistance to extremist movements by men who can transcend their own ego. The Habermasian 'public sphere' has been hijacked by media and mass hysteria in Europe, as it has in our country. This hijacking seeks to render the idea of freedom, choice and agency irrelevant. Both left-wing and right-wing ideologies generate their own violence, though each is motivated by a different goal. In India we have the Naxalites, the Maoists and the insurgents on one hand and various right-wing bodies such as the Bajrang Dal, VHP, the extreme wing of the Akali Dal and some Muslim organisations. Somewhere along the line these organisations have been overpowered by a sense of self-preservation, purist concerns and hatred. Human life has ceased to hold value for itself and the values of neighbourliness, sharing and reaching out have gone overboard. Even the diaspora is insecure. Faced by anti-racist attacks and hardening immigration laws, and a constant blame for being different or behaving differently (such as honour deaths), the diaspora is not necessarily as open-minded or liberal as we would like to imagine. They carry their culture abroad and relay their hatreds and fears back to the home country, going to the extent of funding fundamentalist movements. Stieg Larsson's *The Expo Files* provides evidence of how houses of worship have been used for hate propaganda and have supported violence ('Terror Killings Can Happen in Stockholm', *The Expo Files* 21–29).

Media, of whichever hue it maybe, records the present. The perspective or the angle may be different – prejudiced, objective or one-sided – but whatever it is, it is illustrative and it records the immediate. It draws attention to the people who are assassinated or eliminated, to witnesses who are broken, disappear or go back on their evidence, to voices that question or rationalise, but at the same time it demands a careful scrutiny of the strategy it employs, a strategy not necessarily visible on the surface. There is need to distinguish between recording of events and magnified sensationalism working as propaganda. Aggressive postures of interviewers, their monopoly of time and space, their thrusting of interpretations, all demand scrutiny. Artistic creations are different. Art doesn't have to face the terror and the fear of the immediate, it doesn't have to immediately capture the experience in the street; instead it internalises it and concretises it through locating it in individual histories. It forms a junction between history and politics, between the past and the present, and moves simultaneously to both: the individual unconscious and the collective unconscious. It moves more intimately with abstract values such as freedom and choice, and reflects a long-term perspective as it works with a projection of the immediate into the larger world. Girish Karnad's play *Talé Danda* is a good example. It focuses on the Basavanna episode but addresses the Mandal agitation, and working with Gandhian ideology, it centre stages the interplay between power and rightfulness, between violence and non-violence, between the personal and political and the desired and the possible. In the act of representation, art/literature move beyond the very immediate. The kind of over-writing or collage which is available to Anand Patwardhan or M.F. Husain is not available to journalism or electronic media. The voices in the media, at times, acquire a shrillness. Art has moved very far away from the mimetic act of framing or repeating the familiar or the known, the myth or the fairy tale. It takes a lot more in its sweep, for it depends on memory, thought, experience and personal conviction. The frame is very porous.

Resistance discourse assumes an intellectual and ethical input and, when viewed in retrospect, it apparently forms a counter-discourse. It questions the present and engages with issues such as values and ethics. The first two essays in this collection explore different kinds of art forms, genres and time frames as they address both the present and the future. 'From Gadar to Gandhi via *Anand Math*', places history, politics and ideology in the writing of several kinds of different texts – an eye-witness account, a novel locating itself in the past and Gandhi and Veer Savarkar's work and ideological debates. 'Patterns of Conflict in Border Operations' works with different authors, who work with different histories – tribal, anti-racism and war and civil war – and traces the patterns of oppression, deprivation and injustice, critiquing violence, anti-semitism, the naked display of power and the hidden hand of the state.

There are three essays that work across political issues to issues of alienation and the distancing of a diasporic writer (even as the home country bends backward to claim its own); of shifting historical concerns and introspective attempts to understand history and the act of writing. These are: 'How Strangeness Takes Possession', 'From Encounters to Introspection' and 'Contestatory Relations'. The last is about the 'extractive' attitude of a creative writer to the language she uses. This attitude throws new light on the inventiveness of resistance which works here as a refusal to accept the given. Another essay 'Refracted Nationhoods, Redacted Loyalties' also looks at the culture-language connections, identity formation and a reassessment of the affiliation of loyalties.

Three essays explore the continuities and disruptions in history, the construction of identities, violence and the role of the media. While 'Interrupted Lives, Continued Histories: Punjab Before and After 1984' locates itself in the diasporic role and anxiety for homeland violence, it also looks at the concept of citizenship, the present disaffection and the persecution of a community, worked by the sense of indifference to the human. The personal and artistic reconstructions in film and novel considered here, trace histories and their fall out. 'Mediations Between Collective Voices and Future Time: Politics and Media Representation' explores the dimensions of media interventions in countries with a sizeable majority of illiterate and poor populations. How is opinion formed in these countries, do the leaders get an unthinking following or is there a questioning and an opposition? It also goes on to examine the relationship between transparency and ethics. The third essay, in this category, is 'Explorations in the Historical Subconscious'. This essay works across language, genre and time. *Titu Mir*, originally written in Bengali, is nineteenth century history, 'Andher Nagri, Chaupat Raja', written in Hindi in the nineteenth century takes on the role of a reflected fable in Anand's *Goverdhan's Travels,* written in the twentieth century and originally in Malayalam. They use different creative approaches and are all concerned with resistance and the human action.

'Postcolonial Constructs – Exit?', 'Contrapuntal Narratives: Shifting Paradigms in Comparative Literature' and 'Issues in

Historiography' are directed towards a deconstruction of myths, strategies, resist an imposition of western forms, approaches and conclusions and seek to define our theoretical positions, build up a connection between non-linear narration and, at the same time, reassert the importance of multi-lingual literatures. Similarly, the essay, 'The Fictional Form: From the Endings to the Beginnings', has a fresh look at the formation of the novelistic form while the essay 'Purdah, Patriarchy and the Tropical Sun', is similarly engaged in deconstructing the myth that 'purdah' came to India with the Muslims and goes on to interpret it in relation to tradition, restrictions, religion and its impact on social life.

As I write this, today's newspapers (15 July 2012), carry two very contradictory and yet parallel narratives. The first is of women with covered faces addressing a *Mahakhap* panchayat in Haryana and administrating an oath against female foeticide. Next to it is a news item of the Khap asking the government not to interfere with them and forbidding the use of mobiles to women under forty. These minor dictatorships, existing in patriarchal strongholds, necessitate a constant questioning not only of our social structures, but also of our educational system and the whole legal system. A question which comes to one's mind is that if the lives of these women are restricted, how fair or independent will be their voting? These restrictions enslave the women and place a premium on age while certain professions such as films, electronic media and airlines place a premium on glamour and youth! How topsy-turvy can our world get with 'spirituality' and 'materialism' claiming an equal space.

Resistance is perhaps an act required for the act of living, it is integral to all good art and it is essential for a society to retain some kind of balance between the opposing forces of extremism. It is necessary for history to evolve and for policies to introspect. It connects our everyday life with larger concerns of power and globalisation. As the title essay describes it dwells in all creativity of ideas and ideologies, and goes on to define the role of an intellectual. Censorship, exile or imprisonment are some of the weapons used against the non-conformists in order to silence their voices. But it is a long and hard battle which needs to go on, no matter how unevenly, for human values to survive.

1

Theorising Resistance and Creativity*

Resistance as a term is very hard to define; it has several shades such as non-conformism, protest, propaganda, commitment, criticism; it works in different ways for different people, adopts a variety of means and mediums, is not necessarily always a conscious move and it often ends up in censorship and controversies relating to the obscene or the absence of aesthetics. Furthermore, our responses are even more differently ranged. We react to it from our own location in history, class, religion and ideology. Neither the term nor the responses to it can be uniformly defined or classified. My focus in this paper is, however, somewhat different. I wish to explore the relationship between resistance and creativity on the one hand and the interaction between intellect, imagination and experience on the other. The latter also draws attention to the role of the individual and his socio-cultural contexts. For this purpose my references are going to be to four different artists, writers who have evolved differently but each one has resisted prevalent structures and ideologies.

Moving a little away from this, briefly I refer to the location of resistance in postcolonial studies and wish to free it from these

---

* Presented at a Plenary Session, Comparative Literature Association of India's International Conference at Central University, Gandhinagar, Gujarat, March 2011.

narrow confines. All situations of oppression have pushed artists to resist, if not by all else through exile. I quote only two such examples – Chinua Achebe and Joseph Brodsky. But exile does not always answer the problem. It did not do so for Dietrich Bonhoeffer. Bonhoeffer, a protestant priest and a member of the 'Confessing Church' (formed by the opponents of Nazi interference in Church affairs), was active in his resistance to political injustice and the violence of the Nazi regime. At one point, in order to escape conscription and continue his efforts for a just society, he left the country only to return a month later. He needed to be in his country and continue his efforts from there. Followed a prison term and then death. During his time in the prison he turned to creative writing and fragments of a play as well as of a novel are now available. Both are untitled and more in the form of debates between two strangers or in the case of the novel between three – debates between people either from different social classes or from different generations. It is fascinating to look into the mind of a man who has the courage to resist and to be part of the conflicts he faced, and tried to contend with. Are freedom and equality abstract concepts not meant for the masses? Can man live alone or does he need to belong to a community? In the novel, Christoph, who is the younger man, recalls his teacher who had talked excitedly and passionately about the great revolutions but when he moved on to their aftermath, he became a saddened man. Each of the revolutions had brought about terror, disruption and fragmentation and had ended in some kind of a compromise (Bonhoeffer 226). The two men dwell on the nature of power and the manner in which it creates tyrants and ask: what right does one have to ignore the 'blood and tears of the millions' as we write history? The focus has to shift from the demigods to the ordinary lives of ordinary men and women.

In the play, Heinrich has a visit from a stranger who identifies himself as Death. This 'stranger' is perhaps Bonhoeffer himself, especially, when he says 'I looked Death in the face for four weeks. First uncomprehendly, as on a dark night ... then terror-struck, as though beneath a falling axe, then again with burning desire, ... then full of wonderment' (202). The full price which sacrifice extracts is the need to look death in the face. The two aspects of resistance – courage and uncertainty – create havoc in the individual's mind as all values are weighed against the backdrop of history, leaving behind a feeling of uncertainty even about the nature of value. In all this one is merely trying to grasp the human. Bonhoeffer shifted the focus from religion to faith, and from war to peace thus highlighting the need for a shift in mindsets. Bonhoeffer's life (and death) and that of many of the other members of the Confessing Church, in itself offers a comment on the relationship between sacrifice/martyrdom and resistance – as does exile.

Writers and artists are hounded out through 'fatwas', forced exile, controversies, censorship and exclusion. Salman Rushdie and Taslima Nasreen are examples of one kind and M.F. Husain of another. Husain's work has for more than half a century, aroused controversy. And now for several years he lives in Dubai, has taken up citizenship there and even in the recent Art Summit in Delhi (January 2011) the inclusion of his work had to contend with both fear and opposition. In a private conversation another artist, one who had strong affiliations to right-wing ideology, confessed that personally he had never found anything offensive in Husain's work. If we turn to Husain's life, right from his birth in Pandharpur, a religious centre of pilgrimages, his early training, his readings in Sufism and the Upanishads, his fascination with the *chopais* from the *Ramayana* and the discourses on *Bhagawad Gita*, all indicate a secular mindset, open to ideas and experiences, malleable, restless, impatient to experiment with new forms and new languages of art. He painted billboards, designed furniture, organised a tableau and turned to film-making. In all this he resisted all that was 'archaic' and 'dogmatic', and what was pre-programmed and attempted to present the culture of the streets. Through newness and shock, he wished to provoke response.

To a lay person like me, the sharp lines in Husain's paintings – especially of 'Bharata Mata' and the later one of Mother Teresa, the pro-Indira Emergency paintings, the controversial ones of the Indian goddesses, Gandhi with a missing head, reflect the 'raw primitive energy of folk art'. He constantly brings together opposing styles in order to fuse them and produce something new. In 1991 he experimented with 1,500 metres of white cloth and 300 kilos of newspaper in an exhibition in the Jehangir Art Gallery. Husain called it a 'serious statement', expressing meditation and freedom for the mind (Ila Pal 248).

One may ask – why does Husain attract controversy? And why does he not stay away from religion? They are interconnected. It is the nature of creativity to clear the space around itself. Husain's whole bringing up – the environmental forces of recitations and temples, the in-between space occupied by a Suleimanis, the Indianness of folk art and its heavy reliance on religious figures all were the natural material of art working in a confining atmosphere of growing political violence and right-wing ideologies. At one time, identifying both Phoolan Devi and Amitabh Bachchan as symbols of violence, as also the act of Gandhi's assassination, his paintings drew attention to them. Husain's paintings on the Hindu religious figures are the inevitable result of growing up in India – just as the literary images of Kali and Durga are. It is here that the question which Stephen Slemon asks about the nature of resistance becomes relevant. Slemon asks whether resistance is integral to the work or located in the interpretative act. I would take it further and turn it into a statement: resistance is integral to the meaning of good/classical art, but finds a realisation of its true meaning through a responsive reading and interpretation. It is the question of aesthetic beauty vs obscenity which is located in the interpretative perspective. Any intellectual who does not respond, or does not define his position in response to his environment as he experiences it, fails in a primary responsibility to himself as well as to his art. In Husain's case his paintings are not confined to art galleries alone. His murals and public scaffoldings attracted their own audience. The visual image of a lanky, long-limbed bearded man is evocative of the sharp lines of his paintings, lines which express the cultural past. Other artists too like Sanjeev Khandekar and Vaishali Narkar in 2006 have suffered at the hands of agitationists. And Chandra Mohan's paintings of Durga, a Shiva Lingam and Jesus were destroyed and he (a student of the Baroda school of art) was arrested (Refer internet: artasia-pacific.com/magazine/54Baroda- Authoritiesjailartstudent).

The visual art and its visibility do not admit of any softening or camouflage as does the verbal art. Words have an inbuilt ambiguity and carry within them a historical baggage. Orwell once remarked that while prose cannot escape the totalitarian eye, poetry can, because dictators do not read poetry (and if they do, they do not understand it). One could apply this to Girish Karnad's use of myth for even as he critiques caste, brahminism, religious structures, he does not attract controversy. But Karnad does resist. In both *Talé Danda* and *The Fire and the Rain* he looks at social structures, at the nature of untouchability and the inflation of the brahmanic sense of exclusion. Incidentally the nature of violence also comes in for scrutiny both as violence against the self and as violence against society. Basavanna's twelfth century rebellion against caste, the failed initiative of his followers for a marriage between a brahmin girl and a cobbler's son, the behind the stage support of the king to the movement, the violent rebellion of the king's son against his own father all lead to annihilation and destruction – the revolution fails; Basavanna, caught between his moral conflicts, leaves the village and the king is murdered.

In *The Fire and the Rain* Karnad takes up a lesser known myth from the *Mahabharata*, the myth of Yavakri (*Vana Parva* ch., 135–138), which is once again about several issues – caste, purity, power, anger and the continuity of the revenge tradition. It also exposes falsehood, betrayal and subterfuge. These acts of human beings are worked out through ritual and framed within time and mortality. Aravasu, Raibhya's younger son, is the one who is to marry Nittilai, the untouchable girl, but who ends up attending to dead people, lighting their funeral pyres and having the ritual bath and hence misses marrying Nittilai. His brother is the chief priest of the fire sacrifice. He has stolen away his father's right, who in his own turn had taken away his elder brother's right. This round of dislocations results in betrayals and in the deaths of Yavakri and Raibhya, in the guilt experienced by Parvasu and Andhaka, and in the penance performed by Aravasu. Nittilai also dies, killed by her husband and brother. The play problematises the nature of sacrifice: who sacrifices what? Paravasu or Aravasu? If the pure are to perform the sacrifice: why is it that Aravasu's sacrifice of giving up Nittilai brings rain? Why is it that he alone has the power to liberate Brahma Raksha from the limbo? And why is it that Aravasu, though a brahmin, is now an outcast?

The play works first with a parallel strand of Aravasu forming a performing troupe and this drama troupe meeting up with the fire sacrifice where the play is performed. The play itself is a satire on the behaviour of the gods, their untrustworthiness, the subterfuge employed by Indra to lure Vishwarupa and kill him. For a moment the difference between the real and the make-belief play is blurred. Aravasu enters the real sacrificial garb in his mask of Vritra, resulting in a stampede. Paravasu sacrifices himself, Nittilai is killed and Aravasu is the one chosen to be given the blessing. Finally, though wanting the dead alive, he chooses the course which closes this possibility but sets Brahma Raksha free. And then it rains! Through the course of the play's performance all accepted and stable versions of behaviour, ritual and sacrifice are turned upside down and known realities questioned.

Aravasu is left alone to face his existential loneliness. Man, in order to discover his humanity, has to strip himself of his gods. Nittilai is human; she does not aspire to be other than that. Aravasu's insistence that she think of her own safety goes unheeded as she worries about the hungry children or waits for Aravasu. Karnad's use of myth spellbinds the mind with its super-natural aura, and its familiarity as it plays with deviations; the performative act engages the viewer's attention until it becomes a participatory act. The questioning only comes at the end as Indra pronounces his boon.

But the advantages of a mythical frame are not available to the visual, to painting or to the documentary form. Films may get away with a deal of critiquing and protest but documentaries as a genre proclaim a more open nature and a direct communication with their audience. Saeed Akhtar Mirza has made several films and almost all of them are acts of resistance – *Albert Pinto Ko Gussa Kyun Aata Hai*, *Saleem Langde Pe Mat Ro* and the like – but the narrative helps in softening the statements, attributing them to characters. Structures, dialogues, music all step in to engage the senses of the audience. As contrasted with this, documentaries as instruments of social critiquing follow Brecht's Alienation effect and aim at engaging an intellectual response, and Anand Patwardhan's more than others. One can sense both the anger and the anguish which work behind the scenes. Resistance thus is an act of concern. Patwardhan, over the years, has displayed a wide range of concerns – Hindu-Muslim conflicts, globalisation, nuclear blasts, peace activism, environmental concerns, gender justice and prisoners of war and has debated in them the questions of power and value. His work appears to be clearly intended as a meeting point between the creator and the viewer, the opening out of a dialogue. He wants you to travel with him to listen to opposing perspectives, to hear voices you have not heard, to see what you have not seen, to know what you have not known. In fact, to ask questions, to be disturbed, not to have a good night's sleep and to realise that what is happening outside there, can also happen to you. There is no softening, no blurring, no masks and no narrative complexities. Instead there are disruptive moves which break linearity, and frames which reveal brutality.

Patwardhan sees a direct connection between violence, militancy, aggressive masculinity and fundamentalism. Acts of terror, gender injustice, sati, honour deaths and communal conflict all fall into similar patterns of behaviour. They bypass the individual as well as long-term value. Patwardhan, especially with reference to his documentary *Ram Ke Naam*, has commented that he intended it as a warning to the nation. Documentaries, however, find a limited market. Of all his documentaries only *Jung aur Aman* was released in cinema halls. *Ram Ke Naam* was telecast on Doordarshan only after a court order, and that too much too late for the public approach to be influenced positively in order to stay the flood. Such documentaries act as a counter discourse to soap operas and paid news channels. They allow us to look beyond propaganda.

The ethics of investigation require a basic statement about the differing views and perspectives, the differences which are marked by gender, class, caste, religion, profession or location. It needs to let the individual speak in his/her own capacity before allowing the collective voice to takeover. It is through these individual feelings and perceptions that a connectivity between seemingly divergent events falls into place. It is not to say that documentaries which deal with social problems present an unrelieved reality or are entirely without hope. They are not. They can be poetic despite the struggle, can evoke admiration as well as emotional response, they underline a human concern. In each one of Patwardhan's documentaries I can recall such scenes, such events and happenings. In *Father, Son and Holy War,* when the workers of one community are building the roof of another person of the other community and also when in a group of Muslim women, one of them inspires the others towards self help and fighting for legal rights, are all scenes of coming together, of hope. Again in *Jung aur Aman*, there are Gandhi's bhajans, the Pakistan woman who dances Indian dance forms, the Peace March proceeding to Hiroshima – all these and many more juxtapose not only what men have done to each other, but also what men can do for each other. And as the number of the peace marchers dwindles, our heart goes out to them in their lonely journey. And we hang our heads in shame. How many of us have done even this for mankind, for ourselves as much as for others? Aravasu gave up Nittilai to free Brahma Raksha – not one of us. In another of Patwardhan's documentary, *Fishing in the Sea of Greed,* the underside of globalisation is revealed. The scenario moves from the tales of success to the tales of struggle, the quickly being sucked fish from the ocean waters by the huge trawlers adding to the troubles of the local ill-equipped fisherfolk. This David cannot throw his Goliath down. But then too, the camera captures the beautiful coastal line, the surging waves of the sea, the brotherhood of the community – all these flow to us as messages of hope.

Resistance in art forms is an indication that society is not dying, that there has to be a constant struggle to keep alive. It acts like a fresh infusion of blood and like a constant reminder that in this sea of change, the one constant force has to be the human and all the abstractions we have pursued since our consciousness register their value – the values of freedom, of emotion, of beauty, of love. That leads us to consider the creative and the aesthetic aspects. M.F. Husain's *Meenaxi*: *A Tale of Three Cities* (2004) is a film which can be seen as an elaboration upon the creative process, the manner in which one tries to understand the other, to step across into the other's psyche and is at the same time in danger of being absorbed. It moves between experience and imagination simultaneously trying to expand and to understand the real. Yet it too resists. Nawab is a Muslim writer, Meenaxi is a Hindu woman who approaches the writer requesting him to write her story. How does a man get inside the mind of a woman? And that too from a different background real or imagined, Meenaxi becomes a constant companion. She persists in telling him that he does not understand her, her love-affairs, her passions, her desire for adventure, the fullness of her life. Moving into these experiences, Nawab also realises the power of imagination. At one point the character takes possession of him and she goes on flouting all accepted social mores, she liberates herself from the confines of her background. The film, at heart, is about the nature of reality, of which we can perhaps grasp only the concretely possessable. It is also a search for meaning, for unveiling the invisible.

Resistance is not necessarily about 'newness' but about cleaning up all the cobwebs which prevent us from understanding the nature of reality. It is about unearthing the meaning of what we can value, of what is it that we can sustain in us in some measure. Resistance is not a search for demigods; it addresses the blindness of power. Men and women resist when it is no longer possible to endure, or to breathe pure air. And art, in its attempt at understanding the environment, arises out of it, resists its claustrophobic structures. It is integral to the value of art as much to the value of life as it brings together the individual and the social, the emotional and the intellectual, as feeling and thought are woven together.

2

A Phoenix Called Resistance

Aesthetics versus Meaning*

A national culture is the whole body of efforts made by a people in the sphere of thought to describe, justify, and praise the action through which that people have created itself and keeps itself in existence.

(Fanon, *Wretched*, 188)

I must not suppress the voice within, call it 'conscience', call it the 'prompting of my inner basic nature'. There is something within me impelling me to cry out in my agony .... That something in me which never deceives me tells me now: 'You have to stand against the whole world although you may have to stand alone. You have to stare the world in the face although the world may look at you with bloodshot eyes. Do not fear ...'.

(Gandhi, 'Quit India Speech', 184–185)

Resistance discourse needs to be freed from the confines of postcoloniality and placed within the aesthetics of literature. There is a very thin dividing line between resistance and fundamentalism, between an oppositional stance and a hardened orthodoxy. When the fluidity of the first changes into the fixity of the second, the change takes place. What brings this about are time, history and location. It is proposed to look at three constructs: religion, nation and caste – as they interact and impact

* First published in *Journal of Postcolonial Writing*, Vol. 43, No. 2, August 2007, 172–182.

each other both at home (India) and in diasporic locations, not necessarily in opposition to colonial hegemony or oppression, but as concerns that are more intricately rooted in the individual's relationship to socio-political environs.

1

In recent theory, resistance has come to be closely identified with postcolonial discourse. Jenny Sharpe in her essay 'Figures of Colonial Resistance', takes up Benita Parry's critique of postcolonial discourse as one unwilling to 'articulate a more oppositional politics.' Sharpe herself is concerned with the imposition of western authority upon non-western discourses and, in the course of her essay, problematises 'certain problems' with identifying sites of colonial resistance. Sharpe defines these sites as 'those ruptures in the representation of British colonialism as a civilizing mission', and proceeds to examine the ambivalences and tropes of this discourse, taking it from the 'mimic men' to Forster's punkah-wallah.[1] Sharpe's reference to Forster's *A Passage to India* raises questions of reading and interpretation and location in both time and space. The different readings of the novel, which is located in colonial India, are bound to reflect the changes in our perceptions of India's past. David Lean's film, with its overemphasis on imperial pageantry, reads the novel from an imperialistic perspective. A modern Indian reader, critical of the hollow liberal ideologies of imperial England, would look at the film as the skeleton of the novel which reveals the power and the making of power in an entirely different way leading to a total reversal of earlier readings anchored in liberal ideology.[2]

Moreover this reference to Forster immediately connects up with Stephen Slemon when he asks whether resistance is located in the narrative or is it embedded in the representational technologies, or alternatively located in an interpretative position:

> Is it something actually *there* in the text, or is it produced and reproduced in and through communities of readers and through the mediating structures of their own culturally specific histories? Do literally resistances escape the constitutive purchase of genre, and trope, and figure and mode,

> which operate elsewhere as a contract between text and reader and thus a set of centralizing codes, or are literary resistances in fact necessarily *embedded* in the representational technologies of these literary and social texts whose structures and whose referential codes they seek to oppose? (Slemon 104)

The issues which Slemon foregrounds are multidirectional. The embedding of resistance would foreground textual opposition in both theme and representation whereas interpretative acts take the production of meaning into a socio-cultural world. He draws attention to the relationship between aesthetics and meaning, and the incorporation of resistance into an oppositional poetics. None of these positions is simple or can find a simple answer. If meaning is *there* and integral to the text, thematic concerns, and authorial position acquire significance. Interpretation is an expansion which lacks stability or fixity. The reference to 'technologies' is a return to the question of the 1960s when postcolonial writing was criticised for being concerned with protest, the argument being that protest was not a legitimate concern of art and in order to validate it perhaps a different evaluative standard would have to be applied. Slemon, however, stretches it further to include oppositional poetics.

In Slemon's question about where resistance can be located, the way narrative produces its textual meaning is juxtaposed with referential meaning produced through contextual frameworks. Either/or positions cannot be clearly demarcated. The multiple ways in which meaning can be produced refute the possibility of self-contained texts. Again it is difficult to specify the exact location of resistance, whether it is in retellings, rewritings and reinterpretations, in written or oral literature, in time-bound contexts, or is it reflected in the mode of writing? A focus on oppositional relationships between the imperial and the colonial limits both literature and its interpretation. It ignores the dissidence, non-conformity and resistance within societies and leads to the framing of national discourses within narrow concerns. Fundamentalisms and resistances are both internal and external discourses; locating them primarily within postcolonialism is an approach that seeks to define through 'difference', and any hardening of difference itself becomes a fundamentalism. One needs to remember that fundamentalism in the sense of an orthodoxy came into use only by 1923[3], and is an ideological extension of the 'basic' principles. Resistance, on the other hand, has a much earlier association with power discourse. Like fundamentalism, it also implies a stubbornness, a refusal to shift from one's position or allow an imposition.

2

Literature as resistance works simultaneously at several levels. In 1989 Girish Karnad wrote *Talé-Danda,* a play about a twelfth century revolution in the state of Karnataka in India, when a group of 'poets, mystics, social revolutionaries and philosophers' questioned the hegemony. The movement ended in terror and bloodshed. Referring to this movement, Karnad in his preface draws the attention of the reader to the relevance of 'the questions posed by these thinkers for our age. The horror of subsequent events and the religious fanaticism that has gripped our national life today have only proved how dangerous it is to ignore the solutions they offered'. (i)

Thickly populated, the play introduces as 'sites' of resistance first death, then post-funeral rites, then an intercaste marriage and finally betrayal and murder. Struggles and contestations of principle and ego occur: the play probes the complexity of every act of resistance through its various dramatic strategies. The forces are never represented through binary oppositions of the powerful and the powerless, or the imperial and the colonial; juxtapositions, even when they maybe duplicated, are never the same. Two father-son relationships are portrayed: one of King Bijjala and his rebel son Sovideva and the other of Sambashiva Shastri (a brahmin) and his son Jagadeva (who is a *sharana* and has rejected caste). Trust and betrayal are also juxtaposed in two relationships: Basavanna, the leader of the *sharanas* and his follower Jagadeva, and Bijjala, the king and Basavanna, but the reasons are different in every case. Basavanna does not negate his own principles in the act of betrayal whereas Jagadeva goes back on all his earlier positions. In an explanatory note to the English translation of the play, Karnad gives the meaning of the title as death by beheading. In medieval Karnataka one offered one's head 'either on completion of a vow or in penitence'. This offering can be treated as a sacrifice. In the play both Bijjala and Jagadeva die, one by murder, the other by suicide. And each death is in the form of a sacrifice.

The play opens with Sambashiva Sastri on his death-bed anxiously awaiting his son Jagadeva. Jagadeva, however, is away guarding the king's Treasury against the rebel prince Sovideva, primarily to protect Basavanna who is the leader of the movement but also happens to be responsible for the Treasury in his role as prime minister. Loyalty ceases to be a simple matter of right or wrong; its conflictual nature is obvious. The king, who approves of the revolution, is unable to join it because of his responsibility as a king. Just as the nature of power (with all its limits) and the nature of loyalty (along with its divisions and conflicts) are explored, the next act (Act-II) proceeds to examine the effect of an exogamous marriage, in this case marriage between a brahmin girl and a cobbler boy. What is desirable in principle as a way of dismantling caste constructs carries within it the possibility of unleashing violence and hatred. Both Basavanna and the king are afraid. Basavanna fears for the life of the young couple; the king for his throne. But there is a third concern voiced by others – that of the differences in their upbringing (governed by caste factors). Would the brahmin girl be able to tolerate the perpetual smell of raw leather in her new home? The two rebellions – one a movement for social change and the other the prince's usurpation of his father's authority – end in violence. But this violence links them. Ironically enough, Basavanna and the king, are both reduced in power by the end of the play. Basavanna does not want to impose his will on his followers. The king is held captive by his son. Jagadeva, apparently on a rescue mission, ends up killing the king and committing suicide.

Karnad's play, in its treatment of Indian social constructs and the Indian past, goes beyond the written text and the present moment. The debate that marked India's freedom struggle was between violence and non-violence, the two parallel discourses that interacted every now and then, runs like an undercurrent in the play, which no serious reader in India is unable to ignore. *Talé Danda* ends with the city in flames.

A similar tale of a movement and its decline, of a city that is burnt down was told much earlier – in 1938 – by another writer, in another form. I have in mind Raja Rao's *Kanthapura*, a novel about India's freedom movement. Raja Rao, in his short preface, states the need to abandon both the syntactical pattern of the English language as well as the fictional tradition. His narrator, an old woman, a witness-participant, adopts the technique of a *sthala-purana,* a narrative of the land based on a legend that is native to it. Rao uses the method of the religious kathas (oral narratives) that narrate the life of a saint or the significance of a ritual. The Hari-kathas (stories about gods) yield place to Gandhi-kathas (secular narratives). The women gather in the precincts of a temple and it is from here that they move out to oppose the British through non-violent resistance. The internalisation of this collective strength by the individual member is embodied in *Satyagraha,* the defining principle of Gandhi's struggle. Raja Rao, writing at the point when Gandhi was losing his grip over the other leaders, ends his novel by portraying Moorthy's increased inclination towards the leadership of Nehru. But Karnad has the advantage of the extra half-a-century to his credit in order to evaluate historical positions. *Talé-Danda's* violent ending, is the failure of the movement. In *Kanthapura,* however, the colonisers' violence acts as a spur to the movement.

Literary resistance, throughout the twentieth century, has been interwoven with political events and has acted as an agency both in the spread and the critiquing of ideologies. Representation of history has not necessarily been an interpretation of the past but the historical novel, in India, has outgrown the inherited limitations of the form and proceeded to use fantasy, surrealism, debate and the contrapuntal in order to become a counter-discourse to fundamentalist structures and ideologies.

3

Religious fundamentalism does not exist in a vacuum; its origins can be traced to a variety of sources – struggles for power, identity and nation construction, ethnicity, a search for roots – and can be inflamed by political assessments such as Samuel P. Huntington's *The Clash of Civilizations and the Remaking of the World Order.* Resistance and essentialism are locked in a permanent opposition in an obverse relationship, which reflects contrasting mindsets. Resistance movements, often, create their own essentialisms and harden into orthodoxies as Hanif Kureishi's story 'My Son the Fanatic' (1995) illustrates. The story is about Pervez, a London-based, Lahore-born taxi driver who finds himself in direct confrontation with his young, London-born son Ali. Pervez is increasingly receptive to western attitudes while Ali turns more and more to Islamic norms. The father is perhaps looking for freedom, the son for identity and security; while one gradually moves towards acceptance and erasure of difference, the other nurses a sense of rejection. As they face each other, the son tells his father, 'You're too implicated in Western civilization .... The Western materialists hate us ... how can you love something which hates you'. (106) Ali is willing to lay down his life for Islam and persists in his own ways, until one day Pervez actually kicks him. Ali, through his split lip and with blood pouring down his face, asks him: 'So who's the fanatic now?' (111).

Both of them are right, each in his own way. The struggle is against two different kinds of power structures, one religious and the other racial. Courage and fearlessness are essential in these struggles. But what validates resistance and discounts fundamentalism is the nature of the commitment: is it motivated by a desire for power and supremacy or by the need to establish power in order to be equal and human, that is, is power as an end in itself or is it a means to some wider concern? But none of these distinctions are free of intention, historical context or its aftermath. Any act of questioning or assertion is a way of resistance in constant danger of freezing into a fundamentalist position. It is this fluidity which would be the basis of defining resistance against the fixity of essentialism. Kureishi's story reflects upon the condition of many an immigrant who is caught between the need to belong to the culture of adoption and the need to project an independent, recognisable identity. Except that in this story the conflict is represented through a generational opposition.

Resistance discourse is not of recent origin. It has existed since the beginning of human history. All attempts at change have begun as resistance movements, whether it be the Buddhist questioning of hegemonic structures, Aristotle's response to Plato or the successive rewritings of the *Ramayana*. Intellectual resistance is innate to human growth and existence; the seed needs to push against the weight of the earth in order to sprout. All resistance defines the very organicity of human life; intellectual resistance goes further in its recognition of the human agency.

The writer does not begin with an ideology or necessarily work within a collectivity. The role of intellectuals vis-à-vis the establishment has never followed a straight line, yet whether as prophets, elites or as common protestors, intellectuals have invariably carried the burden of wisdom. The primary right of an intellectual to be in the position of an interrogator places him outside a hegemonic structure. Gandhi unhesitatingly changed his views whenever he felt that they had outgrown their utility or relevance; Arthur Koestler reviewed the communist ideology over and over again. Writers of our times have also done this, time and again, as they look into history and analyse the relationship of the past to the present. Thus the need to question, to evolve, to review, the refusal to be limited by an ideology is one characteristic of literary resistance. The individual being needs to be located in a contingent world, one which is sensitive to emotional responses and conflicts lest literary art becomes propaganda and an unfeeling, unthinking medium.

Why does one resist and how does one define 'essentialism'? Resistance is born out of anger, frustration or/and despair; a basic unhappiness pushes people to it. Race, colour, caste, class and religion are all categories that seek to bind and cohere. As such their boundaries seek to include as well as exclude giving rise to control on the one hand and discrimination on the other. When Fanon asks: 'What does the black man want?', the emphasis is on the word 'black' that a black man has struggled to arrive at the category of manhood, of humanness. The white child's wonder, 'Look mama, a Negro' is indicative of a racial construct. The moment the situation is framed within human categorisations, the framing is a protest against commodification. Protest brings to the forefront both the historicity of time and the significance of the present. Protest is also indicative of the writer's ability to move ahead of his times. Essentialisms, in contrast, seek to imprison men, subtract from their dignity, individuation and personal space. The writer, then, even as he moves with his times, forms collectivities and supports ideologies, does not surrender his right to question. How then does he express himself? How does he put across his dissent, his recognition of the right to transgress, without getting locked into fixities, in the face of censorship, control and, at times, imprisonment? Books have often been banned: Gandhi's *Hind Swaraj* (1909) and Veer Savarkar's *The First War of Indian Independence* (1907) were both proscribed. Ismat Chugtai, Mridula Garg and Amrita Pritam either had to contest court cases or were threatened with censorship. Mulk Raj Anand's *Two Leaves and a Bud* (1937) was also banned with the ban being lifted only after independence. Plays and films on Gandhi have been the subject of controversy; Rushdie's *Satanic Verses* (1988) was banned and those who spoke against censorship sidelined. States have tried to contain forces of resistance; religious heads have frowned upon personal freedom; the challenge facing a writer is always there as to how far he wishes to go.

Returning to Slemon's question about the location of resistance whether integrally generated by the text or produced through interpretation (Slemon 104), both, text and interpretation, can be said to be sites of resistance. Historical specificity and relationships of affiliation or otherwise with collectivities do impact the 'meaning' and 'reading' of a text, but resistance is embedded in narrative strategies and often shares its referential codes with essentialisms. The relationship of the writer with the reading community provides an additional context. The 'embeddedness' of meaning is clear when texts are censored or proscribed but writers can escape such censorship primarily through the use of myth, legend and fantasy. These become aesthetic means of creating both meaning and acceptability. For example Rokeya Shakawat Hosain combines dream and fantasy in 'Sultana's Dream' (1905) wherein she makes fun of the masculinist position. But when Mukul Kesavan disrupts the linearity of historical time by transferring the unnamed narrator living in the 1980s to 1942, in *Looking Through Glass* (1995), he uses fantasy not merely to reinterpret history but to resist a monolithic construct of the nation. Resistance to a dominant essentialist thrust also marks the narrative of Manzoor Ehtesham in *Sookha Bargad* (1986), where resistance is firmly embedded in the structure of the text, its historical underpinnings and experiential base. Ehtesham uses both dreams and surrealistic narrative strategies to deconstruct the nation-construct which marginalises the Muslim identity. Rashida, the Muslim girl-narrator details the history of her family. Her father, who grew up in pre-independence India, chose to stay on, rather than move to Pakistan, and attempted to give his children a secular modern education but in the process he is isolated from his own community. Without the necessary acceptance by the mainstream, her brother Suhail, who is frustrated by the constant suspicion that a Muslim was subjected to during times of crises like the Indo-Pak wars of 1965 and 1971, and a failed relationship with a Hindu girl, drops out from his engineering studies while Rashida herself is caught in the popular perception of Muslim girls being ghazal singers. The individuals are frozen into stereotypes. Suhail's recurring dream of seeking protection under the shade of a banyan tree turns into a nightmare, as he realises that the tree is already dead. The tree is a symbol of the nation which defines itself through exclusion and as it is dead, it can no longer grow:

> I notice that the area the tree covers has expanded .... In order to protect myself from the sun, I move towards its shade but the moment I step under it, I sense that its heat is worse than the heat of the sun .... It is dead. Honest to god, it is absolutely dead! It has gone dry while still standing on its roots! (198, translation mine)

Narration of failed dreams is a form of a resistance to monolithic nation construction just as the nourishing of a dream has the potential to become a resistance narrative. Giriraj Kishore in *Pahla Girmitiya* (The First Contractee, 1999) describes the awakening of Gandhi's resistance movement, by juxtaposing his dream to the imperial dream of conquest. The first line of the novel 'The white man had his dream' is countered by the first line of the third chapter, 'Mohandas also had his dream.' (52) Then step by step the sense of brotherhood and nationhood merge in the word *hum-watani* (fellow countrymen) and the multi-lingual nature of the signature sheet which the Indians plan to present to the authorities as a protest against discriminatory law, brings home to Gandhi the multi-lingual nature of India. Kishore's novel is of significance in the discourse of resistance for several reasons: it recalls history using it to establish continuities and project counter images, it reminds the reader of the difference between subjection and subjecthood; it defines assertion of one's right as a method of resistance. Published at a time when policies of exclusion and slogans of extinction were rampant, it projects the nation as one of plural identities and differentiates between aimless terror and legitimate resistance.

Retelling of myths and inventing new ones also constitute resistance narratives. Mahasweta Devi's novella *Operation*? *Bashai Tudu* falls into this category, when Bashai the man is lost in Bashai the legend. Bashai, as Samik Bandhopadhyay has pointed out, has been constructed out of several tribal heroes of the actual Naxalite movements. She 'lets him grow into a myth' and 'Even as the magic of the myth runs through the narrative and lends it coherence and unity, one has only to read between the lines to discern the revolutionary project that keeps the myth alive as a strategy. (xi) Bashai's physical death does not terminate the movement; the moment he dies, another steps into his role and the cycle goes on until the individual is submerged in the collectivity and grows larger than life. Devi's short story 'Draupadi' is equally evocative in its meaning as the tribal woman, who has been raped and violated, refuses to put on her clothes; her nakedness thus becomes an act of resistance not only to exclusionary, freedom-denying mainstream essentialism but also to male hegemony and false morality.

Literary resistance is not necessarily a militant voice: it functions subtly through literary modes such as humour and farce, emotions such as anguish and despair and narrative strategies like interiorisation and contrapuntal expositions. Resistance discourse has a socio-political context but at heart it is humanistic: it recognises the *essence* of man as a need for freedom and it questions the legitimacy of monolithical power structures. It interprets the term universal in a changed context – not as a single normative principle or as an all-absorbing, all controlling ideology or power structure but as an undercurrent of the new humanist discourse which emerges through resistance struggles – whether this be in Sartre's *Men Without Shadows* or Fanon's *The Wretched of the Earth,* or through the figures of men like Kali Santra in Mahasweta Devi's *Bashai Tudu* or a woman like Draupadi (Devi's story 'Draupadi'). Resistance discourse parallels, reflects and supports resistance movements, movements that do not insist on submergence of individual dreams but become, in themselves, an enlargement of them.

Hanif Kureishi's story 'My Son the Fanatic', demands examination of the difference between the sense of commitment that resistance to an opposing force demands and the commitment which manifests itself as an essentialism. Why is one defined as resistance and the other as essentialism? Is it that while resistance permits both objectives and strategies to be fluid, essentialism frowns upon any deviation and remains anchored in a fixed point in the past, wary of any fresh reinterpretation? This distinction may explain religious fundamentalisms but is not an adequate explanation of dictatorial power which refuses to be human and rejects rationalism. A Hitler or a Stalin cannot be explained through this formulation. Yet their commitment to specific goals is beyond question. One could debate it further by examining the nature of power. In *Hind Swaraj,* Gandhi refers to power as 'soul force', a term that lends itself to multiple interpretations and can cover a wide range from the ethical to the spiritual and could be hijacked by any essentialism. At best one can define the difference as a recognition of the human and the possibility of change in one kind of resistance, while the other sidelines both these values.

Resistance in itself has been an integral component of literature – at least all meaningful literature – ever since literature emerged as a discourse. Draupadi's questioning of the slave's right of ownership in *Mahabharata,* Cordelia's of Lear's paternal right to the total subjugation of the child are not merely voices of lone women. They raise issues of philosophical, moral and political import. Protest is simultaneously a dialogue, a deconstruction and an assertion – while also being a defining strategy. Furthermore being value-based, the applicability of this value makes protest both flexible and universal giving it both power and continuity. Literature enables the protest of an isolated situation to cross boundaries of time and space.

Today the publishing trade and the over-hype that the media creates also raise issues of visibility versus invisibility, of repetition and volume rather than meaning. The politics of awards provides another dimension to the confrontation between resistance discourse and essentialist constructs. I refrain from categorising essentialism as 'discourse', for if it attains the status of a dialogic discourse, its 'essentialism' will be deconstructed and softened. Because it allows no voices of dissent or questioning it has been frozen in its ideology unable to negotiate shifts in time and space. We, as readers, with our discriminating agency, have the responsibility of keeping the questioning image alive, through response, debate, action and ideology. By limiting literary resistance to ideological frameworks, we miss the point – the very organicity of resistance to human life – and fail to comprehend its 'essential' presence in all good writing.

Notes

1. 'Mimic' men is a term, she obviously borrows from V.S. Naipaul's novel *The Mimic Men* (1967), which is a novel about the difficulty of breaking away from a colonial past and the powerlessness a new nation experiences in the face of neo-imperialism. 'Punkah Wallah' is a minor character from E.M. Forster's novel *A Passage to India* (1924), where the figure of the native with his handsome body, becomes a symbol of a mindless obedience, oblivious to all else.

2. For interpretations of *A Passage to India,* as part of a liberal discourse, despite the failure to connect the East and West, see Lionel Trilling, *E.M. Forster: A Study* (London: Hogarth Press, 1944). Also refer Peter Burra's introduction to the 1979 edition of *A Passage to India* (Penguin). For alternative, post David Lean interpretations refer Arun Prabha Mukherjee's *Oppositional Aesthetics* (Toronto: Tsar Publications, 1998) and Iqbal Masood's article in *The Indian Express,* 5 May, 1991, 'The Lean Legend'. The film brought about a sudden change in Indian interpretations of Forster, primarily as Lean's film begins in England and foregrounds the British perspective. The above references, for both kinds of interpretations, are just a sampling. One could produce a long list in support of both sides.
3. *Shorter Oxford English Dictionary* (2 volumes), mentions it as 1923. An online entry defines fundamentalism as, 'A type of militantly conservative religious movement characterized by the advocacy of strict conformity to sacred texts. Once used exclusively to refer to American Protestants who insisted on the inerrancy of the Bible, the term fundamentalism was employed more broadly in the late twentieth century to a variety of religious movements.' 'Fundamentalism', *Encyclopedia Britannica.* 2007. *Encyclopedia Britannica Online* 28 April, 2007 (http://www.britannica. com//article.9390025).

3

Unstable Meanings, Multi-directional Journeys and Disrupted Continuities*

I have a long title, in itself a text to be decoded. I wish I could have made it longer and added 'unreliable memories'. But it still manages to say a great deal as it brings contradictory elements together, moves through several disciplines and points towards several clues which can serve both as entry points and outwardly directed inquiry in the concerns of the text's relationship with discourse. It points towards language, travelling discourses and interventions in the linear development of thought. More than all else it imagines the possibility of decipherment. Language may be lucid, but it is at the same time polysemic and ambiguous. In fact, its strength and ability to transgress lie in these characteristics. At times, it is not even fully equipped to express the congregation – the coming together – of ideas. Alternatively, it may be deliberately pared down to compress meaning, or convey a state of being. Simple or complex, it carries with it the writer's engagement with a variety of discourses, past readings and future implications. It hardly ever stops at being a statement. Again, discourses may have a commonalty of thought, even though generic differences cloak them differently. Text and discourse do not present a one to one

---

* Keynote address delivered at the seminar 'Texts and Discourses', University of Burdwan, Burdwan, 18 December 2009.

equation or any identifiable mathematical proposition. The title of my paper is in itself an attempt to explore the several meanings of discourse. It works like a dramatic segment compelling us to ask as to who is the speaker and who is addressed, and what is the occasion. Moving across multiplicities, it resists singleness as much as termination.

Text does not inhabit discourse as a smaller circle or world would inhabit a larger one. They also do not present two independent worlds linked together by language. Discourse, again, does not constitute a text or emanate purely from it. Surface clues as picked up through linguistic analysis do not necessarily reveal the text in its fullness. Discourse analysis by focusing on the semiotics of a text, perhaps suffices as one approach but it unfortunately carries within it the limitations of New Criticism. The current emphasis on general semantics is an attempt to include philosophical debates within the scope of meaning, seeking to arrive at a more defined relationship between word and meaning. At times I wonder how one can adequately visualise the relationship between text and discourse. Is it possible to draw three separate circles – the writer's world, the reader's world – each with its own socio-political ideas and epistemological formulations – and the connection which comes into being in their meeting? No matter how we visualise or project the relationship, no single, uniform definition is likely to emerge because discourse is marked as much by its multiplicity as by its fluidity. Moreover, engaged as the text is in a constant negotiation between reality and representation, it has the capacity to generate new discourses.

The problematics of this issue – discourse and text – I think were set in motion by the upheavals of the early decades of the twentieth century when accepted knowledge systems were destabilised and several new disciplines emerged as a result of human attempt to hold on to some semblance of meaning. The 'newness' of knowledge was both disruptive and destructive and the category of the 'human' was placed under a question mark. [Freud's *Civilization and Its Discontents* (1929), Ortega Y. Gasset's *Dehumanization of Art* (Spanish original 1925, an enlarged edition including *Other Writings on Art and Culture* came out in 1948), and Walter Benjamin's, 'The Work of Art in the Age of Mechanical Production' (1935).] I am aware that one could debate the use of the word 'human', as defined by the west became a category to be deconstructed for with the surfacing of colonial knowledge as the debates about cultures and civilisations demonstrate.[1] What matters more than the problematics of the human are the social and political revolutions set in motion through the dynamics of new knowledge.[2] The resurgence of art movements – such as surrealism, dadaism, theatre of cruelty – like the new researches were all attempts to make sense of the outside chaos.

It was at this time that the Frankfurt group of thinkers – Adorno, Habermass, Horkheimer and the rest of them – pushed the 'text' into a social existence, liberating the term from a placement in a written document. It was at this point that the ongoing debates about the relationship of art with reality culminated in a fullsome acknowledgement of the interconnections between the two. Foucault in his essay, 'Structuralism and Post-Structuralism' (1983) acknowledges the school's contribution to post-structuralism and goes on to admit how the French academia continued to live in ignorance of them as it struggled towards similar positions (440).[3] Adorno in his work *Minima Moralia: Reflections from Damaged Life*, commented on the dissolution of the 'subject' – the subject as human being, as a thinking person, as a voice – was no-longer-in-itself. The concentration camps, he pointed out, had annihilated the existence of the individual subject.[4] Adorno writes, 'Though the subject still feels sure of its autonomy but the nullity demonstrated to subjects by the concentration camp is already overtaking the form of subjectivity'. It was through this double movement – the loss of the autonomous text and the loss of the autonomous subject (more fashionably talked of as death of the author) that criticism sled into critical theory and the text was placed in a continuum of time, in the flow of history.

Space and time are of importance to both text and discourse. Paul Ricoeur in his essay 'Human Sciences and Hermeneutical Method: Meaningful Action Considered as Text', works through these tempero-spatial dimensions and describes discourse as located in the temporal while language as virtual. Foucault throughout his work reflects an ongoing concern with space. In his essay 'The Thought of the Outside' (1966), he defines discourse as a 'to and fro' between interiority and exteriority, the point of intersection is situated in the moment when language arrives at its own edge, engaged with its own invisibilities and un-graspabilities and moves into a spatial outside (152–154). Self-reflexity of both text and writer is a contributory factor. Text and discourse, as they connect, bring alive the Heideggerian concept of *dasein*, 'being-in-the-world' as the text comes alive within discourse.

Returning to the literary text and its linguistic dimensions, I draw attention to two passages. The first of these, written in 1947–48, reads as follows:

> Given the existence as uttered forth in the public works of Puncher and Wattman of a personal God quaquaquaqua outside time without extension who from the heights of divine apathia a divine athambia divine aphasia loves us dearly with some exceptions for reasons unknown but time will tell ....

You would have recognised this as the beginning of Lucky's speech in Samuel Beckett's *Waiting for Godot*, a speech without any punctuation marks with lots of meaningless interventions and interminable in itself. How do we read it? Is it intended to make meaning and connect up somewhere? Perhaps one could weed out words and phrases like quaquaquaqua, one could treat repetitions as points of fresh beginnings like 'reasons unknown' and 'time will tell', or one could go ahead to open out the incomprehensibility of all knowledge and the flow of time as it unfolds its meaning. Apparently meaning is there, even if it is in the distance. *Waiting for Godot* is a performative text; Michael Lindsay-Hogg in his film frames Lucky's speech, placing Lucky in an upright position, out of his servile bending, with his white hair flowing, standing atop a hill-rise, and speaking in a prophet-like manner. Performance too is a language to be read, imagined or seen. Then there are proper nouns like Puncher and Wattman: who possibly are they? Philosophers, scientists, publishers – producers and conveyors of knowledge? Would it make better sense when we go down the speech with its recital of the discoveries and inventions of man, directed towards human immortality – all the medical and physical sciences? Incidentally, in 2005, an Australian publishing house (David Musgrave) adopted Puncher and Wattman as its name providing an example of discourse reaching out into the future. No mere close reading is enough to comprehend the passage. We need to go outside into the world of religion, existentialism, psychology and the functionings of the brain. The prefix divine used to mark apathia, athambia and aphasia words that describe lethargy, disengagement, loss of memory – words of disconnection, do they signal a disconnected disinterested god? There is a reference to time eternal and existence of a personal God, there is also an inbuilt uncertainty and distancing. The evidence is second hand, is it to be believed or not? Divine love is not available to all for some unknown reasons, thus once again referring back to the word 'personal', to the story of the two thieves mentioned earlier on in the play on several occasions, to incomprehensibility and the state of limbo. Where is the rational connectivity? Why are the public and the personal contrasted? Our questions lead us deeper both into the text and outside the text, to loss of faith, to a host of other things including the location in space, in bondedness and a life without personal choice. The white beard resurfaces at the end of the second act. Lucky's speech sets itself in a central focal point in the text and against the background of the contemporary world – heavily loaded with happenings that bode ill and take away the possibility of action. It also hearkens back to Beckett's novels written before the play and his enigmatic, monosyllabic heroes. Lucky's speech poured out without a pause contrasts with the monosyllabic, forced conversations of the two friends. There is simply no way it can be summed up in an explanatory note or pure textual analysis or a contained one.

The second passage is from Foucault from the first of his 'Two Lectures on Power' (7 January 1976). Reviewing his own work, he describes it as fragmentary and diffused and says:

> None of it does more than mark time. Repetitive and disconnected, it advances nowhere. Since indeed it never ceases to say the same thing, it perhaps says nothing. It is tangled up into an indecipherable, disorganised muddle. In a nutshell, it is inconclusive. (78)

Uncannily echoing the Beckettian stance, the very first question one is prompted to ask is: do we take his statement at its face value? The innocent listener/reader may be tempted to do so. But the mature reader resists. The speaker apparently is posing a challenge and inviting the reader to come forth and participate in the task of unearthing the meaning by decoding the text, to ask the significance of repetition and why repeated journeys are necessary. The words which stand out are 'repetition', disconnected and inconclusive, words which project movement, aimlessness and an ongoing search. The passage works perfectly well as a manifesto for Foucault's work and spells out the need for deciphering both the linguistic text as well as the philosophical discourse. Its embodied circularity is a representation of the nature of power which is neither a possession, nor extricable without effort and, like power, it has the capacity to shift. Once again it creates discourse at multiple levels – the discourse of the text, the whole philosophical discourse from the Enlightenment onwards, the writer's own philosophy as expressed in his other works, the shifting political scenario of his times, – the 1960s and 1970s – when 1968 was a period of turmoil in France. Going beyond the present, the passage invites the reader to participate not merely in the text but also in the context of our times. The use of linguistic schemata creates a methodology and helps the unearthing of clues, of picking up openings and identifying polysemic nuances. But they work from outside inwards. There is another way of entering a discourse where linguistic analysis may be summoned later, after first initially entering the text – the hermeneutic way – which works with ideas, origins and exegesis.

Every text attempts to say something; it seeks to communicate. And all communication does not employ language; it does not have a definite signified or referent. The writer's relationship with language may very often be one of grappling with the inexpressible. The efforts to express then seek other forms: epigraphs, repetitions, intertextualities. Through these the text spills outside its confines and invites the reader to take them as clues and explore her relationship with all earlier contacts with them – with sayings, quotations, observations and earlier statements. Intertextuality is introduced stirring up old memories and constructing new ones.

Each one of the encounters needs to be brought back to the text in question – layer after layer of memory, of discourse, of meaning. Many nineteenth century writers use epigraphs and peritexts as do twentieth century writers. These epigraphs are not superficial attachments; they are not even representative of 'abstracted' ideas. Instead they acknowledge the outside and recall the reader to the historical flow of time in its continuity, circularity and simultaneity. Nayantara Sahgal's 2003 novel *Lesser Breeds* has several epigraphs – the title from Kipling's poem 'Recessional' recalls in association his other poem 'The White Man's Burden', as well as the civilisational discourses including J.S. Mill's '*On Liberty*' and Macaulay's 1835 Minute. A second opening epigraph is from Gandhi's favourite hymn *Vaishnava jan to tako kahiye, Jo pir parayi jane re*. The juxtaposition of the two is a confrontation between two opposing ways of life, two opposing civilisations and ideologies. The hymn has another layer – that of going across to the other. It brings into the circle of memory the history of India's freedom struggle. There are several other epigraphs but I think the point has been made. Again maps too serve as a connecting point between the interiority and the exteriority of the world of the text in the novel. Maps and iconography have the capacity to make complex statements about the conflicts in society and summon the reader to engage with socio-political discourses. Fairly early in the novel we have a reference to an elongated map in Bhai's study, indicating the spaces showing natural wealth and the European possession of these areas. Mineral and natural resources such as tin, timber, copper, lead, oil and rubber were the targets of western control (79–80). Then follows a whole chapter reflecting upon maps and spaces, visibility and invisibility and discussion about China, Philippines, Japan, and India and reflections on the strategic moves of the British during the Second World War (169–198). Later, in Mr Jenner's library in the States, there is once again a Map of the World where 'Early medieval Europe floated in unnamed seas surrounded by blank lands lettered Peopled by Monsters' (220).

Lesser Breeds also works with and within different time periods – 1932 to 1968 at one level but subterreanily moving from 1757, the Battle of Plassey, to 1988, and through this expanse works through power, subjugation, resistance, deceit and love. As it traces the story of the growing capitalistic powers, it also examines the strength of fairy tales and Gandhi's vision of combating imperial power with non-violence. Fairy tales have their own complex mixture of terror and enchantment. Leda is a character in the novel who is engaged in collecting fairy tales of all kinds and narratives with fairly tale ending with rewards and punishments fairly meted out. Fairy tales have a great deal of violence and sadism built in as well as a great deal of suffering before the happy ending can be arrived at. Gandhi's belief in non-violence does not appear to be very different from a fairy tale. Houses are another category in the novel which open out in different ways – refuge, gifts, inviting houses, houses which connect. Leda is gifted a house as is Nurullah – houses which have been loved and lived in and symbolise relationships.

One must stop to ask the question whether these are merely interpretative strategies or do they formulate a discourse? The point is when does an interpretative strategy become a discourse? I'll venture a guess. It is the nature of reading which brings this about, when the reader becomes a participatory reader in the contingent world of the text as well as her own. When this reading enables the recognition of difference in approach, in histories and values and turns self-reflexive, it becomes discourse. Discourse places a greater responsibility on the reader as more than knowledge and perception it demands a degree of consciousness.

I am tempted to work with different kinds of texts, in order to explore the possibility of generating discourse in other ways. For instance a text like Gandhi's *Hind Swaraj*, which on the face of it is a political statement from all perspectives, but moves on to reveal itself as a personal statement at the same time as well as a blueprint for political action. Over and above the message which the title sends abroad, what kind of discourse does it build? The language is simple, the style dialogic. Written primarily with a need to communicate, it is transparent. Moreover the English text is a translation from the original Gujarati text and the transference has simplified it further. Written virtually mid-sea on his journey back from London to South Africa, it is concerned with India. Gradually it dawns on us that Gandhi's 'Editor' (the policy-maker) and the 'Reader' (the

Listener) are not the only listeners. In fact, it is Gandhi himself split into two. He is debating these issues with his own self, evaluating the choices, working out the logic and the logistics, carefully considering the likely hurdles and oppositions. It is also almost a judge's document carefully weighing and balancing his arguments; it lacks all the rhetoric of a public speech.

For a first-time non-Indian reader what does the text reveal? Are there any clues to be picked up by the non-initiated? There is a constant juxtaposition with the west in terms of civilisation and its manifestations, there is a fierce will to stand on one's own premises, no matter where it leads and there is a projection of soul force. *Hind Swaraj* focuses not merely on the nation or its subjugation, but goes beyond it to define civilisation, posit alternatives, redefine the notion of modernity and work on the possibility of a developed conscious self – the individual who goes to make the nation. Religion too has been shorn of its pretences and worked out in its moral essence. A full awareness exists of the economic scenario. Where does one go from here and how does one read it? *Hind Swaraj* is part of the many discourses about colonisation as well as of several resistance strategies. It branches out into multiple discourses both contemporaneous and distant. Directly placed in opposition to the violence of the revolutionaries, violence which had just taken place in London, and written after his talks with them, the text also moves away, through its redefinition of religion, from the conservative thought of his time. *Hind Swaraj* belongs simultaneously to several discourses, including ecological ones. It resists terms like exclusion and hierarchy and is both self-reflective and self-critical.

The relationship between text and discourse is a relationship of inter-dependence. Texts are not isolated events, and events too become texts as they flow in historical time and are re-enacted under changed circumstances or changed intentions. I cite here one example – the Dandi March with its transparency, purpose and strategy. Place it alongside other political marches, rath yatras, pad yatras and their purpose and impact vis-à-vis mobilisation, the nation and the self – Advani's several, Sunil Dutt's peace marches and several others carried on for harmony, ecology and solidarity in order to unfold its location in the political situation of

1930s and the political situation of the 1980s and 90s. Inbuilt into the yatra discourse are endurance, community, dislocation, comradeship, discipline and motivation. Where and when do they get dislocated by ego, power, camouflage and publicity – provides an important entry point.

The discourse enveloping or existent in oral literatures despite the lack of any single stable version, is richer than literary texts in its reflection on community, kinship patterns and even political happenings or changes. Oral literature is spontaneous and, as it is not overtly concerned with addressee or readerships, tends to be forthright in its statements. It reflects upon morals both public and sexual, explores psychological levels of desire, critiques social practices and often singles out deviation as praiseworthy. Their different versions reflect social change and become time markers. *Kanthapura* works with the constructs of the *sthalapurana* and the embedded Hari-kathas soon to be transformed into Gandhi-katha. Oral literatures have often reworked themselves into written narratives – we have Raja Rao, Girish Karnad, Suniti Namjoshi, Gabriel Marcia Marquez as well as a host of other writers who bring orality into their writing either as a story or as a method, as they seek to work through similitudes, across psychological and social discourses.

Discourse, in fact, is the spilling over of the text and constantly demands a detective-like skill from the reader – involved yet sceptical, the mind and eye of a Hercule Poirot, the quality of disbelief, and a persistence in distrusting memory recalls. Even the morphology of the text places it in a horizontal discourse, and opens out the suppressed layers of interaction – I'll just give two examples – Ondaatje's *The English Patient* with its isolated camp of exiles, and the discourse of the village narrative vis-à-vis the outside.

No text locates itself in a single discourse – texts carry forth human complexities into the outside and into the future, constructing our worlds and future ideologies, unveiling unknown realities, tentative meanings, unsettling us in our responses, pushing us into unexplored areas of knowledge and thought and reflection, in fact, literally helping us grow up. Texts in their turn, generate other discourses, which converge into new meaning patterns.

Notes

1. Western humanism has come in for a degree of criticism for central to it was the 'white man's burden'. Dividing the human between white and black on the basis of colour and between civilised and barbarian on account of the difference in culture, it limited and degraded the human. Resistance movements have attempted to redefine the human in terms of relationships, sensitivity and compassion. Both Gandhi and Fanon have contributed to the formation of a new humanism though in entirely different ways. The Gandhian contribution has been an ethical one, while the Fanonian works through strategies of self-assertion. Dignity is a category central to both.
2. My reference here is to the philosophical questionings and artistic experiments made in art in order to define and interpret reality – Bergson's *Creative Evolution* (1911), William James's *A Pluralistic Universe* (1902) and Henry James's 'The Art of Fiction' (1884).
3. Foucault admits that had he been familiar with the Frankfurt School, he would 'have avoided many of the detours' he made while trying to pursue his path. ('Structuralism and Post-structuralism', 440).
4. Adorno repeatedly insists that the exile forced on many intellectuals had completely mutilated them. *Reflections From Damaged Life* is about the descent of the human into inhumanity.

4

The Untapped Seam and the Indian Interventions in Theory*

When pressed by the seminar organisers to provide a title, I opted for a working title. The one which I use does not meet the requirements of what I wish to say. Closer to my intentions may perhaps be a title like 'The Confines and Possibilities of Theory', for I come to the subject with a number of queries, several doubts and a lurking hope of some shift. I begin with a couple of issues: are we out of the postcolonial syndrome or still waiting for someone to announce that it is over and done with? And what, if any, has been the extent of Indian intervention in theory? There are a couple of big names and several small ones, but is it the right trajectory that we are tracing? One can mention names like Gayatri Spivak, Homi K. Bhabha, Arun Prabha Mukherjee, the two Mohantys – Satya and Chandra Talpade – and the in-and-out of India brigade of critics and theorists. There are the critical introductions by Ania Loomba and Leela Gandhi. Aijaz Ahmad's *In Theory* also counts; it attracted a lot of debate when it was published. Debates at home have also taken place and many of them reflected in the volumes edited by Trivedi and Mukherjee (*Interrogating Postcolonialism*), Prafulla Kar's edited anthology *Critical Theory,* and Jain and Singh's *Contesting Postcolonialisms* amongst several others. What need attention are not the names or their visibility, but the theories which they have formulated or dialogued with and even more than that the question

* Presented at a Conference in DAV College, Yamunanagar, 2004.

of what we have made of them as critics and readers. Beside this engagement with postcolonial theory – a term I shall return to a little later – we also have two other parallel trends, one which began with the seminar on 'Nativism' in 1984, followed by Ganesh Devy's *After Amnesia* (1992), another seminar in 1995 (at Kanpur, organised by the Sahitya Akademi), the papers of which were edited by Makarand Paranjape.[1]

Both *In Theory* and *After Amnesia* appeared in 1992. One looked outward from an Indian location and critiqued Said and Jameson, going on to emphasise the need for interrelatedness of language literatures. The other looked inwards and projected the theory of a national forgetting which had disrupted the linearity of native narratives. Critics have interpreted this amnesia in different ways but Devy succeeded in drawing attention to the differentiation between *marga* and *desi*, reproducing the east-west polarity on the home scene. The 1995 seminar, in some ways, was the passing away of 'Nativism' as it appeared to be dangerously close to right-wing ideologies and mistakenly located itself in region and language instead of continuing a search for a pan-Indian contemporary idiom. Prasanna's articulate critique of *Desivaad* states the case loudly and clearly. In 'A Critique of Nativism in Contemporary Indian Theatre', he observes that his own experimentation with it had lead him toward an exclusionist, regional audience. *Desivaad*, if it wanted to project itself as a viable alternative, 'had to find a better way of understanding Indian creativity' (Prasanna 100). There has to be a choice between separatism and invisibility, between going to the west, or returning to the past.

A third major trend has been the persistent preoccupation with the revival and retrieval of Sanskrit aesthetics, which conveniently falls within the scope of comparative and influence studies. It has been more dominant in the South than in other regions, with scholars like Ayyappa Panikar, Krishan Ryan, C.D. Narasimhaiah engaged with the process. The research going on in some of the universities in the South provides evidence of this. A number of volumes of theoretical positions have also appeared like Satish Aikant's edited volume *Critical Spectrum*. But the theoretical positions lie scattered across disciplines – the subaltern historians, the sociologists, the psychologists. Significant statements are made but are not necessarily as visible as Bhabha and

Co. The critical theory scene, on the face of it, appears to be a stream run dry. If we look at it closely it is possible to discern, that all the three main trends are, in some measure, defensive. And defensive strategies are freedom denying and constraining. If we do not want to be confined to a world made by others, we need to step out of this concern with polarities, with centre and periphery, and walk out of the legacy of colonialism and get on with the business of disrupting the linear discourse of subordination.

Bhabha opens *The Location of Culture* with several questions, and one of them is: 'Are we trapped in a politics of struggle where the representation of social antagonisms and historical contradictions can take no other form than a binarism of theory vs politics? Can the aim of freedom of knowledge be the simple inversion of the relation of oppressor and oppressed, centre and periphery, negative image and positive image?' (Bhabha 19) And he goes on to expand on this in his work of the third space, of interstitial spaces and of hybridity. Though Bhabha is often cited for these concepts, the complexity of his concept of hybridity, of his desire to find a way out of this polarity of distinction which he makes between cultural difference and cultural diversity are not necessarily examined in detail or employed as routes of interpreting texts. They have become resting places and defining concepts instead of ways of generating new formulations.

What is theory? Writers and critics have bent backwards to dwell upon this. Rajeshwari Sunder Rajan in a 1997 essay lists four main ways in which one tends to regard theory from a commonsensical standpoint: (i) mere *theory* in opposition to reality, (ii) to the empirical, (iii) to a pragmatism that grounds meaning and intention in the individual 'self' or the autonomous text and (iv) as 'not "historical"'. She goes on to elaborate, 'Historical analysis is specific to a particular situation, recognizes contingency and thereby circumscribes its explanatory force' (Rajan 80). In the subsequent discussion she sets out to upset some of these formulations by looking at the anti-foundational approach of Tharu and Lalitha in *Women Writing in India,* where they approach the text not with any preconceived assumptions but with a desire to explore. Ahmad on the other hand repudiates theory 'through a sustained engagement in theoretical terms'

(90–91). The first allows theory to emerge from reading, the second narcissistically works with itself. The opposition between the two methods is important (though both have their own uses). The significance of allowing the text to generate its own theoretical framework cannot be ignored, but the relevance of theoretical awareness and the need to question other theoretical positions also cannot be disputed. And there remains a lurking doubt that the confrontation as it is framed is not on equal terms.

My own essay, 'Destabilising Meaning: *In Theory* and *Orientalism*', views the formulation and the questioning of theory as a desire to intervene with history and the historical process. Thus theory is not ahistorical at least not in its inspiration. Even as it adopts a radical or a subversive position, it is engaged in a backward look at history (108–109). Both Tharu and Lalitha and Ahmad, in their different positions are engaged with history. Theory, despite its ruptures and hiccups, flows in a *continuum*. Why else should there be debates and questionings? It is this *continuum* which interests me. Theory is an attempt to understand the past, to perceive its impact on the present, to produce knowledge, often also an attempt to resist other theories and to work out a method or process. The context is crucial to its every stage: formulation, acceptance, questioning/rejection and closure, a closure which often is an absorption, a transformation, or an overlaying. It has a direct relationship with philosophy, culture and psychology. The persistent presence of a Nietzsche or a Heidegger, of a Freud and Lacan, of a James Mill or the Orientalists is evidence enough in itself. Every new theory looks for a guiding principle. Rorty and Ricoeur are philosophers, Fanon a psychoanalyst, Foucault a historian of thought. Again we need to ask: does ideology have a role to play in the formulation of theory? Does it define the basis of our perspective and how far are political ideologies rooted in other disciplines?

It is evident from the above that theory in order to come into existence, needs to cross disciplinary boundaries and interrogate cultural texts; it is equally evident that it emerges from the interaction between practice and representation. In a literary context these have widespread implications. Theory is also a way of perceiving reality. As such it is not in opposition to reality. But reality is not and cannot be in the singular. Can one derive from this that the theoretical propositions need to take care of at least the known pluralities, if not the unknown ones? In view of the above discussion, it is possible to review the interventions of Indian thinkers. The scene throws up a strange mixture. If we return to a theoretical and historical continuum, one exists in Indian thought and philosophy, one which is diverse, divergent, interrelated and dialogic. But the moment we search for the visibility, it is either very selective, or minimal. Anthologies of theoretical essays, writings of western theorists and even our own diasporic writers have other concerns. It is not that the third world does not find a place but it is India that remains marginal. The desire for visibility leads to an engagement with debates emanating in the west and on their own grounds. At worst there is a surrender to it, at best the native cultural image is suitably framed and marketed.

Homi Bhabha's *The Location of Culture* does contain references to Indian history, the 1857 war, subaltern historians, a stray reference to Tagore, but I failed to locate any to Gandhi, Radhakrishnan, Krishnamurthi or any other major Indian writers (other than Rushdie that too under 'racism'). As against this there are at least thirty references to Fanon, several to Kristeva, Foucault and Freud. Mohanty's *Literary Theory and the Claims of History* has passing references to Ahmad, Bhabha and Spivak, an unlimited number to Fredric Jameson and Derrida and some to Lacan, Paul de Man and Althusser. Ania Loomba and Leela Gandhi's introductory works on Postcolonialism – both published abroad and in the same year are equally west-oriented. In Loomba's work Aurobindo, Ramabai, Rakhmabai and Indulekha get one mention each, Gandhi five while references to Fanon, Said, South Africa, Africa abound. Spivak ranges with them. Leela Gandhi gives four references to Gandhi, none independently to *Hind Swaraj*, some to Partha Chatterjee, a few to Ranajit Guha, two to Tagore while Bhabha, Fanon, Said and Spivak get several. In India, both the volume on *Nativism* (ed. Makarand Paranjape) and *Critical Theory* (ed. Prafulla C. Kar) carry no indices (a fact which says the unsaid). *Nativism* by virtue of its subject could not avoid Gandhi. There is also a reference to Daya Krishna and Gurbhagat Singh writes about the Adi Granth in Paranjape's volume. Concerns may differ from theory to theory, but it is obvious that the location and readership of the writer have a great deal to do with the thrust, that Gandhi is a marginal name in postcolonial theory and when explored, his ideas are seen to reflect a counter modernity (as Robert Young has observed), that he appears to have little visibility in oppositional theories and resistance discourses. Along with him we can dismiss most of our philosophers, past and present and go on to discard the interventions of our intellectuals in the formation of cultural texts.

In 1989, W.J.T. Mitchell had used the colonial metaphor of production, raw material versus finished product with reference to literature and theory. He had commented that while the most interesting literature was being produced in the colonies, the most provocative literary criticism was being produced in the erstwhile imperial centres, a situation which reflected the earlier division of labour. Colonial relations had not really ceased to exist instead they were more concealed and insidious.[2] Fifteen years down the road it still continues to be true and is an issue which calls for an intellectual review. Nativism was not able to sustain itself, and the business of research often ends in fragmented statements or descriptions. Theoretical frameworks often stand apart from what they contain. A doubt begins to surface that perhaps we are not at home with theory.

Between the theorist and the text is also the young scholar critic, a person who does not make original formulations but by making intelligent use of existing theories and applying them critically in order to open their implications prepares for the onward journey towards independent thinking. Theory apparently has a multiplicity of functions and one among these to enable the unearthing of meaning and to help trace out histories of cultural genealogy. We theorise also for collectivity and a continuity, to discern a pattern in the flow of events and the mysterious link it has on the actions of men. It does become, at one level, a hermeneutic code.

Continuing with the *bhasha* specific argument of *Desivaad*, translations across languages have a crucial role to play in the construction of any theoretical position. It is simply not possible to rely any longer on single language histories. In order to recognise the full meaning and impact of India's plurality, the simple metaphor of separate and independent existence, the 'thali' does not appear to be adequate. But assimilative, mainstreaming tendencies are equally unpalatable. Nevertheless, it is apparent that India does not easily lend itself to polarities. I draw attention to an insightful essay by Gurbhagat Singh (an essay which has not received the debate it deserves), 'The Betrayal of Polyphony: Blocked Possibilities of Criticism in India'. Singh projects his theory in three stages. Rejecting a unitary identity, he elaborates upon the concept of 'migrant ontology' – those recognisable features which travel to alien semantics and phonology and conduct themselves in opposition to the imperial metanarratives' (90). Next, he distinguishes between 'difference' and 'differential'. While the first stresses dissimilarity and perhaps uniqueness, the second emphasises distinction and recognises plurality. It automatically rejects a unitary structure. The third step he advocates is the emergence of a differential criticography which seeks to interpret the ontology of each *bhasha* literature as a product and negation of its own genetic geo-culture (93). Singh's theory rejects the imagined unity projected by Gandhi, Nehru and Kabir and projects a confederative one. Singh critiques the hegemony of Sanskrit aesthetics which has led to separatism and enclosures, to the indifference to other languages like Pali and Apbhramshas and its failure to meet the challenge from Muslim cultures. There are living traditions, more flexible and porous. He gives the example of *Adi Granth* and its composition which established the right of the languages traditions to intervene in a major way. Homogeneity privileges power, polarities lead to subordination and inequality in terms of value, but plurality enables exchange and interaction. Any move of a migrant ontology leaves behind a residue. As one travels from one part of India to another, from one language to another, residual elements are traceable even though socio-economic histories differ.

It is exactly in this polyphonic discourse, in the crossing of borders and boundaries that the possibility of a new interpretative discourse lies, for despite all these differences there is an identifiable degree of commonalty in history, in the sense of time, in kinship patterns and in the relationship to land. Another writer whose intervention deserves attention is Agyeya. At a time when the neo-postcolonialists were engaged in defining their positions and the *desivaad* school caught up in its own language euphoria, two lectures were delivered by him under the Samvatsar series in 1986, coinciding with Rajiv Gandhi's call to the nation to take a 'quantum leap' into the twenty-first century. These two talks responded to the political situation of the time in cultural terms and framed an indigenous position. In *Smriti aur Kal* (Memory and Time) and *Smriti aur Desh* (Memory and Space), Agyeya works out the affiliates of time and space. There is no single measurement of time. Agyeya moves backwards and, in accordance with the Samvat, locates the beginning of the twenty-first century in 1942, the Quit India period – a movement which was also important to us as a nation. The imposition of the Gregorian calendar, (which is now referred to as the Common Era), pushes us into oblivion, our histories into pre-histories, and dismisses the intellectual debates of an earlier period as irrelevant. He argues for the simultaneity of multiple time frames. A logical mind immediately perceives that by this recognition the notion of uni-directional, linear progress is also dislocated. In India there are several time-frames which live side by side, the Hijri, the Zoroastrian, the Sikh calendar and so on. Again if the marker of A.D. is once dislocated the line drawn between *itihaas* – that which is known to be so, and the *puranas, mithihas,* that which is believed to have happened, is also blurred. Agyeya argues that distant pasts, like the birth and identity of Christ, also have plural versions and are veiled in uncertainties. The relationship between reality and imagination is not as final as one would like to believe. The imagined begins differently, it takes us out of oneself, but sooner or later the imagined begins to become a part of the real. The rejection of the imposition of the Gregorian calendar, to the singular time flow, of the arbitrary dismissal of the *puranas* as prehistory, also unsettles the time-lag theory and historical periodisations.

Going on to dwell on the nature of memory, he points out that it is never concrete or real. Earlier memories get overlaid by later memories, memories can be transformed through dislocation and disrupted through imposed or willed amnesia. All perceptions of reality are also perceptions of memory. Further the limits of one's memory are the limits of one's identity – just as Wittgenstein had pointed out that the limits of one's language are the limits of one's world. It is amazing to think of this in these terms, connections which we are all aware of, but have never put them in these terms.

Memory is the *active* principle in literary creativity. By dismissing the division into history and prehistory and erasing the difference between the imagined and the real as constructs of memory Agyeya frees the contemporary writer from the burden of imposed frameworks, prioritises multiplicity and connects the projected reality of a literary text with memory, rather than with 'protest'. By emphasising the significance of location, he offers us a counter-theory for engagement with diasporic writing. The journey outward in the case of many of our intellectuals like Gandhi, Jiddu Krishnamurthi and several others, and of diasporic populations is a shifting of location where a disjunction has been effected with memory, a disjunction which brings about a sense of insecurity, bewilderment and existential awareness, a disjunction which pushes them towards crystallising memory. When I read Agyeya's second talk on '*Smriti aur Desh*', the whole debate about the diasporic writer's concern with memory, history and homeland acquired a new perspective. They were the substance with which identities were fortified.

The anchoring in a location is not merely a comfortable security, it determines 'perspective' – the way one looks at the past and the imagined 'real'. Agyeya's essay can be read in several ways, and at several levels. It is concerned both with the physical presence of space and with the unconscious limits or expanses it makes available to us. One is led into an awareness of both power and reality in a 'space-time continuum' (116). Just as memory limits one's identity, the limits of space limit our being. They act as 'confines', they assert or deny our authority. 'Exclusion' and 'Inclusion' thus are defined by the kind of authority one can exercise in a given space. But beyond these social and physical dimensions, there is also the access to cultural space and to the expanse of imagination. Spatial dimensions can be imagined both inversely and reversely, and through this imagination has the power to subvert the tyranny of space, to deconstruct rigid constructs and to accommodate modernity. In fact, the moment we place tradition within the continuum of time, the static position of both tradition and modernity are challenged.

I refer to these two essays for more reasons than one. They stand between the limiting ideology of '*desivaad*' and the 'raw material-finished product' syndrome. They also refute the need for the one kind of mainstreaming recognised by the dominant dialogue with western theories. Instead they offer a hope for horizontal interconnections between our multi-lingualism and multi-cultural inheritance. They create the possibility for journeys across the barriers of time and language, and for the use of polyphony as a strength to facilitate work towards an interpretative discourse. Agyeya's essays are of importance to post-postcolonial theorists not because they talk of time and space but because they (i) emphasise the interconnection between culture and memory, and time and memory (ii) also because the simultaneity of time which is not merely a parallel awareness of more than one kind of time but one which (a) destabilises power relationships, (b) is dismissive of the 'theory of lack', and indirectly of the time-lag theory, and above all because (c) it pushes one to locate outside 'postcolonial' space. I also refer to them because there are other writers and thinkers who, like Agyeya, have made important statements and worked out philosophical positions, which are either not visible, or not applied in critical practice. They constitute the untapped seam which the young academia is missing out on. Theory is meant to initiate the mind into a direction of inquiry, and not an attitude of submission. I end with a quotation from the philosopher Jiddu Krishnamurthi, which provides us a methodology for research:

> To understand the fact, you must come to it inquisitively, not positively. The positive mind, the positive attitude in one of determined opinion – a conditioned outlook, with a traditional point of view which is established, to which you automatically respond. (32)

Notes

1. Also see Sudhir Kumar's 'Nation versus Nativism' Kumar argues that nativism as a language-specific literary theory is 'too narrow a discourse to be tenable for long'. Though he also advocates a falling back upon the 'positive saliences' of Sanskrit tradition (122).
2. Mitchell wrote this in the *Chronicle of Higher Education*, 1989. My reference is through Darshan Perushek's citation in 'Postcolonial Realities, Poststructuralist Diversions. An Unamused Exchange,' *Economic and Political Weekly*, January 29, 1994.

5

Issues in Historiography*

When one thinks of Srinivasa Iyengar,[1] one automatically thinks of historiography. The two go together as he was a pioneer where the history of Indian writing in English is concerned. The persistence, the devotion, the ongoing additions, expansions, new editions all bear testimony to the tremendous effort he spent on not only writing the literary history but also responding to its constantly changing demands. He first brought it together in 1943 as *Indo-Anglian Literature*, following it up two years later by *Indian Contribution to English Literature* (1945). The next version was to come nearly fifteen years after independence in the form of *Indian Writing in English* (1962) when he put together the lectures he had delivered at Leeds in 1958. An enlarged edition appeared in 1973 and subsequently several reprints have followed. Despite the fact that several other histories of Indian Writing in English have appeared since then, the authority and the comprehensive range of his work go unmatched.

The centenary celebrations naturally call for both: an evaluation of the problems that beset historiography and the importance of literary history in its own right. For in no case is it possible to treat it merely as an account of literary happenings or a recording of literary publications. Instead it spills over into every

---

* Srinivas Iyengar Centenary Celebration, Inaugural Address delivered on 10 December 2007 at Andhra Pradesh University, Visakhapatnam.

sphere of life and its ramifications touch almost all aspects of socio-cultural life as caste, class and language, education and the power structures it nurtures, the idea of nationhood and that of tradition with its multiple strands all find a reflection in the literary artifact.

Literary histories have followed different courses. Early histories based their interpretation on linguistic identities and equated Sanskrit with Indian tradition. We have accepted this all along, but there is an another aspect to be foregrounded, that of the claim of Tamil as an ancient literature and a formulative influence upon the making of literary traditions. The division of languages into Indo-Aryan and Indo-Dravidian brought about an unnatural division in literary culture.[2] But this equation of Sanskrit with India demonstrates how language – in this case of the elites; power vested in the upper classes, and nation as represented by a territory come together to constitute the basis of literary history. I draw attention to this in order to work out the basic framework and also to problematise the same. Apparently this three-fold base does not work in the case of IWE (Indian Writing in English), which in any case has journeyed through several avatars. It began as Anglo-Indian and was concerned with the writings of the British about India, then moved on to Indo-Anglian. It foregrounded the national identity and the constituents also changed. Later when the concern was with Indians, it slid into a clumsy description as Indian English which was neither hyphenated nor a description of the language in use and this had soon to be replaced by the circuitous description 'Indian Writing in English' disrupting at one stroke the accepted relationship between nation and language. Srinivasa Iyengar's history as embodied in his lectures delivered at Leeds recognises this rupture, though the writer does not talk about the many problems that may have confronted him or account for the choices he made. I propose here first to list the various issues that clamour for attention then move on to the manner in which some writers have addressed them, and finally work out the priorities of historiography in our times.

Literary historiography owes its development to the growth in the reading public, the fostering of national sentiment and the onset urban life in the eighteenth century – factors which impacted the role of the writer. It coincided with the growth of imperialism as well as with the expansion of the notion of freedom. The contradictory impulses – attraction towards the west and simultaneously a resistance to it – made power a negotiable term. Scholars in India have largely accepted the idea that literary historiography is of western origins. This misconception is due to our adherence to form; there is a need to realise that literary history is written and has been written in several different ways: Ganesh Devy in *Of Many Heroes: An Indian Essay in Literary Historiography* (1998) has traced out some early beginnings in India by moving out to plural histories and working through different categories of writing such as the *suta* and the *mantra* literatures and drawing attention to the commentaries on classic texts which successive generations of scholars have indulged in (29–35).

Historiography as a discipline needs to be freed from any single or fixed model primarily for the reason that there is none. Different scholars have evolved their own strategies and worked out different priorities – chronological, ideological, genre-based divisions or bibliographical approaches; some have worked through reception theories. It is difficult to define or lay down normative parameters of literary historiography. One way as well begin with the question: Why history? Is literature not good enough in itself? Why is a literary history necessary? Who is the likely reader and what does this history say? These questions need to be addressed before one can determine as to what are the likely methodologies or sources that can be appropriated for this purpose.

Why does man historicise? Apparently to trace lineages, establish continuities, extract some meaning from the happenings around him and relate them to the present, acquire authority and if not authority, at least an overwhelming sense of cohesion. History is a record. And Gandhi in *Hind Swaraj* said that history is ordinarily an account of conquests (*Hind Swaraj* 89).[3] Struggles and processes often have no history. India and Indians have often been targeted as a historical people, people without a history or a sense of history. [See Romila Thapar, *Time as a Metaphor of History: Early India*. New Delhi: OUP, (1996), 2006]. Applying the same analogy to literary history, one may take it to be the visibility and influence of certain texts. Whereas this would be a record of shifts in style, in subject matter and concerns, this record may be a misrepresentation and the canon thus formed a truncated one. A literary text is often misjudged by its own contemporary readership. The manner in which failed texts phoenix-like rise out of their ashes, compels us to consider a wider role for literary historiography.

Both history and theory flourish in, and because of, the academia. They have been treated as rival claimants for space in the academic syllabi.[4] One is seen to push the other out. This was also one of the major fallouts of the close textual reading propagated by new criticism. The historiographer today has to review and explore their relationship to each other: do they merely impinge or do they – that is, history and theory – feed on each other in order to redefine themselves? In fact it is the literary artifact, the primary work of literature, which happens to be at the centre of both. And this work is not autonomous or self-contained. It relates to life, imagines it, fictionalises it, moves out from the page to external happenings, socio-cultural issues, political power structures and inwards into the human mind. Literature works through narratives; in the same measure literary historiography is a narrative, a constructed narrative, organised towards leading to a particular meaning. Like the writer, the historian selects certain events, builds up his plot, works it towards a climax and relates it to temporality. It is not for nothing that Hayden White borrowed the idea of emplotment from fiction. Histories have their plots, their frames, their core ideology as they relate to the outer event in history, reflect the change in cultural reception and continue with the specific objective they may have in mind – nation construction, recovery of tradition, new definitions or providing a source for future research.[5] It is on account of all these factors that histories have to be written. Those who do not have one, invent it. American academia had to make a concerted effort to separate their literature from that of the mother country. In the beginning it was an invention. In India, we are differently placed, especially when it comes to English language writing. We use the language but not the culture or the social milieu. And our political history is different. One of the factors which needs to be problematised is the nature of this difference.

Let me return briefly to Srinivasa Iyengar's monumental work on Indian Writing in English. It is a work infused with national pride, it is a response to the 'civilisation discourse', histories written by the imperial rulers and, in 1958, the assessment is guided by the need to project the literary tradition of an erstwhile colony, now an independent country, to a foreign, non-culture audience. Therefore it problematises difference. It looks for its own strengths and like Swami Vivekananda's speech in the Parliament of Religions,[6] Iyengar's main stress is on spiritual strength. But his objectivity and training as a scholar push him to look at the beginnings, at Hindu College and the ensuing debates. The debates in nineteenth century Calcutta were also part of a rising national consciousness. The literature of self-definition is prioritised above all else. Writers like Sri Aurobindo – of whom he was a lifelong devotee – and then Gandhi and Nehru are taken up for building up a sense of national worth. These writers were engaged in looking for alternative traditions, alternative power-structures and in discovering their own inner strength. Iyengar's history, being a response to the imperial perceptions of culture, fell comfortably in place with the requirement both of the academic mission as well as that of a newly independent nation. It progresses along a genre-based chronological narration. Within the genre divisions, it is a writer-based history as some of the writers are discussed at length and in fair amount of detail. Bengal Renaissance interests him though nowhere does he use that term; there are two chapters on Tagore and three on Sri Aurobindo. The latter are also an elaborate discourse on Indian spirituality. From there he moves on to political prose before taking up the development of the novel. There is a single chapter on women writers though the account covers both the beginnings of the novel in the late nineteenth century and the modern period till the late sixties – from Krupa Satthianadhan to Anita Desai. In itself it is a monumental work. A huge amount of research has gone into it; a great deal of information is provided, minor writers, beginners, dropouts are also briefly mentioned especially wherever Gandhian impact is traced. These are writings which are not easy to trace and Iyengar continues to remain our main source of information. Faithful to its time, today when we place it side by side with certain other literary histories, we are in a better position to gauge its merit. Srinivasa Iyengar presents a record not only of the writings but also of the major ideological flows: the spiritual as well as the political. With the sole exception of the chapter on women writers, others are placed together in ideological clusters. It is a storehouse for future researchers. But its own growth from a base to its superstructure does not indicate the major problems a historiographer faces.

Any attempt at writing the history of Indian Writing in English is beset with problems primarily because of the rupture in the relationship between language and national culture. Invariably it has been perceived as a response to a new culture, and in its relationship to the language of the imperial rulers; it has laid claim to the literary tradition of England. It is born of a twin parentage and is hence divided between language and culture. As a result the cultural half gets an advantage where historiography is concerned. Sujit Mukherjee in 'Indo-English Literature: An Essay in Definition' had asked the question 'where do we accommodate translation?' Mukherjee refers to V.K. Gokak's use of the words 'Indo-Anglian' for works originally written in English and 'Indo-English' for works translated into English. Mukherjee seeks a further division and asks for a separate treatment for works translated by the authors themselves, as Tagore and now Girish Karnad do (205), on the ground that a self-translator accommodates the claims of language, while when the work is translated by another it is more closely rooted in the language of original composition. In another work, Sujit Mukherjee questioned the periodisation of Indian literature under the time-lag theory (Refer *Towards a Literary History of India* and *Some Positions on a Literary History of India*). Here one is able to see that Indian Writing in English is closer to other Indian literatures than to the writing of British authors. Iyengar's history, however, does not work along these lines hence the problem does not arise for him.

What happens when the outsider writes literary history? Despite a better grip over the language, the outsider is distanced by the cultural density of the literature. William Walsh, a respected scholar in the field of Commonwealth Studies, brought out a history – *Indian Literature in English* – in 1990. Obviously the book is meant for students of Indian Literature all over the world and having been written by a Britisher and published in England (William Walsh is Professor Emeritus at Leeds), it has greater visibility than the various other histories that have followed Iyengar's. I want to look at it briefly on two counts: its organisation and its ideology. It follows a genre-division but drama is totally absent. It also includes a chapter on British writers who have written about India. One wonders whether the last chapter beginning with Kipling and ending with Farrell has a legitimate place in it. Again R.K. Narayan, on whom Walsh has a separate book, finds a place of pride in this. Almost all his novels are discussed in detail while Anand and Rao get a quarter of the space – their work is discussed in ten pages while Narayan has as many as twenty pages devoted to him. Is this the making of a canon, a critical evaluation, a personal preference, or a shortcut? Where is the balance? *Auchitya* as we call it. Does the literary historiographer have the right to define literary preferences in this manner?

As for the ideology, right in the 'Foreword', Walsh takes up a superior position – when he writes about the making of the Empire, and describes English as a link language which is a 'powerful testimony to the expressive and creative capacities of the English language itself' (vii). But as one reads the book not only is Walsh's history one-sided, replete with political generalisations, but even his sense of geography is inaccurate. For him the Indian National Congress developed into a powerful Hindu Socialist party to which the Raj was compelled to hand over the government of 'non-Muslim India' (28); William Bentinck is a *large minded* Governor General (31) (one wonders for whom?). Then again 'There is no word either for religion or spirituality in any of the Indian languages' (36). Bengal becomes the Sikh heartland (16). I would rather not go on listing the many biases that the work is replete with, and which are not visible to the outsider, or even to many of the younger generation of Indian scholars. But I refer to it primarily because it substantiates my point that historiography faces many pitfalls, especially the difficulty of being objective. In Walsh's work the nature of emplotment is based on imperial ideology.

The writing of any literary history is problematic, but these problems are manifold in India because we have a multi-lingual tradition; there is a long tradition of oral literatures and also because we are still caught up in colonialism in two entirely different ways. First, we address the west, work through a system of responses as if the stimuli is somewhere else. Thus we forego our agency. Sisir Kumar Das's two-volume history of modern Indian literature, subtitles the first volume as a response to the west. Part of this is historically true, because we work through the history of British encroachments in India and follow the course of their control: that is, our methodology is wrong. We fail to turn our attention to all else that falls outside it. The second reason is that we look for similar structures and quickly come to the conclusion that literary history – like the term nation, the ideology of resistance, of feminism, and literary forms like the novel – has come from the west. But if we were to look around and notice the different concepts available to us in our traditions, and the narrative forms that have evolved over a period of time, we suddenly realise that these forms have contributed a great deal to modern writing. In fact, the forms and concepts that are said to have been imported have been stretched to accommodate the native forms in ways that compel us to realise the limits of our initial premise. Edward Said in his essay 'Traveling Theories' has elaborated upon the idea how theories and concepts travel but falling on different soils they do not remain the same. Again, Homi Bhabha's essay on 'Postcolonialism and Postmodernism' in *The Location of Culture* explores the dependence of postmodernism on postcolonialism. In fact, they are not only parallel in time, they have an almost incestuous relationship in this that they have used similar materials like oral traditions, non-conclusive endings and magic realism; materials are similar, but the impulses are different. It is to work out these parallels, interactions and interdependence that literary histories have to be written time and again covering the same ground but interpreting it anew. Every new history demands a re-evaluation of the earlier formulations; it intervenes with earlier assessments. No two literary histories are the same. The historiographer is constantly called upon to define his location – in time, in culture, in ideology – and to define a framework.[7] The latter demands the principles of inclusion and exclusion to be adopted. There is a constant tussle between the hermeneutics of interpretation and the compulsion to relate to a larger socio-cultural narrative. What then are our basic expectations from the historiographer? We turn to history in order to get a sense of time, to be able to see things in continuity, to trace traditions, to mark the shifts in sensibility, the crisis in society, the transformations of form and to be able to pick up the missing links. This, in itself, is a tall order. Often, the question is asked is literary history a substitute for literary criticism? Is the historian a judge? Then it is very likely that a great deal may be excluded, understated or abandoned. As a literary critic he may be inattentive to the overall atmosphere of ideas. But on the other hand if no evaluative norm is applied, it is reduced to a mere record, existing in limbo for future investigations.

Iyengar himself did not use the word 'history'. Others have also often stayed away from it. But histories are being written all around through selections, anthologies, hagiographies, and comparative studies. Selections help both in canon-formation and its destabilisation, while comparative studies move horizontally into similar yet different structures. Selections, through the act of repetition, keep literary memory alive, and through newness call for the expansion of received ideas and existing perspectives. We have a variety of examples where methodology is concerned. In English literature, Legouis and Cazamian progress through literary periodisation, Boris Ford's multi-volume history is a collaborative effort, but it is very consciously set against historical and cultural specificities marked by the flow of time; other histories are specific to a period like the Victorian Age or the eighteenth century, still other work with ideas – like Basil Willey's background studies. These work through observation, recording, interpretation, reception and a host of other narrative techniques.

Do we have something similar happening today in our own country? We too have histories working with the pluralism of India and its multi-lingual traditions – the multi-volumed history being produced by Sahitya Akademi; and then mono-language histories of all literatures, there are also several interventions by theorists. Susie Tharu and K. Lalitha in their two-volume work *Women Writing in India: 600 B.C. to the Present*, have provided a historical view of women's writing across languages. The biographical notes and the lengthy introduction use chronology, social background, biography and theory. The selection is also an evaluation. The missing elements are the sources for the researcher to investigate and pursue. Sisir Kumar Das in his two-volume history from 1800 to 1956 has also worked across languages but through genre developments. He has put the work together through a collaborative effort, provided chronological details, included minor writers and has given a chronology of publication details and political events. But one has to turn elsewhere for information on translations.

My own three-volume work not only moves across languages but the middle volume is written in Punjabi (and not English). I work with the purpose of reperiodising and reconceptualising the nation with the purpose of bringing in the women writers more centrally and constructing the nation as marked by pluralism, moving away from the dominant idea of a Hindu nation. The first volume concerns itself with narrative origins, the second with relocating modernism in historical time, the third in moving beyond postcolonialism, the widespread engagement with which is increasingly leading to literary myopia, and stalls our moving ahead to explore native concerns. *Beyond Postcolonialism* goes on to work with classical aesthetics and experiential aesthetics. The latter brings one to subaltern history and subaltern writing. Subaltern writing finds a place in English through translation while history is initiated by a group of scholars, some of whom are located in the west. Dalit writing is experiential, political and ideological. As literary representation it asks for a whole new framing and conceptualisation. In fact it calls for a revision in our aesthetic norms.

When it comes to the writing of history of Indian Writing in English, in some measure we move outside both mono-lingual and multi-lingual frameworks. While single-language histories are concerned with a region and a language, multi-language histories look for interflows and influences that help to construct the nation. In a larger sense they set out to recover the past, self-worth and agency, IWE constitutes a third category. This is because it rides astride two different entities: one, a linguistic tradition, the other a cultural specificity. Here the legitimate constituents of a literary history are heightened. Power relationships are also double-edged – it may be still elitist vis-à-vis the other languages and it needs to demarcate its territory vis-à-vis the diaspora which, more often than not, is distanced from the raw reality of life in India. English language writing even as it constructs the nation, presents different facets of nationhood, both here and abroad. The diasporic frames need to be opened out for their perception and nature of representation. The way in which India, its culture and history are being used becomes in itself an important question. More than the physical location of the author the emotional affiliation and authenticity should be placed under the scanner. Ordinarily territory and language may go together; or a travelling language and strong affiliations with a cultural territory may be at work – but at times the perspective is that of the outsider – distanced, non-comprehending or misrepresenting. It is a pity that western recognition, awards and reception are making inroads into our evaluative structures. I have no intention of attacking the writer's freedom to write or use material in any way, but I am critical of the manner in which we tend to be blindly guided by trends set in the west – whether it is the reception of a text, a theoretical formulation or a critical opinion. The centre has to be where we are; interpretation and questioning of theoretical formulations also have to flow from here. If the text is no longer a self-contained autonomous structure, critical evaluation is also guided by perception partly determined by location and affiliation. Literary histories by working as overarching narratives may allow us to discern the centre more clearly. It is obvious that there cannot be two centres; even as we work for a decentring of positions a power relation is involved and our dominant concerns have shifted over the years from influences and nation construction to resistance, margins and indigeneity. The effort has been even in the past to look for an equal relationship. If we worked with influences, we also worked with 'Indian contribution' to western literature. An interaction was also visible in the response theory when several noted scholars worked with 'Indian Response' to a particular writer like Whitman, Emerson or Steinbeck. It indicated a question of sensibility, of an emotional approach rooted in culture.

The emplotments of literary history are variously framed. R.S. Crane in *Critical and Historical Principles of Literary History* (1971) traces the main forms as (i) organic – which explains causation; (ii) historical which traces continuities and (iii) the atomistic which works through moments of change, the epicenter of crises (Devy 99–100). Perhaps all three approaches can work together as cause and effect explain shifts of power, dislocation of agency and go on to revive an undercurrent.

The literary historiographer today may not delve deep into the interpretation of texts but he has to work with an evaluative framework. He is not a mere recorder, he is also an interpreter of trends both ideological and literary. The challenge before him is two-fold: how to attain objectivity and how to retain balance, that is to prevent his personal preferences of writers and ideas from carrying him away. If the 'histor' is a judge as the Greek origin explains, then he too is to be judged by posterity for his imbalances. In fact, the responsibility of the historian is greater than that of the writer and the critic. The writer is accountable to himself and his contemporary reader, the critic can afford to be subjective and impassioned; but the historian carries the burden of continuity as he stands between the past and future. His response to the moment thus becomes extremely important as the work is going to be read contemporaneously and is also likely to frame future receptions. It constitutes a benchmark in itself; future scholars are going to use it as a point of departure even as they rewrite his text. Thus he has constantly to negotiate his role as a recorder, moving between history and literary history, between experience and representation, between an abstract idea and a linguistic expression, and has to learn to discriminate between marketability and authenticity.

Nothing, and least of all knowledge, is to be taken on trust. In order to make both the writing and reading of literature dynamic, there is need to be constantly engaged in the task of interrogating texts, ideas, theories and choices. Departments of English (and Comparative Literature) are the centres of debate and it is here that new directions for historiography have to be worked out. Where are we heading in terms not only of employment or acquisition of knowledge, but production of knowledge, becomes an important issue which should concern both the academician and the historian.[8]

Finally, I return to Srinivasa Iyengar's *Indian Writing in English* which works within a nationalistic framework and ask myself the question what has it done for me, and for hordes of other scholars; what were our expectations from it and were they fulfilled? Its greatest strength is that even as he writes at length about spirituality, he does not allow it to descend into a religious debate; again, with the detailed references to now-forgotten writers, or non-available material, he has created a source for future researchers if they can hunt in the public libraries for the plays of Kailasham and the novels of Venkatraman; yet again he has not fallen into the west-initiated periodisation and the excessive glamourisation of the Bengal Renaissance. In fact, he has worked through writers and formulated a thesis on the basis of his own interpretation. But perfection is not human: his responses to the modern sensibility are timid. Modern writers are an appendage to the work, the real strength for him lies elsewhere. Fully aware of these limits one still admires the task he has performed and the spirit that egged him on.[9] It is worthy not merely of our admiration but also our homage. I am glad that I am part of these centenary celebrations which have provided the opportunity of doing a whole lot of rethinking on literary history and its multiple frames.

Notes

1. K.R. Srinivasa Iyengar (1908–1999) served as professor of English and later as Vice-Chancellor of Andhra University (1966–1968). Among his several publications are works of criticism, biography and poetry. I especially want to draw attention to his works on Sri Aurobindo, Swami Vivekananda and the Mother, which form a dominant current in his writing.
2. See K.S. Srinivasan, *The Ethos of Indian Literature: A Study of Its Romantic Tradition* (Delhi: Chanakya Publications 1985), where Srinivasan questions the sole identification of Sanskrit as a literary language representative of India by British historians and scholars. Tamil and Prakrit 'too have a heritage of considerable antiquity'. He goes on to critique the Orientalists' selection of texts to be translated and the separation between Sanskrit and Tamil leading to 'tomes on literature, in isolation, e.g. Sanskrit or Tamil, not Sanskrit and Tamil.' Srinivasan explores the etymological roots of Dravida, *dravita* and Vindhya and the misinterpretation of these words. He writes, 'The harm done by such "knowledge" can't be estimated; but it is not difficult to see that partial perception, which led to partial truths, supported by unfounded etymology has led to the rousing of passions that fly, mounted on words' (1–5).
3. Gandhi in his search for a definition of history (and for the history of passive resistance), writes 'The Gujarati equivalent means. "It so

happened". If that is the meaning of history, it is possible to give copious evidence. But, if it means the doings of kings and emperors, there can be no evidence of soul-force or passive resistance in such history .... History, as we know it, is a record of the wars of the world ....' *Hind Swaraj*, 89 (In *Hind Swaraj and Other Writings* Ed. Anthony J. Parel, Cambridge Univ Press, 1997, ed. used New Delhi: Foundation Bks Pvt Ltd. 1997, 2005).

4. See Edward W. Said, 'Secular Criticism', *The World, the Text and the Critics* (Cambridge, Massachusetts: Harvard University Press, 1983). 4–5. Said foregrounds the 'connection between texts and the existential actualities of human life, policies, societies and events' (5).
5. Though Hayden White's emplotment basis itself on Northrop Frye's four-fold division in *The Anatomy of Criticism* into Romance, Tragic, Comic and Satirical, yet it is a useful approach for the examination of literary history and compels one to recognise the relationship between the two – history and literary history.
6. Swami Vivekananda addressed the World Parliament of Religions in 1893, where in he projected India's unique strength as characterised by its spirituality and pursuit of moksha and went on to conceptualise Hinduism as a search for perfection (uncannily echoing Nietzche's belief in the superman). For the addresses, refer *Swami Vivekananda: An Anthology.* Ed. Bimal Prasad (New Delhi: Vikas Publishing House 1994, 1996). 1–20.
7. A useful perspective is provided by Veena Das's article 'Subaltern as Perspective', *Subaltern Studies VI.* Ed. by Ranajit Guha (Delhi: OUP, 1994) In fact the whole volume is of significance.
8. See M.K. Naik's 'Preface' to his *A History of Indian English Literature* (1982), wherein he writes, 'while the needs of a systematic chronological survey have been kept in mind throughout, the responsibility of rigorous critical evaluation has not been sought to be evaded'. Also see the introduction to *India's Literary History: Essays on the Nineteenth Century.* Eds. Stuart Blackburn and Vasudha Dalmia. (New Delhi: Permanent Black, 2004), where besides periodisation and the cultural meaning, literary histories it is maintained also help reinvent tradition.
9. Srinivasa Iyengar also published a work in 1961, *Drama in Modern India and the Writer's Responsibility in a Rapidly Changing World* (Bombay). I have not been able to lay my hands on it. But the work gone into it is reflected in Iyengar's chapter on drama. I also draw attention to another lesser known work by the same author. *Literature and Authorship in India.*

6

From Gadar to Gandhi via *Anand Math**

The present paper sets itself the task of tracing one aspect of the 'resistance discourse' in nineteenth century colonial India. In itself the term 'resistance discourse' appears to be very simple and straightforward and uni-directional, signifying opposition, a questioning and a defiance, all at the same time, but the moment one seeks a definition, it becomes complex and elusive. Both the words 'resistance' and 'discourse' immediately relate to the world outside the text – not only in its immediacy but also historically and through memory. And as both are located in language, in the speech-act, they summon the notion of 'meaning', of cause and purpose and also of reference. Commenting upon resistance discourse, in the postcolonial context, Jenny Sharpe has defined it as a 'rupture in the representation of British colonialism as a civilizing mission' (Sharpe 99), which immediately brings in the issue of identity and subjecthood, as well as the need of projecting an alternative. Not only does 'resistance' reflect upon an opposition, but it also foregrounds other socio-economic inequalities, differences and dissensions. This move towards 'difference' simultaneously seeks to negotiate with 'sameness' as well, (because all inequalities rest on the premise of difference). The formation of identity and the acquisition of an agency become primary concerns even as the power-conflicts play themselves out.

* Presented at a Conference at Saurashtra University, Rajkot, Gujarat.

The term 'discourse' is equally invested with multiplicity (of meaning and purpose). Paul Ricoeur in his essay, 'Human Sciences and Hermeneutical Method: Meaningful Action Considered as Text' (14–15), examines not only the medium of discourse but also its tempero-spatial inferences. His view is that discourse is realised temporally and in the present whereas the language system is virtual and outside time; while language is a condition of communication, discourse is an exchange of thought. The moment a text is written, a disassociation takes place between the author's intention and the meaning of the text. The two cease to coincide. The text becomes free to be interpreted in different ways, ways which are governed by the present context. Apparently the text is perhaps never wholly autonomous (in the new critical sense), instead the author's relationship to it becomes complicated. Further to this, one needs to take the Foucauldian view of power into consideration as any problematisation of 'resistance' needs to confront the concept of power.

For the purpose of this paper, I propose to move between several texts ranging over a period of fifty or more years, across languages and across cultures in order to enter the discourse they have created among themselves and to investigate the manner they spill over into the stream of ideological thought to enter our contemporary discourse. Together they present continuity in the act of opposition and the rupture in the dominant discourse of the Empire. The first of these texts is *Ankhon Dekha Gadar,* a Hindi translation by Amritlal Nagar[1] of a Marathi travelogue *Majha Pravas* by Vishnubhatt Godse Vassaikar. The travelogue is the account of a journey undertaken by a brahmin in search of financial gain. Beginning from a place near Thane, Vishnubhatt travels all over the major cities of central India – Gwalior, Jhansi, Lucknow, Kanpur, Allahabad, Baanpur, Bithoor, Kalpa, Ahmadnagar, Indore, Pune – and describes the various battles, the shifting power-centres, the kinship patterns, royal affiliations, acts of bravery as well as of betrayal and cowardice. Vishnubhatt by virtue of being a brahmin and a traveller is an outsider and does not have to live under the fear of loss or dispossession of any wealth and dislocation. He is outside the immediacy of the struggle, even as he is caught within it. As an observer, he can sense the undertones, the different affiliations and at times the shifting loyalties. But to some extent he is also an insider as he has access to the strategical planning and performs the religious 'yagya' considered necessary for all kinds of beginnings. And his travels provide him access to the different political affiliations and support structures. Dates are not mentioned, but there are abundant references to seasonal changes and months. It is, however, not an immediate record, it is a recollection, written at the request of the historian Rao Bahadur Chintaman Vinayak towards the end of the century, thus dialoguing with the aftermath of the defeat. Vishnubhatt died in 1903 and the travelogue was published posthumously in 1907, fifty years after 1857. It is history, yet not history. There is a mental and an emotional transference to the past and a graphic description of the living conditions, of the instability and uncertainty of the period, the fear and terror let loose, the reprisals and the hangings (109, 129). It remains outside history by its refusal to impose a pattern on the events or to apportion blame or praise. The language, however, constructs a frame as does his religious location. The narrative catches the religious references and the writer's own comments underline them even further. There are constant references to the 'role of destiny' (*Kal vash, grah acche nahin the*, 106–107) and the final defeat is also perceived as a punishment for their sins and suffering as an act of penance. The emphasis on mahurats and horoscopes (42) further reinforces this as do the events ascribed to miraculous divine interventions. The vedas come in for their importance. Temples are built and also demolished (of course by opposing agencies). When a mosque and a temple are built side by side, the fact of religious harmony is foregrounded. Language controls his view of reality as the terms like 'kala' and 'gora' are used, or caste nomenclatures and words like 'Hindustan' are used for the land of his travels, distinguishing it from Maratha country.

What enriches the travelogue even more than this social description is the day by day account of the battle in Jhansi, very much as it happens in the *Mahabharata*. The role of rumours, and the circulation of the chappatis as messages serve to provide a counter system of communication as letters are censored and intercepted. An element of prophecy is also added by reference to the 1757, Battle of Plassey, arousing the hope, that the day of liberation has dawned. The emplotment of the battle scenes is marked by the proclamations of authority – *Khalak Khuda ka, mulk Badshah ka, amal Laxmibai ka* (90) and on the eighth day after the battle had been lost, there is another proclamation *Khalak Khuda ka, mulk Badshah ka, amal angrez sarkar ka* (128). These proclamations become a discourse of power and strategies of psychological control.

As one goes through it, a sense of objectivity becomes evident in the narration. If accounts of loot by the British are presented, similar accounts of Indians indulging in loot are also described. Again, due credit is given to Hindu and Muslim alike – to Begum Hazrat Mahal and to Azimullah Khan as to Laxmi Bai and Nana Saheb. Acts of courage and of consideration of leaders and soldiers alike are admired. But traditional cultural values are in a state of crisis. What does 'loyalty' come to mean in such a context? And where does the conflict between the act of self-preservation and patriotism take us? Help and support are not forthcoming from several areas like Gwalior and Nepal and the South but no judgement is offered on these.

The discourse of an event takes place through a convergence of differing views on the same event. There are several other accounts specially British which focus on the happenings of 1857 both in its immediacy and through retrospection. Of these I would like to focus on two – one written in the form of a diary by William Edwards, a civil servant, published in 1858 and the other by an army officer, Iltudes Thomas Prichard, published in 1860. Edwards's narrative begins in July 1857, two months after the main uprising had surfaced. During these two months he was a wanderer and a fugitive often protected by Indians of all shades (89–90, 161), motivated by different reasons: reward (37), compassion (137) or a mistaken sense of loyalty (helping him to escape through various means 153). Underlying this informer role of passing on the information from one camp to the other, is also a humanistic discourse when the British are perceived as individuals and not as the impersonal enemy (85). Edwards perceives this dislocation of traditional loyalties and the weakening of the bond between landlords and their tenants to be the result of absentee landlords or the new landlords and their indifference, a situation for which the British are responsible.

As the uprising begins, prisons are broken into and the prisoners released adding to the social instability of the period. Edwards is constantly on the move in search of safety, compelled to seek protections from various Indians – Rajputs, Sheikhs and Nawabs, but at the same time somewhat suspicious of them. His hosts may, at any moment, set about to murder him (49, 89–90, 161). This humanistic discourse exists not at a racial level or within a power-relationship but outside them, often drawing attention to relationships, feelings of gratitude or sheer compassion. [Ruskin Bond's *A Flight of Pigeons* (1980), offers another example. The story is based on Ruth Labadoor's account]. For the moment it destroys the gap between 'them' and 'us'. Any query related to the motive behind this compassion is likely to throw up different answers.

Prichard's account is less personal and more descriptive than Edwards's. But his use of language immediately attracts attention. Words like adventure, exciting, rebellion, campaign frame the narrative. There are descriptions of the hardships undergone but for the rest, in Rajpootana (*The Mutiny in Rajpootana*), they merely drifted in and out of the rebellion, partly because there were several principalities who had stayed out of the 'Mutiny' and also because the Rajputs had never wholly associated themselves with the Mughal empire. The soldiers also did not attack them, they simply told them to go. The feudalistic social structure was another restraining factor (229). It is Prichard's conclusion which is important. He points out that it is not only the Indians who are unhappy, even the British are unhappy as they realise the gap between what they profess and what they do and the breach of trust they are constantly a party to (277). The ordinary Indian had encountered the Anglo-Saxon perhaps only in unpleasant ways (278–279) and the lower rungs of the British had been corrupt and avaricious. The Indians really owed them nothing. Malleson in his history of the mutiny has referred to the 'barbaric methods adopted by our forefathers' (Karl Marx in an article in the *New York Daily Tribune* had written about the British incomes in India which drew a picture of discrimination and exploitation).

The British went ahead with their policy of reprisals and adopted several measures to rule out the possibility of any recurrence. The strength of the British forces was increased, the country effectively disarmed and potential disaffection controlled. The fact that the Indians who had initially every advantage and yet failed to succeed, in Prichard's opinion, merely proved their racial inferiority (277). Various terms have been used to describe the events of 1857 – mutiny, *kranti*, uprising, outbreak, insurrection, revolt, and rebellion (Marx and Engels used the word 'revolt'). The shift from mutiny to rebellion took it outside the army and extended the movement to the people. But Veer Savarkar's work *The Indian War of Independence, 1857* went on to frame it as an armed conflict. This change of the terms used was in itself an indication of the changing nature of the discourse. The way the people looked at the British was undergoing a change. Completed in 1907, on the fiftieth anniversary of the rising, it was proscribed by the British government even before it was published. Both the writing of it and the struggle to get it published are amazing achievements in themselves. Relying almost wholly on British sources, it still goes on to create a new discourse, first by stressing the widespread nature of the conflict, and except for a few exceptions tying up the whole country together; second by recognising and highlighting the diplomatic efforts made by men like Azimullah Khan, and third by acknowledging the legitimate place of the Muslims. In fact, the impulse of nation-construction is at work. In the Author's Introduction, Savarkar establishes a continuity with the past: 'the nation that has no consciousness of the past has no future. Equally true it is that a nation must develop its capacity not only of claiming a past but also of knowing how to use it for furtherance of its future' (ix).[2]

At about the same time another book appeared – Gandhi's *Hind Swaraj* or *Indian Home Rule* – which was also proscribed by the Bombay government. *Hind Swaraj* was written in response to the agenda of the revolutionaries with whom Gandhi had had talks in London (*Hind Swaraj* 13). While Savarkar modelled himself on Shivaji and Baji (as Rao Solanki has observed), Gandhi worked through debating methodologies and ideological routes. Strangely enough, Savarkar and the other revolutionaries did not take count of the post-1857 scenario and the measures which the

British had taken to render consolidated armed action difficult; Gandhi on the other hand drew attention to the honing of the human material by working on the concept of *satyagraha*. Both evoked cultural alternatives to the western code and both tapped the religious subconscious even as they posited violent and non-violent methods on the national scene. It needs to be noted that both these polarities had coexisted in Bankim Chandra's *Anand Math* – one of strengthening will power and character through an ascetic discipline and the other of a violent resistance.

Anand Math goes back into history while simultaneously entering into a discourse with the present. But through the fictionalisation of the Sanyasi rebellion of the 1770s as anti-Muslim, the text went on to become the construction of a truncated, inward-looking nationhood.[3] A classic by itself, the novel however does not even emotionally take account of the events of 1857, of the Muslim role in it, or the lessons of diplomacy and vision the struggle has laid before the present. It also ignores the symbolic value of Delhi as the site of contest. Through a division of the nation on religions grounds, the role of the insider informers, the disassociation from the struggle by Hindu governed principalities and kingdoms, the part played by the elite class and landowners is all brushed aside. The code in *Anand Math* uses abstinence as a preparation for warfare and nationhood is framed by the mother-son relationship. While Gandhi went on to use the first to work towards self-reflection and soul force, Savarkar in spelling out the programme of the Hindu Mahasabha used the mother-son relationship to reinforce the holy-land concept as a pre-requisite for nationhood. Again while Gandhi, through expanding his religious consciousness worked towards a humanistic discourse across race, religion and caste, Savarkar drew the boundaries sharper and worked toward Hindutva. The latter fostered masculine value-structures while the former privileged the feminine (Nandy's *The Intimate Enemy* 51–53) and affiliated with the non-Brahmanic discourse. The subsequent discourse which emerged was centrifugal in Gandhi's case and centripetal in Savarkar's case; each discourse went on to develop its own terminology. Tagore's *Home and the World* which has been read as a critique of the concept of growing nationalism by Ashis Nandy, is in fact also a work which problematises the division in the nationalistic movement. Discourse works both through exclusion and inclusion and the various nuances of the world 'swaraj'[4] demonstrated these possibilities. Memory has to be a major trope,[5] even if it is unreliable and selective, because discourse is an attempt at recontextualisation, working through conflict and dialogue. (See Sara Mills's analysis of Michel Pecheux's work in *Discourse* 13).

The nature of resistance discourse is such that it constantly moves between the past and the present, between memory and imagination, and between the actual and the desired. The rights or imagined rights, a people have had at a time in the past are constantly juxtaposed with the present state of deprivation and denial. The memory of battles lost and struggles miscarried is also important to it as is mourning, which consists a major trope in Urdu poetry.[6] It is not for nothing that very often 'resistance' discourses acquire the face of a 'jihad', a religious warfare. In order to rehabilitate the resisting force, or even to widen its area of freedom, references to history become necessary as do the imagined prospects of a new identity and relationships. Very often the boundary between legend and history is blurred, because just as power inscribes its own resistance, resistance generates its own refer myths, Mahasweta Devi's *Operation*? – *Bashai Tudu* (1990) and *Titu Mir* (2003).[7] In fact, it feeds itself and draws its inspiration from earlier resistances. The Sanyasi Rebellion was a rebellion of the peasants and the masses, both Hindus and Muslims, against the British imposition of taxes and revenues. It unleashed a reign of terror; later peasant insurrections fed into it and in the 1830s the Wahabi Movement, once again was an attempt at redefining freedom and the role of religion. Titu Mir's stand was, against injustice and economic disparities. In this chain of events and intermingling of discourses, 1857 – both the conflict and the writings on it – went on to outline new possibilities in nation construction and the role of the individual moral strength. Despite the professed belief in destiny, the people were not free of blame. Gandhi's civil disobedience within a discourse of civility is seen as a 'spectacular resistance' (Bhabha 181) which went on to forge a new concept of heroism.

As discourse relates to the present, and also depends on the trope of memory, the meaning of a text is not closed within it. In its coming into being and passing on into the world – the categories of 'representation' and the 'real' are relevant. Even as it absorbs earlier discourses it feeds into newer one. And in the process it creates a mixed representation and a partial reality. Power – the power to control, to articulate, to interpret – becomes a significant participant. This underlies the need for heterogeneity – the meaning comes to be vested in it, and it goes on to signify that discourse, by its very nature is not unidirectional or monolithic – constantly in motion, constantly fluid, it interacts, generates and permeates reality: Gandhi and Tagore, Ambedkar, Savarkar – were all the time carrying on a continued discourse: when discourse is muffled, conflict begins. Power becomes a dead end, an end in itself. Therein lies the difference between power and resistance. The question to how far is the author responsible for the afterlife of the text remains unanswered.

Notes

1. The text was commented upon in 1948 by N.R. Pathak and subsequently a reprint was brought out sometime in 1950s. Nagar's translation (1949) precedes this reprint and in a second reprint, Nagar went on to confer a new title.
2. In sharp contrast to this are Savarkar's Presidential addresses given to the All India Hindu Mahasabha (1937–1939) brought together in *Hindu Sanghatan: Its Ideology and Immediate Programme* (published by the Presidential office, Mumbai, 1940), N.K. Damle in his Introduction refers to as the Geeta of the Sanghatan. A period of thirty years had transformed the writer of the history of 1857 who had spoken of an integrated India to now concentrate on Hindudom. Nepal which had stayed outside the Indo-British war, was now hailed as a close ally in the pursuit of a Hindu kingdom and religion perceived as the main tie. A common language, a common culture, a common history and a common father land – are the essential characteristics. On these grounds he excluded the Indian Mahomedan, the Jews, Christians and Parsees (6–7). Identity formation, at this juncture, has come to identify itself on almost German lines. There is a 'perfect' merger of religion and motherland

(!) he writes that in *Hindu Sanghatan* the 'Revolutionary Rising' of 1857 was led mostly by Hindu leaders. (56)

3. Bankim Chandra Chatterjee was an employee of the British and while the novel was being serialised he was transferred. The ending of the novel can be accounted for by the desire to keep his employment.
4. In *Hind Swaraj,* Gandhi defined freedom is above all a mental attitude. 'It is swaraj when we learn to rule ourselves. It is, therefore, in the palm of our hands'. (58–59) Savarkar in 1937 defines it as political independence of the Hindus, 'the freedom to grow to their full height' (*Hindu Sanghatan* 18). For Gandhi the journey begins with the individual, who is to be an active agent, for Savarkar, it is the religious community. Also see, 137 for a continued definition of swarajya.
5. Another kind of discourse exists in recollection through proxy. See for example Amritlal Nagar's *Gadar Ke Phool,* (Information Section, Uttar Pradesh, Lucknow, 1957) published on the centenary of the 1857 war, which is a series of interviews with people whose families were in some way or the other involved with the Mutiny) a slender substitute for living memories. Resistance discourse can be constituted even through silences, a dress code or a linguistic strategy. Robert Young with reference to Gandhi has pointed out the effectiveness of such strategies. The cultural code of the period needs to be paid greater attention in order to trace in it the presence of a withholding and a resistance.
6. The loss of Delhi was mourned by many a poet – Bahadur Shah Zafar, the dethroned Emperor himself was a poet whose ghazal कितना है बदनसीब ज़फर, दफन के लिए, दो गज़ ज़मीन भी न मिली कुए यार में। Refer the Introduction and the poems anthologised in Jaan Nisar Akhtar's *Hindustan Hamara* Vol. 2. Resistance discourse is also a lament and a mourning – an 'impossible mourning' (in the Derridean sense), a permanent dispossession, Akhtar mentions the comment of Professor Bari on the rebellion of 1857 as the last breath of feudalism (7). He also gives a long list of poet-martyrs (12). Akhtar's collection historicises the concept of a nation. The world 'Hindustan' struggles with the concept of a mono-religious nativity and the poems reflect the political history through the whole period. The poet has always played a role as inspirer, motivator and recorder. Quoting Shamshur Rehman Farooqi (referring to Farooqi's article '*Hindustan Ki Jange Azadi Mein Urdu Shahri ka Hissa*') he expresses the belief that despite a distancing from the actual

struggle, the poet, through an imaginative leap projects the velocity of the storm in his poetry. Several Urdu poets participated in the struggle (13). Just as the war cry has surfaced in this poetry, there is also mourning, a sense of helplessness and frustration. Zafar's ghazals mark this more than anything else they express the agony and the anguish of the captive emperor. Other poets of these times are Wajid Ali Shah Akhtar, Mirza Asadullah Khan Ghalib, Zaheerudin Zaheer Dehlavi, Mirza Daag ('Mersiye Delhi') and Khwaja Altar Husain Hali ('Delhi-e-Merhum').

7. One needs to ask, apart from the position adopted by subaltern historians, whether the peasants' acts of insurgency feed into a national resistance or do they run a parallel course. The war of 1857 was dominantly supported by the people, including the peasants.

7

Explorations in the Historical Subconscious

Nineteenth Century India and After*

The road to indigenous history lies through several routes – oral traditions, myths, memoirs, travelogues and fiction. And the act of reconstructing indigenous pasts requires a constant resistance to the dominant hegemonic structure. For the moment I focus on the difference between the historian and the writer. History, as Gandhi commented, is a record of conquests. It does not take note of resistance and of the impact events have on human lives. The main staple of history are facts, statistics and treaties; it aspires perhaps for a certain neutrality and objectivity, but lost in a cause-and-effect account, it cannot be said with any certainty whether it achieves it. Literature, on the other hand, shifts its focus to the lived realities and weaves in abstract questions related to justice and morality. Moreover, literature works with a variety of modes; it can have shifting perspectives, it engages with the unexpressed intentions of men and women, their conflicts and subconscious desires. Increasingly, the relationship between history and literature is becoming a dialogic one as each expands its boundaries and encroaches into the other's field. Hayden White in *Metahistory* (1973) and later in *Tropics of Discourse* (1978), worked the various kinds of emplotment historians adopt, the choice depending on their

* Presented at a Conference on 'Memory and History' at Veer Narmad University, Surat, 9 March 2010.

individual perspective. In *Tropics of Discourse* he spells out the different stages of representation beginning with *mimesis* (description), and progressing through *diegesis* (the argument or narrative) and culminating in *diataxis* (the combination of mimesis and diegesis, 4). The writer's attempt involves more than a representation as the interpretative act also differs from the historian's, for rather than focus on objectivity, the interpretative act becomes, for the writer, an act of entering the psyche of the generations of the past, their lifestyle, relationships, values, aspirations and failures. It works with multiplicities, with both dreams and nightmares and is interested in capturing the moment-to-moment debates impacting their choices. The canvas is vast.

I have selected three novels for my purpose today – each tells a different history, in a different language, about a different set of socio-cultural environment and yet interconnects with the others as colonial struggles are analysed. These are Mahasweta Devi's *Titu Mir* (2003), Krishna Sobti's *Zindaginama* (1979) and Anand's *Goverdhan's Travels* (1995, Tr., 2006). Each one is different from the other in its narrative structure and ideological concerns, and it is this difference which is important for capturing their indigeneity. One needs to pause for a moment and ask oneself, what is indigenous history and how is it different from subaltern history? Does indigeneity have any relation with language and status? Or is it more a question of 'power' and 'nativity'? The problematisation of the term is necessary. Indigenous is definitely a wider term than 'subaltern', which is primarily defined by its 'position' in the hierarchy of power; the term indigenous, applies specifically to the 'nativity' of its origins – and thus it also includes a large degree of freedom of allowing itself to grow in different directions. The focus on 'indigeneity', goes on to emphasise the firmness of its location in the land and works with cultures, rituals and relationships. It also goes on to dwell upon the ways in which people come together, encounter external forces, the way movements are consolidated and communities relate to each other. Why they get to be written is entirely another matter, one which needs to be considered on its own merit. More often than not it is the compulsion of a period to reassess itself, to know its past beyond the projection and to uncover the invisible – all that has slipped out of official or known versions.

Titu Mir, though the last to be written of the three novels under consideration, takes up the early decades of the nineteenth century and is located in Bengal under the Company rule. Ostentiously the novel is about a revolution built on a dream but at a deeper level it is also about the indomitable spirit of man, about the economic laws that create schisms, the power manipulations and the moral corruption that begins to work within this duplicity, the struggle between the power-wielders and the powerless, about religious strengths and reforms. Above all, it is about the way nations are constructed and are betrayed. *Titu Mir* depicts the personal transformation of a village boy into a revolutionary leader, who on his way to this role also becomes a Wahabi. It is about the subtlety with which both land and power were taken away from the indigenous populations for the indigo plantations, which have been the bane of the nineteenth century. These plantations impoverished the farmer, destroyed the fertility of the land and the acquisition of land for these led to absentee landlordism, severing the intimate connection between land and its people, between the attachment to the motherland and the construction of a nation. The inevitable going across of the power-seekers provides an archetypal pattern of Indian polity. From this perspective *Titu Mir* goes on to illustrate Gandhi's observation that the British did not conquer us, we ourselves submitted to them or allowed them to conquer us, consciously playing into their hands, betraying our loyalties and values for purposes of material greed – the flaw lies within. The meeting point between the reader and the writer's imagination is often through an image, or a shared distant memory kept alive through similar happenings. *Titu Mir* projects two memorable ones – one of the bamboo fort housing Titu Mir and his men, and the other of a young boy in search of a leopard, eager to capture him and make him his pet. Both point towards the power of a dream and the courage to confront a formidable enemy. Later, these images are reversed: the fort can be easily ignited, and the law turn Titu into a fugitive, torn away from home and compelled to be on the run.

The novel spans Titu's lifetime, but goes back in time through his mother and grandmother's memories to the great famine of 1770–1771; it works with a socio-cultural background which is not so strictly split along religious divisions. The divisions largely economic are also based on moral distinctions – the good versus the bad. The capitalistic venture of the East India Company is supported by the native landlords who transfer their allegiances in self-interest. The relationship between the two is based upon 'revenue' collection (34–35). And the marshalls of law are as exploitative in their dealings as the Company. The middlemen extract their dues, the zamindar's managers enter into private contracts, the peasant is deprived of his share in the crop; this is contrasted with the way 'fakirs' and the 'sanyasis', men who have withdrawn from worldliness, become revolutionaries, leading crusades against the exploitative encroachments. Mahasweta Devi brings alive, through this history, the connection between religion and politics, where the insistence on the moral 'right' is of significance. Else, why should men of religion intervene in this worldly state of affairs?

Located at the juncture of the sliding of political power from the Mughals to the Company, the novel offers a study of the way in which a people-oriented flexible system of revenue collection when 'the landlords lived with their people and shared their lives', was superceded by a highly collection-oriented regulated and fixed system, and goes on to project issues related to the Zamindari system and the Permanent Settlement (34). Thus several histories – of class, of land rights, of power shifts and of revolutions – are presented side by side, deeply interconnected and impacted by each other. Muslim culture, its religiosity and moral strengths also surface alongside, dismantling the pro-Hindu novelistic projections of the late nineteenth century writers such as Bankim Chandra Chatterjee (*Anand Math*), R.C. Dutt (in his early historical novels), Pratap Narayan, Radhacharan Goswami and several others (See Sudhir Chandra, *The Oppressive Present*, 119–130).

The slow deterioration of the inter-religious relationship, as it travels down the years to the post 1857 period, is thus markedly visible to the social historian. It is evident, that it is partly caused by the deepening economic gap. The Muslims are largely peasants, while the Hindus are landlords; it is partly also caused by the shift in the imperial power from the Mughals to the Company; and partly it is the result of Hindu insularity and its caste system. But more than all else it was the Company's policies, its need for more and more wealth – teak, rubber, precious stones, ivory, rice – and its territorial greed that was responsible (55). And as it pursues these goals, it incidentally, through its expansionist policies, sows the seeds of rebellion (56), and pushes the humble sepoy and the peripheral villagers into the recognition of their rights and the courage to assert them. Inevitably, it is through the consciousness of this injustice that the nation is being constructed, in opposition to territorial annexations and the parallel reformation based on changing geographical boundaries. Lineages of movements are traced through the leaders – Shah Ismail, Syed Ahmad and Titu Mir and through the spread of the Wahabi Movement, which was at one level a crusade against the British and as such a liberation struggle based upon religious reform. It connects the country, like the Bhakti and the Sufi movements, moving through Rohilkhand, Patna, Calcutta, Gwalior, Bareilly, Punjab, Bombay, Hyderabad (63–64). The battle against the English is in the nature of holy war, a fight against injustice, torture and oppression being fought with whatever resources they possess (64). The movement also sidelines those godmen who channelise the people's energies into being fearful, building dargahs and mosques and spending money on elaborate death rites (66). Religious reform – rooted in economic realities and aiming at separating faith from consumer-oriented rituals – is a necessary step towards bringing people together for a common cause (74–75), across religious divisions. (This reform is in direct contrast to the reform movements of the later half of the nineteenth century – Brahmo Samaj, Arya Samaj, Prathrana Samaj and the like – movements that came up in response to British criticism, and with the idea of bringing in a strong element of rationality, movements which were separatist enclosures, mostly middle or upper class and which interrupted the spread of the Bhakti and Sufi movements, the movements which were indigenously grounded and resistant to dogmatism and conservatism). Amidst all this, the tentacles of the Company Law spread over the land through the indigo plantations and the people through its oppressive laws which created fear tainting both – the land and its people (96). It is in opposition to these that Titu Mir and his band rose up in arms with their only weapon, the lathis that they had (101). But the infighting between Indian principalities was another front to combat for the revolutionaries, a situation where the leaders were fighting not for freedom but for power, in fact 'to lay their bit of freedom at the feet of the English'.

In this retrospective historical representation of a revolution, Mahasweta Devi working through multiple perspectives, traces the changing patterns of social interaction and outlines a positive aspect of Muslim contribution. The Wahabi revolution falls into place in the history of both violent and non-violent revolutions, pointing towards the non-cooperation implied in the non-payment of taxes and the link between faith, courage and fearlessness but it is its concern with justice which forms the central concern of Anand's novel, *Goverdhan's Travels*. Originally written in Malayalam in 1995, *Goverdhan's Travels* is altogether in a different mode. It moves freely across space and time, travels back and forth from Ibn Buttata, Galileo, Kepler, Kepler's mother, through India's history of invasions, its myths and religious scriptures, back to the lives of Satyakama (from the *Upanishads*) and Siddhartha (Gautam Buddha), wandering through villages and roads, forests and ashrams and prisons and houses, in pursuit of 'justice'. For framing this question he begins with Bhartendu Harishchandra's play *Andher Nagri Chaupat Raja* (written in 1881) and picks out a character condemned to be hanged. The man is innocent, and is merely a substitute for a whole relay of innocent culprits chosen to be punished by an erratic ruler. The portrayal of erratic behaviour of the ruler is not without cause, it is an ironical move mocking the very idea of British justice. Bhartendu classified it as a play about a town where everything is priced at a single rate; no importance being attached to the value of the commodity. Later, a travelling mendicant, despite his Guru's advice to the contrary, is charmed into staying there by the apparent equality the place projects. Finally he is put in prison because his neck happens to be of the right size for the hangman's rope. But through a clever turn of events, the king himself is persuaded to become a volunteer for the hanging. The play ends there completing the full circle of an absurd idea, problematising the notion of seemingly just punishment and the hollowness of abstractions like equality and justice if seen only in terms of appearances. But the novel picks up the point where Goverdhan is taken prisoner and rather than be rescued through the wit of the Mahant, is set free by Bhartendu Harishchandra himself. Anand also reverses the need for a thick neck to that for a thin neck, thus transforming Goverdhan's image from a well-fed mendicant to a thin, undernourished man. Bhartendu Harishchandra's entry into the novel is significant for it permits discussion on the nature of creativity, on the relationship between writer and a fictional character created by him, over whose life he ceases to exert control beyond a certain point.

Anand is not concerned with any linear projection of history or historical events; instead he is concerned with ideas which have motivated men, and with men who either aspire to live up to their ideals or fail to do so. Ibn Buttata, the fourteenth century Moroccon traveller and Bhartendu the nineteenth century writer discuss freedom: who is free to act? And what does freedom mean? (86–89) We are all anchored in some unknown compulsions. Bhartendu's act of setting Goverdhan free is duplicated in reverse when Umrao Jan, a real-life woman inhabiting fictional space, sets her writer free. The right of proprietorship over the other, and the power to set the 'other' free do not always work in a similar fashion. This also points out the difference between fact and fiction, between history and imagined history. *Goverdhan's Travels* are travels in time, across disciplines, across cultures, problematising the meaning of persecution and oppression. The central image is of prey and predator, an image reinforced by the jailor David Butler's passion for hunting turned into a job of hunting men. Goverdhan's role of a permanent victim is also reflected in the lives of rulers and residents alike. The ruler of *Andher Nagri* makes an appearance and justifies his absurd notion of justice as being motivated by the intoxication of power. (142) The action of the writer, in contrast, signifies the abdication of power – but each case presents its own moral dilemma. Every right has a wrong attached to it; every act of justice incorporates a moral imbalance. Characters from the pages of history, known writers like Ghalib and Amir Khusrau, characters from Bhartendu's play and the fictional characters created by Anand, all jostle with each other in the pages of the novel, bringing up their experiences and reflections out of their own time to connect with the present of the other character. For a moment one can find Kalidasa, Amir Khusrau and Bhartendu talking about creativity, power and moral right, about human dignity as the only shield against being looked upon as a victim (250). (Also see Kalidasa's conversation with his characters, 252–258).

What kind of an indigenous history does the novel tell us? It speaks about the absurdity of history, of the resurfacing of similar persecutions and prejudices across time and space; it seeks to analyse power and freedom in political as well as in creative contexts; it goes on to discuss literary genres and imagined creativities on the same plane as trade and governance; and more than all these it points towards the inadequacy of all abstractions – reason, justice, freedom, creativity. And while hinting at the resurfacing of the past it places the present on the tip of the nib, making it important. In brief, it works as a philosophical construct located in Indian pasts and epistemologies alike to show our greatness as much as our failures. Is there a reinforcement of 'karma', of destiny, as a concept? Not quite so – human vulnerability is of another kind: protest, will and desire on the one hand and compassion and courage on the other match with the illogic of faith.

The three works I have selected move on two different time directions. Sobti's *Zindaginama* was written before the other two, but in terms of its primary focus it works with the first two decades of the twentieth century. Located there it makes numerous forays into history and into geographical spaces, reflecting the culture of society subjected to invasions and wars, and migrations to different lands. Like *Titu Mir*, the image of the masculine patriarch is dominant but unlike *Titu Mir*, the women in *Zindaginama* are also visible. There is a strong acceptance of the feminine, of the act of birthing, of procreation. The association of the farmer to the land is metaphorically enhanced to include the notion of a motherland, of a mass of territory inhabited by people bound together in pursuit of similar goals. *Zindaginama* is very different from both *Titu Mir* and *Goverdhan's Travels*. Both of them have a central figure through whom the narrative is woven together, not so *Zindaginama*. Here the whole community with all its social hierarchies and a range of occupations, is at the centre. Mahasweta Devi reflects on the concept of revolution, Anand works with the epistemology of abstract values but Sobti goes on to unravel the ways in which history percolates down the ages, the ways in which it inhabits oral traditions and is disseminated, debated, discussed, interpreted and questioned. Through location in a time-space, Sobti's community is free to depend alike on heard and recorded memories, on family histories, and at the same time move horizontally across space into the mainland – Lahore, Delhi, Calcutta – and other countries such as Canada through migration, and Europe because of the war. The community has its refugees, migrants and fugitives. Land rights and revenue systems are once again the main link between governance and the people, indicating control of one over the other. The novel itself works with two different time frames – one from 1905 to 1919 while the other is free and works with historical memories. We have many markers of both the time spans. The 'present' of the novel is marked by references to the 1905 partition of Bengal, the 1911 bomb blast in Chandni Chowk, the 1913 formation of the Gadar Party in Washington, the 1914 Komagata Maru incidence when twenty-seven Sikh immigrants were killed and the recruitment drive during World War I (51), Gandhi's resistance to the South Africa regime – all these are mentioned. But none of them is an isolated event; they impact each other as well as the lives of the human beings located at a distance. They invoke patriotism, provoke revenge and excite passions. Often they create parallel movements, disrupting families and power structures alike.

This community saga, through its very narrative structure and claimed title, adopts a dominantly oral narrativity as it shifts voices, episodes and linguistic registers, prefers 'told' and 'heard' accounts to eyewitness accounts or documents. Through a poetic prologue divided into two parts, the first of which is brief and in the form of a statement, and the second of which goes on to form part of the opening chapter, is a lyrical homage to the land and its people. Let me dwell briefly on each one of them. Defining history in the first part, Sobti rescues it from the heavily documented version of the rulers and relocates it in the memories of the people, where it grows, expands and comes alive in culture. The second part goes on to describe the land of five rivers (undivided India), using maternal metaphors and to describe its lush fields. In the next phase it is the masculine strength that its peasants present and the produce their daily labour yields which is commented upon before moving on to its festivals, vibrant community life, the many invasions the region has faced, the exile which, at times, is forced upon its people and then comes the reference to the rivers of milk turning into rivers of blood. The poem hints at the violence of partition and the fact of human mortality. It marks the changes in historical terms, the shifting cartography, and the changing equations amongst the people.

Despite being community-centred and space specific, *Zindaginama* moves freely into the many cultural pasts – scriptures, history and folk culture. In that measure it is decentred and serves an ethnographic purpose as it captures the community's equations, relationships, revenge motifs and dialect shifts in a way that no historical record can. It is through these strategies that the historical unconscious is explored and captured. Historical time does not flow in linearities or within exclusively defined borders. The connectivity both with the present expanse of space and lives of people in far away lands as well as with past events is evident. This village community is not an enclosed space. The narrative thus leaps out of this time span to memories of other pasts, of wars won and lost. The great Kohinoor won by Maharaja Ranjit Singh in 1813, was lost due to the defeat in Chillianwala in 1849 (181). Throughout the nineteenth century, the borders of the Sikh Empire were constantly shifting, either expanding or contracting, remarking on the inherent instability of power and thus of history. Memory is pushed back to Alexander and Ghazni's invasions (358–359), exploding the myth that villagers are ignorant and simultaneously reinforcing the strength of the oral tradition. Legends, myths, romances and bhakti poetry provide role models, patterns of moral behaviour and knit the people together in a common bond. Rabiyan sings the *kafis* (poems) of Bulle Shah and Waris Shah in *Zindaginama*, Anand works with Kabir's poetry while Mahasweta Devi's Titu Mir has Sohrab for a hero. It is the historical unconscious which selects its heroes and role models and reconstructs them in the imagination of the present. It is through the discussions of the villagers that the past is remembered.

The references to the canals dug during Shah Jahan's rule, the farsightedness and welfare policies of earlier rulers, are placed side by side with British policies for land development. The comparison critiques the British economic interest. Other targets of criticism are the missionaries, urban lifestyles and corruption (*Zindaginama* 264–266). Progress is not a gift brought home from abroad but a home-grown product, dependent on the people, the land and the inheritance of the past. Contemporary revolutionary activities both in Punjab and Bengal are relocated in the past with a reference to Guru Gobind Singh:

> When all other paths have come to a dead end, then it is legitimate to pick up the sword.

The intimate connection between freedom and power – though not spelt out as independence and sovereignty – is perceived as the mainstay of any governance. Rulers come and go, territories may change hands but the land belongs to the people (*Apne mulk ki dyodhi to rahe Kabul Kandhar*, 99). A passage in *Zindaginama* asserts that though thousands of invaders have come and gone, 'Lahore belongs to the people of Lahore and Kabul to its people'. What I wish to point out is that kings and rulers, Sultans and Shahenshahs come and go, political regimes change but no one can displace the population of these countries (99). A truth, which now stands partly eroded by the exodus during the partition, but which lives on in the idea of homeland. Over and above this expansion into space, *Zindaginama* works with a variety of embedded interventionist and supplementary narratives – riddles, folk songs, *swang* (a performative masquerade), letters, customary get-togethers like *trinjan*, a gathering meant for women, especially young girls on the threshold of marriage, and festivals like Lohri, celebrated by young children by going from door to door asking for firewood or money and thus demanding community participation. Then there is the ceremony of being initiated into school curbing one's ego and teaching one the lesson of humility. The men's *majlis*, the gathering where politics is a staple diet, where comparisons between the past ways of governance and the present are made, where the illiterate become co-sharers in the knowledge disseminated through the written word, and where grassroots democratic procedures are followed – these all work together to bring together the various strands of history. Similar to the religious openness of the early part of *Titu Mir*, when oppressor and victim are not identified on basis of religion, *Zindaginama* also projects a picture of non-discriminatory social interaction despite economic hierarchies. As Sobti redefines history as people's history, revolutions and revolutionaries also engage her attention.

Hayden White in *Tropics of Discourse* commenting upon the burden of history, which is, in other terms, the burden of the past, points out that philosophers, writers and historiographers have seen it as a medium of 'educating men to the fact that their own present world had once existed in the minds of men as an unknown and frightening future, but how, as a consequence of specific human decisions, this future had been transformed into a present ...' (49). History is perceived less an end itself and more a 'preparation for a more perfect understanding of the individual's responsibility in the fashioning of the common humanity of the future' (49). Likewise, history points out not only to continuities in terms of genealogies of political patterns but also towards discontinuities, disruptions and dislocations, in fact to the Foucauldian ruptures.

The historical unconscious embedded in the memory of a nation carries these contradictory forces within it. In the case of nations which have lived through phases of subordination and invisibility, have been fixed in stereotypes and misrepresentation, the surfacing and recollection of the past serves a very important function surfacing as it does time and again in some new incarnation: each time the writer hopes to capture this as he enters the relationship of the individual with the complex burden of his memories and conflicts and helps bring it to the collective unconscious.

8

Patterns of Conflict in Border Operations

Devi, Ondaatje and Phillips

It is no longer possible to begin with any well-defined points of origin or identities, or to work within the polarities of 'self' and the 'other'. Cultures and peoples have travelled across national boundaries and wide-scale migrations and dislocations have resulted in the disruption of the notion of an anchored self. Power is both invasive and pervasive irrespective of its nature, whether political, economic or cultural. Despite the revolutions and insurgencies, and despite democratic ideals, the hierarchical power relations continue to persist.

The three writers I wish to focus on are Mahasweta Devi, Caryl Phillips and Michael Ondaatje, writers engaged in the exploration of the idea of a self resistant to the systematic onslaught on its very being, the strength which the self still finds in consolidating a value system no longer recognised by 'modernity' as well as the continuity of history as manifested in the acts of remembering and forgetting. Devi's novella, *Pterodactyl, Puran Sahay and Pirtha* appeared in an English translation in 1993. It is, in Devi's own words, an abstraction of her tribal experience of nearly three decades and her deep understanding of their situation and agony. Caryl Phillips in *The Nature of Blood* (1997) works with the narrative of a young Jew girl as she grows up in pre-war Germany subjected first to enclosures and discrimination, then to the disruptive effects of hatred, the journey in the overcrowded train to the concentration camps, and then her slow recognition of a world outside as she recovers in a British refugee camp and lives with her intermittent bouts of hallucinations and journeys into the past. Michael Ondaatje in *Anil's Ghost* (2000), is once again concerned with the refusal of the past to be buried and forgotten as the young Anil Tesseree is back in Sri Lanka, the country of her birth, but as a forensic expert on a Human Rights Commission. Here, among the long-buried skeletons of the past, she finds one which is a more recent one and provides evidence of a political murder. The rest of the novel is the story of the search for the dead man's identity. Bit by bit his life history is put together. Ananda, an artist, is hired to reconstruct his face and this unknown man, for purposes of identification, is given the name of Sailor. Anil is not alone in this search. Others like Sarath, Gamini and Ananda are with her. The search leads her to the heart of Sri Lankan culture, the Buddhist influence and Buddha's statue, the serenity that he spreads form a main strand in the novel.

All these three narratives are about victims, about the struggle for social justice and of determined but perhaps blind resistance to the forces of the brutal system. They are about struggles with the presence of the past, a past which cannot be wholly rejected or wholly sustained. These are all internal conflicts within a nation state and are about people in borderlands. Gloria Anzaldua in *Borderlands* (1987) describes the border as the thin edge of barbwire, an image immensely suited to the anguish and helplessness which pervades the being. Borders offer both security and insecurity and constitute an ever fluctuating space like the waves of the seashore, subjected to eternal renegotiations. The borders are inhabited by people who are refugees and rejectees and are forced into a constant struggle for survival. How do they cope with this reality? The borders are also visited by people who are not of them but are with them – what kind of a trust can invest their relationship? Victims and their sympathisers transcend polarities and inhabit conflictual situations. Individual concerns and pursuits are absorbed in collective anguish and collective struggles. Border operations are a constant state of siege, very different from active war. The complexity of this struggle is overwhelming in its multiplicity. Cultural loyalties, value structures, human concerns are tangled together in an effort to resist absorption into the mighty 'Other' which concedes no place for any difference. The reader is powered by the nature of this reality which is so compelling in its truth.

The recurring tropes are those of memory, mystery and knowing, concerned with the several ways one remembers. Memory and reality are selective and subjective. The act of remembering is the genesis of both: hatred and revenge on one hand and forgetting and forgiveness on the other. Every act of remembering is an extension of the self and becomes also a search for definitions, rootedness, belonging and non-belonging. And knowledge both of the self and the other is equally elusive.

Pterodactyl, Puran Sahay and Pirtha is about a bird – now extinct; a man – Puran Sahay, and a place – Pirtha. The story opens with Puran Sahay's life – his father's aspiration for a full life for his children, his marriage, the birth of a son Arjun, the death of his wife and his withdrawal into celibacy. He is a journalist but with a rare ethical sense and prefers the truth to sensationalism. Even in the 'telling' of this truth, he does not want to treat the tribals as 'objects' or as the 'other'. In fact, his whole behaviour is an attempt at belonging to them, to know what they know, not merely as a curiosity but as an experience. Puran's story is the outer framework, linked with the interior through his childhood friendship with the Block Development Officer Harisharan. Harisharan, is apparently a representative of the system, but in fact his concern is primarily to find ways and means of hoodwinking its heartlessness and use its resources to the advantage of the people. He too, like Puran, is keen to build a human relationship.

Within this framework which links two worlds is the story of the boy Bikhia who has seen and then drawn a monstrous shadow, the shadow of a bird. The vision drives Bikhia into silence: 'Why is Bikhia not speaking? Why is he remaining mute?' Why does he feel that it is tremendously urgent to keep his knowledge to himself? (156). Perhaps Bikhia's silence is an act of protection from the outside world. Communication is visibility, and visibility without understanding or compassion is dangerous, it exposes one to pursuit and elimination.

> 'Today' does not know the 'past', the ancient. 'Today', 'the present times', 'civilisation', becomes most barbaric by the demands of getting ahead. Yet he doesn't know that today desecrates the ancient peoples' burial-grounds by building roads and bridges, cutting down forests. (156)

History is never a mere progression; it is in fact both a continuity and a discontinuity and carries within it tales of aggression and dislocations. There is no possibility of going back; time moves ahead, erases and obliterates the weak. Computers cannot process the truth; they can only deal with data. Even nature is endangered by man-imposed substitutes. The vision is a warning of the dangers of non-recognition, non-acceptance, of the development which has a brutal face manifested in its engagement with those epistemological structures which do not involve the whole being – 'modern man is afraid to know life by entering life. It is much safer to know life by reading books' (159).

The tribals are in danger of being wiped out not merely by the encroachments of the development agenda into the area of their means of subsistence but also by the insensitive political agenda aimed at capturing votes. Instead of declaring it as a famine area, huge family planning posters are sent to them ignoring their need for health-care centres. As the tribal is deprived of his food, of his forest and his land, driven further inwards into caves and death, Puran, whose name means 'complete' finds himself to be a 'halfman', a rootless weed (160). The tribal is being trampled in the fast track race of development. The danger as always is from the 'other'. But this internal enemy is different from the previous 'others' – the foreigners, the aggressors who could be identified with the non-human and whose greed had a visible face, but the present 'other' has several faces, many of which are invisible, others disguised as friendly. The exploitative side of development, the policies in the hands of people who know nothing of their problems and needs, agencies such as the World Bank and the International Non-Government Agencies, and for the tourists is search of exotic places, the journalists hungry for news, the politicians, the bureaucrats, the underworld mafia all go to form this other. How does the tribal deal with that? There is no meeting point between the two streams of life: they run on parallel lines, there is no communication at all between them. The only possible way is 'to love, love beyond reason for a long time'. Love, excruciating love has to be the first step (197).

Caryl Phillip's *The Nature of Blood* works simultaneously with several narratives and though the novel is surfeit with images of blood and bleeding the title signifies much more than the mere act of physical bleeding: it defines human nature – the need for revenge, and the need for relationships, the blood of sacrifice of the innocent, and the blood which purifies. The outermost frame is of Uncle Stephan's life, a German Jew, who has discarded his wife and daughter, let them go to America and has pursued the dream of carving a new country for the Jews, Israel, a country not yet on the map. It is like beginning life anew from scratch. There are memories of being closed in by the Nazi administration, of the spread of fear, and the denial of freedom. Uncle Stephan appears only intermittently in the main narrative which works through the consciousness of Eva, his niece, now rescued from a concentration camp and placed in a refugee camp by the British. Eva's inner world is choked with memories – of her name, her parents, her sister Margot, the annihilation of the parents, the sub-story of Margot's host family's treatment of her, of the journey in the packed train towards death (reminding one of Sylvia Plath's poems), the links between forgetting and survival juxtaposed with the need to remember, for the act of mere survival. She hallucinates, imagines her mother's presence, recalls her grandparents, withdraws into silence, refuses to take food and finally travels to London in response to the soldier Gerry's promise of marriage. Gerry however is now married and outside her reach.

For the victims of the Nazis, death is a constant companion. 'To become weak is to disappear', the solution is to live from day to day, not to think of tomorrow, to become indifferent. They are locked in the present. Victimhood destroys the dignity of the victim; it destroys all idea of normalcy; it alienates one from all gesture of life – 'How to use a toothbrush .... How to say hello and goodbye, How to eat slowly'. (32) It also feeds one's self-centred, selfishness. The narrative movement does not remain locked in the present; it moves to and fro. There is a journey back to the fifteenth century, the month of March in 1480, and April of the same year – when Jews are said to have sacrificed an innocent Christian boy as part of a religious ritual and when the Christians hold their leaders captive and condemn them to torture and death on this false accusation. The continued hatred, the lack of tolerance of earlier years, of earlier places, of 1349, of 1424, resurface once again in this event of 1480.

The Nazi persecution of the Jews is a continuation of this hysteria of fear and hatred compelling the Jews to inhabit a permanent foreignness, which recalls the crucifixion of Christ and drives them into ghettoes and enclosures, stressing their separateness. European civilisation based itself not merely on exploitation and inferiorisation of the other but also on its exclusion from professions and places of power. Locked in their houses, or hoarded together in death chambers, the attempt is to wipe out all signs of their existence (71).[1]

The Jews are caught in a vicious cycle – they are incapable of successful mourning, because this act of self-expression involves a 'letting go', and therefore a forgetting of the dead .... 'Naturally, their suffering is deeply connected to memory. To move on is to forget. To forget is a crime. How can they both remember and move on?' (157) Eva lives between dreams and nightmares, hallucinations and intolerable reality, attempts suicide but survives and continues to live a divided self – trying to escape her double but invariably being chased by it. Uncle Stephan too similarly lives between dreams and reality – remembrance is a form of madness – but how does one forget? The fears, doubts, suspicions which drive one to utter loneliness give birth to the 'other', a soul riven in two in its very essence, 'split down the length of their body' (Anzaldua 2).

The conflicts of the self with the conscious reality are shifted to a triangular contest in *Anil's Ghost,* where it is not war but civil war, with the separatist guerrillas in the north, the anti-government insurgents in the south and the government in the centre. Once again it is the 'other' within the nation state, negotiating with the confused histories of power. And the forces which converge are many – Anil, a woman, who has purchased her masculine name from her brother at age thirteen, which the astrologers had advised her to change to Anile, the feminine version, Sarath Diyasena, an archaeologist and Gamini his brother who is a doctor and in love with his brother's wife; Ananda, the sculptor, who has lost his wife and has gone through other losses and the many unknown, absent, living and dead victims of violence, a great deal of which is generated by the outdated and now totally irrelevant governance which has not been able to outgrow its colonial heritage.

The narrative has several frames. There is first the burial site, a mass grave in Guatemala where the living have come looking for their loved ones. This italicised beginning is connected later with other italicised passages (91–93, 172–175) which describe similar events and connect through clock time 5.30 a.m., 5.15 a.m., 6.00 a.m., but in different locations and different calendar times. Then fairly early in the novel there is a reference to the ritual of 'Netra Mangala', which Palipana, the blind sage, describes in detail to Anil and Sarath:

> *Netra* means 'eye'. It is a ritual of the eyes. A special artist is needed to paint eyes on a holy figure. It is always the last thing done. It is what gives the image life. Like a fuse. The eyes are a fuse. (97)

It is this act which transforms a stone statue into a god. The artist has to duly prepare himself the night before and paint the eye at five in the morning, the hour the Buddha attained enlightenment. Without the eyes 'there is no Buddha. There is no existence'. And this ritual has to be performed by looking at the reflection in a mirror, for 'no human eye can meet the Buddha's during the process of creation' (99). Towards the end, with Anil gone and Sarath dead, Ananda is engaged for performing this ritual on the reconstructed face of the Buddha statue. In the scene when he paints the eyes, he transforms the statue not into a god, but a god with a human face. With it the statue comes into life with the 'pure sad glance Ananda had found', to see the world with human sight.

With the performance of this act the meaning of *Anil's Ghost* falls into place. Sarath is the ghost which Anil and Ananda will always carry with them. Gamini, as he writes his report on the dead bodes, identifies one as that of his brother Sarath, who had been tortured and whose bones have been broken as were the Sailor's, the skeleton which they had unearthed together and pursued right to the very end in search of justice. But the pursuit ended in failure, in the flight of one (Anil) and death of the other (Sarath). Sarath's hands had been broken in several places (290). Just as one victim can speak for others, this repetitive tale of torture becomes in itself an evidence of murders committed by the authorities that be (reminding one of Guatemala of the opening scene). There is a casual sense of massacre. Sarath who had always 'side stepped violence' (289) was now dead and violently put to death. As Gamini lovingly patches up his brother's body to bid this last farewell, he is conscious of their lives being lived on 'this borderland of civil war among governments and terrorists and insurgents' (289).

None of the three narratives closes on a note of hope except by highlighting the human capacity to hold out against the inhuman and the non-human. They all, as Gayatri Spivak has commented with reference to Mahasweta Devi's work, 'imagine' an 'impossible undivided world' (*Imaginary Maps* 199). For Spivak, there is a need to move away from uninstructed cultural relativism and to 'open the structure of an impossible social justice glimpsed through remote and secret encounters with singular figures' (199). Spivak also talks of supplementing 'hegemonic notions of hybrid global culture with this experience of an impossible global justice' (199).[2] The latter would pause to reflect on specificities, and refrain from pushing a monocultural agenda across to others; it would also pause to 'see' and to 'know', not with preconceived notions of the normal and the correct, but with humility and patience.

Puran Sahay is conscious of not knowing enough, of not knowing at all with his fear of jumping into pain and suffering and life. The 'other' the objectified victim, the stereotype of the Jew, needs to be subjectivised and discrimination seen for the ugliness it actually represents. And like Ananda, the face which he reconstructs does not have to represent the fear of the victim or the agony of the tortured body, but the serene, yet to be created Buddha, the god with a human face.

These voices of those who are placed on borderlands and who have perpetually to live not merely with hostility but also with insecurity and uncertainly are voices which critique blind power and reverse the meaning of western Enlightenment. Progress, reason and the hegemonic application of universal norms is countered by exposing the false notion of progress, and stressing the need to 'love beyond reason', of going and living amongst these neglected residues of history to build trust, to get to know them. The need is not to look for sameness but to understand the difference in order to replace structures of hierarchy by equal ones. The search is for an 'ethicality' which moves beyond reason, beyond political gain and beyond resistance and is underlined with 'knowing' the other. These conflicts are neither of the individual nor of the collective. They represent both private and public battles, fragmented, and atomised at multiple levels.

Notes

1. Another narrative from the past is woven into this complex web, the story of a slave taking up the generalship of the Venetian army for war against the Turks, a story pointed to be one of the sources of Shakespeare's play *Othello*. This story acquires significance (i) through the foreigner's shift from the margin to the centre, (ii) the introduction of the Black element in the narrative, (Caryl Phillips's own origins), (iii) replicating the outside image of the utility of the outsider – but despite this usefulness, a constant rejection and discrimination.
2. The recurring use of the word impossible reminds one of Derrida's reference to 'impossible mourning', which Vijay Mishra problematises in his essay, 'Diasporas and the Art of Impossible Mourning,' (*InDiaspora.* Edited by Makarand Paranjape. New Delhi: Indialog, 2001.) Mishra's interpretation supplements Caryl Phillips's statement in *The Nature of Blood* when he says that mourning would lead to a new beginning, a letting go (qtd. above). Mourning involves an acceptance of truth (Mishra 30).

9

Interrupted Lives, Continued Histories

Punjab Before and After 1984

There is no single lens through which terrorism can be perceived, no single cause for its existence and no single solution. Even as it exists at the heart of society and manifests itself in what we commonly label as anti-national and anti-social activities, even as draconian and inhuman laws are made to control it, wars are fought, security mounted up, we need to realise that much of what we see as legitimate and acceptable activity is either responsible for feeding terrorism or is in itself an act of terrorism disguised as policy. It was the German persecution of the Jews which dramatically brought the nation state into a direct confrontation with its own people. This reversed the image of popular uprisings such as the French and the Russian revolutions. Juxtapose the image of the Fall of Bastille with that of a concentration camp – in between this reversal lies the birth of modern terrorism.

In the present paper my case study is the Punjab militancy, through its rise, fading out, dormant currents and the manner in which it has affected life and attitudes of the people of Punjab. The literature on Punjab is limited. It is only in the last decade or so that creative writing has turned to it. I work with Gulzar's *Maachis* (1996), Shonali Bose's *Amu* (2006) and Anita Rau Badami's *Can You Hear the Nightbird Call?* (2006), the non-fictional account of the 1984 events by Manraj Grewal and Blaise and Mukherjee's account of the Air India crash in 1985.

In the written version of *Maachis*, published post-film, Gulzar has a Foreword where, commenting on the militancy, he writes, 'It was not a sudden happening. Events had been building up and we had all watched – perhaps too silently and without protest – the build up of scandals and corruption. But in the 80s it became clear that what had inspired us just a few decades ago, had all been sidelined'. In fact the militancy followed close on the heels of broken promises, economic exploitation and political marginalisation. Manraj Grewal in the Introduction to *Dreams after Darkness*, a work on the happenings of 1984, traces the history of Punjab from pre-partition days to the present through the lives of many victims, instigators and rebel leaders. And even as these lives are explored for their psycho-social motivation, the survivors also come in for their due share. The disputes were over language, over a capital city and over river and hydel power. Punjab watched as other states were carved out of its territory and its prosperity levels gradually fell. Increasingly, the people's citizenship rights were held in abeyance (Grewal 2–11). But the final straw was Operation Bluestar, June 1984. There was hardly any difference between the Jallianwala massacre and Operation Bluestar as disproportionate violence was employed and innocent people were attacked, shot at and caught in a stampede, pilgrims and all. Further, Sikh generals were asked to lead their troops, that too on a day when the Martyrdom Day of Guru Arjan Dev (the founder of the Golden Temple and the fifth Guru of the Sikhs) was being observed (Grewal 13–15). Sikh identity, the concept of nationhood and the rights of a citizen – all were now destabilised. Before and after Operation Bluestar, we have a history of attacks, murders and bomb explosions scattered all over the country.[1]

While Badami traces the history of this violence right from Partition through Punjab and Delhi politics, moving towards the international scenario, *Maachis* works through the lives of two Sikh families of rural Punjab and the psyche of the Sikh youth trapped between the hostility of the authorities on one hand and the violence of the aggrieved victims on the other. The narrative begins with a suicide in a Punjab prison and then moves back in time to trace the beginnings of this violence. An ordinary police inquiry results in Jassi being whisked away to an unknown prison and returning home after a gap of weeks, broken in body and spirit. Meanwhile Paali, childhood friend and his sister's fiancé, had unsuccessfully searched for him and is now converted to a life of violence. The collective memory goes back to the Partition as they begin to wonder whether this is their own land (Gulzar 111). In his sheer frustration, Paali is on the lookout for a way of retaliating, of hitting back and it is in this mood that he meets Sanatan from whom he learns two things. One, that his own cousin had been killed by the militants, when they suspected a possible betrayal, and two, that militancy had roots more in the sense of being discriminated against than in any commitment to a political ideology. Sanatan tells him:

> I don't belong to any party .... I am not fighting for any religion or country either. I'm fighting to end my helplessness, my lack of control over things that affect me ... the sheer uncertainty .... (132)

There is a strong resentment against the term 'refugee', used almost as *muhajir,* a term which treated the migratory population from West Punjab as outsiders, forgetting alike their struggle and their sacrifice (Gulzar 132). If we go beyond this text, history tells us that populations were shifted from East Punjab to the canal area (which lies in West Punjab), in order to develop that forest land. If these very people have come back after Partition, merely because some documents have been signed, it does not make them outsiders. What follows in the narrative is Veeran's search for her fiancé, her landing up with the group of these runaways and replicating family and kinship ties. Back home in the village, Bebe – Jassi's mother – and the old man, Paali's grandfather, languish alone while the young people live on the borders of habitation, entering it now and then, for purposes of revenge. Humiliation and suspicion drive them further and further into an abyss. Soon the hastily put-together family of aggrieved people, breaks up. One by one the family scatters, as its members are killed or imprisoned. Finally, it is Veeran who pulls the trigger and kills Sanatan. It is she who smuggles the cyanide pill to Paali in the prison to free him from suffering. *Maachis* is a narrative of human loss, of the linear journey which violence takes, unable to effect a return; it is about a felt need for human dignity and of rightfully belonging to the land. The word 'land' has several connotations – of belonging, rootedness and nation.[2]

Bose's *Amu* shifts the ground to Delhi and looks at the events of 1984 through the life of a young woman who returns to India after a childhood abroad, totally ignorant about her origins. Amu is completely overwhelmed by Delhi's street life, the fun and the noise, the grand monuments of history and as she moves about Delhi with her camera, she catches on to the traces of the past. Somewhere she has a connection with this past for below her Bengali identity and the American location, is her childhood phase of another submerged identity. The film works through adult memories, personal guilts, compromises and lost normalcy. As Kaju, the protagonist, unravels her past through sheer persistence, she learns that her father had been dragged out of his home to be brutally murdered, that political leaders had directed the genocide, openly vowing death to every Sikh, that even her young brother had not been spared and her mother had finally ended her own life in the refugee camp. She also learns that fear had played a strong role in leading people to betray each other, to divide them along religious lines and hold them there. But when human beings relate to each other they learn to confess their guilt. It is in the recovery of her childhood name Amu (for Amrit) that she validates her search.

The desolate farmhouses, the isolated hide-out of the militants, the scampering from one place to another in *Maachis*, the refugee camp in *Amu*, the widowed Nimmo with her ghastly memories that drive her insane in Badami's novel, the bereaved survivors in *The Sorrow and the Terror* are reminders of the catchment areas of terrorism. They project the ruins for us to see the difficulty of rehabilitation. One needs to extend one's emotional being in order to comprehend the indignity, dependence, engulf these clusters of people brought together through a sense of helplessness, they are truly bereaved but have none of the comforts of shared family memories or community outlets. Instead they are required to shift all attention to the act of sheer survival. *Amu* was awarded an 'A' certificate on the ground that 'why should young people see what is better buried and forgotten' (the blurb on the CD). But histories cannot be forgotten or erased, especially not the history of violence. *Amu* ends with the burning Godhra train which led to the Gujarat riots of 2002 – another genocide but now targeting a different community, a genocide which draws attention to the conflictual relationship between the concept of a nation and the political effort to redefine it; the individual's sense of nationhood, and the role of the nation state either as participant in the reshaping or as a non-active observer. Both *Maachis* and *Amu* move away from an abstract idea of violence, to concentrate on individual lives and bring out the sense of fear, the uncertainty, the helplessness, the anguish caused by the suffering of loved ones and a gradual move towards using the body as weapon or nurturing the suicidal impulse. They work with relationships, which no matter how strong, cannot be abstracted from the surrounding violence. Who is responsible? Amitav Ghosh in his essay 'The Ghosts of Mrs Gandhi' asks: 'Who are the guilty?' a question which has no single answer. State, governance, policy-makers, the law-maintaining arms of the government, the religio-political leaders who distort the idea of nationhood and shrink the space for its minorities, who is it that one can really blame?

One of the epigraphs with which Badami prefaces her novel, *Can You Hear the Nightbird Call?* is a quote from Agha Shahid Ali's poem 'Farewell' – 'My memory keeps getting in the way of your history'. It is a statement which counters hegemonic master narratives with personal memories. A decentred narrative – more about a people than about individuals – works dominantly through the consciousness of Sharanjit Kaur now called Bibiji. Her father was one of the passengers of *Komagata Maru*, later she marries a man from Vancouver, and still later takes her young grandnephew with her to Canada as a gesture of making amends to a sister whose interest she had bypassed. But Jasbeer gets involved with the Khalistan movement. A parallel narrative is that of her niece. Nimmo, who had been hidden in a grain of bin during the Partition riots, and it is her son Jasbeer, who is now in Canada with Sharanjit Kaur.

Nimmo is a fervent admirer of Indira Gandhi, but this admiration offers her Sikh identity no protection during the 1984 riots. Follows a replay of the Partition violence with all its brutality. Nimmo hides her daughter in a steel almirah and throws away the keys to save her from an attacking mob. But when the house is set on fire, the trapped child cannot be rescued as the keys are lost. *Can You Hear the Nightbird Call*? analyses the growing sense of alienation and the disaffection with a state which refuses to act. There is also a reflection on the role of the diaspora and seems to ask the question: at what point does legitimate nostalgia for a homeland descend into interference in its political concerns? How does one keep this imported violence with an indigenous strand out?

Terrorism is born out of sheer helpless rage and is stoked alike by the political power wielders in international politics, as well as by acts of the nation state. The level of political interference in the generation of mob violence against the nation's minorities calls for a serious review of the quality of leadership as well as the level of education and political awareness of the voting public, though in the case of Punjab militancy educational and economic levels were not really material. Why has vote politics generated violence? Or is it, as Arundhati Roy has stated, that violence is a necessary accompaniment of development? In an essay 'Listening to Grasshoppers: Genocide, Denial and Celebration' she states: 'Armed with the reading of history, is it reasonable to worry about whether a country that is poised on the threshold of 'progress' is also poised on the threshold of genocide?' (*Outlook*, February 4, 2008: 54).

Stealthily violence walks in from the outside into homes, from the collective mindless mob into individual lives causing suffering and bereavement. And as it leaves behind permanent scars, it alters identities as in Amu's case where it is a complete turnover in language, faith and family. It is an unending sequence of cause and effect, of hatred and revenge. Incapable of building bridges it places all known realities such as community, faith, love and relationships on hold. No effort at rehabilitation or restricting it can restore the erased past or negotiate with the dead. The past lingers on in the collective unconscious – just as the grain bin and memories of the Partition riots resurface in Nimmo's life (in Badami's novel), and it also organises individual lives around a feeling of guilt. Bibiji's life is a narrative of trying to make amends for the mistakes of the past. She reaches out in various ways to her relatives, her neighbours and the community at large. Guilt to that extent is a healthy emotion. But a sanitised humanity bereft of guilt and conscience is immune to all feelings. The schizophrenia it develops between power and feeling is a permanent one; it has none of the agony and the conflict of the real schizophrenic. The police officers in *Maachis* are hardly disturbed by the acts of violence they commit: the object of their torture is merely an object. The above may be equally true of the terrorists, except for the fact that all other routes are barred for them. Veeran is left with no other option than to kill Sanatan, assist Kirpal (Paali) towards his end and herself commit suicide.

Young lives are interrupted – Jassi, Paali, Veeran and a whole lot of others; all the young talented people who were on board *Emperor Kanishka* were all looking forward to the blossoming of their careers in medicine, music or dance. In many cases they left behind a single surviving parent to mourn their unlived lives. Blaise and Mukherjee, in *The Sorrow and the Terror*, give real life accounts of this tragedy, which crossing the boundary of two nation states, Canada and India, took place on the coast of a third, non-involved one, which had to enter into the tasks of recovering, storing and identifying the dead. It also had to arrange for the incoming relatives and the counselling of the bereaved. Three hundred and seven passengers and twenty-two crew members died. Over ninety per cent of the passengers were Canadian citizens (Blaise and Mukherjee vii). Yet the Canadian officials were slow to come forward and the society at large failed to fully acknowledge it as a national tragedy, an attitude which made a statement about the role of adoptive states in times of crises.

With the origins of terrorism located both in the act of the margins staking a rightful claim on the national imaginary as well as through their operations from other territories, opens out larger questions than one can address. One is pushed towards examining the nature of democracy, the rights of the citizen, levels of political awareness and participation, ability to resist injustice and, more positively, the creation of a communicative approach across religions, race and ideologies. Both the terror and the sorrow are human emotions. They inhabit our minds, our sentient beings and finally, it all narrows down to the quality of human life – in administration, life, religion, in community solidarity, in sympathy and in reaching across to the other. Potential strongholds of terror are the exploited and angry. In a recent issue of *Seminar*, devoted to a debate on effective governance, Kiran Bedi criticises the role of the civil servants who never really are held accountable for their mistakes while Harsh Mander, in the same issue, stresses the need for the civil servant to resist illegal orders.

In the meantime, one needs to recognise that acts of violence are never self-contained or isolated episodes. The social fabric of Punjab has become distorted. We have large-scale migrations (some of them illegal), greater drug addiction, and a greater susceptibility to the influence of outside interference. At home, there is an increase in female foeticide and the sex ratio is disastrously unequal and a patriarchal orthodoxy continues to exist. Militancy, is for all practical purposes, controlled and considered to be over but it is difficult to say that the scars have healed or open structures are in place.

Notes

1. Refer Manraj Grewal for more details such as the attack on Rajiv Gandhi, on General Vaidya and several bomb blasts and bus burnings.
2. A sense of alienation was also responsible for sending this homegrown disaffection abroad.

10

Mediations Between Collective Voices and Future Time*

Politics and Media Representation

Public sphere is an area which is without margins and lacks a clear definition. Invasive of privacy and simultaneously catering to the need and desire for 'visibility' and participation, it is beset with several contradictions. When Habermas debated the whole issue of 'structural transformation', his reference was to the bourgeoisie, the rising middle class. The public sphere was viewed as one constituted through discussion, legal enactments and judgements, and went on to include visible aspects such as insignia, demeanor and rhetoric. It consisted of interaction through a huge variety of mediums, which in recent years has greatly multiplied through technological revolution. Habermas's exploration is, however, restricted to a class category and remains focused on the imperial powers in Europe, powers that had gradually worked their way to find space for democratic processes and participation. What happens when we shift the Habermasian formulation to the erstwhile colonial space, which at the time when Habermas was formulating it (1961) were countries young in their freedom and democracies?

The moment we do that, a whole new series of factors come into play – class, religion, languages, literacy, levels of education,

---

* Presented in 'The Virtual Transformation of the Public Sphere', Forum for Contemporary Theory Conference, Chandigarh, December 2010.

access to media vis-à-vis censorship restrictions; the motivation levels are also different. For protest or resistance, and even for power, mass followings, support structures, and collectivities of a kind are more evident. Also the degree (and nature) of intervention of the Big Powers, especially during the Cold War phase, is far in excess of the external pressures the European powers had to contend with. For them it was a more equal playground. Additionally, one cannot afford to ignore the role which religion and tradition continue to play in the construction of public sphere. Hence, I extend the meaning to include all the above categories and to work with three kinds of public protests, resistance or assertion movements, vis-à-vis the authorities in three different political environments: Gandhi's Salt March, 1930 against an imperial power, Benazir and the PPP's anti-Zia protests against authoritarian rule and, at times, under conditions of Martial Law, and Advani's Rath yatras in democratic space. The last two have directly been entwined with the electoral process. My concern overlaps into the personal ethics and the public semiotics of these movements. These movements have thrown up slogans, images and icons and have both a visual and an imaginative aspect to them. None of them is an impulsive move: they were coordinated to make an impact on the flow of history. The attempt in all cases is to alter a construct already established in the minds of the people and to mobilise opinion to swing it to its opposite. Each has generated its own legacy, and each reflects a choice for the public they wish to woo. The degree of gap between professed intentions and personal expectations may have varied in each case. The more important issues are as to what is at stake in each of these movements and how does it affect the larger community. The role of the media has varied considerably in the period from 1930 to 1990 and after. The new sensationalism, the paid channels and party-owned press over and above the party organs like Gandhi's *Young India*, PPP's *Megawatt*, Shiv Sena's *Samna* and others – all have played a significant role. Both pro and counter literature has followed and both pro and counter media representations are there. These are what weave these issues further into future discussions and discourses.

Before moving into a detailed discussion of these three, it needs to be mentioned that in the course of history both in India and abroad there have been several uprisings and demonstrations. Jaya Prakash's movement against the Emergency was one such but it was spontaneous and born out of the moment of aggression, which it wished to resist, not a pre-meditated demonstration. Further the media was muzzled. Public opinion forged a link only through personal values of ethics and freedom. The three under consideration are all planned movements with specific and long-term objectives. A quick recall of the main events and the political environment each worked in and created would throw more light on the difference. Gandhi's Salt March was a well-considered and thought-out plan, a honing of his earlier experiments, transparent and inclusive of the common man's interest. It bypassed all divisionary categories like class, caste or religion. The symbol chosen was 'salt'; a commodity essential for survival and the act was to extract it in violation of the law. Beginning on 12 March, this 352 kms march of 78 volunteers reached the coast on 5 April 1930. En route there had been many halts and plenty of interaction with the villagers. The iconic image it threw up is that of a pilgrimage. Charles Markovits, commenting on the Gandhian iconography, observes that he is almost always pictured half-naked, either spinning the wheel, or, with his pilgrim's stick, leading the Salt March (Markovits 14). Gandhi's visible representation of himself reflected his objectives which, amongst others, included the need to raise the peasant's consciousness of his political rights. Simultaneously, it was also an exercise in dispelling the fear of the powerful and the brutal 'other' (the *mai-baap*, the *sarkar*). The March was covered by three different documentary makers and by the international press (Markowits 108). Webb Miller was the journalist who reported on the Salt March, and served as the original of Attenborough's Walker in the film *Gandhi* (1982). The March is also very graphically portrayed in the film. The scene presents a multi-pronged movement – the non-violent satyagrahis crumbling as skulls are fractured and blood is spilt, the khaki-clad policemen anonymous in their brutality, the sari-clad women as they rush to give first aid, the young children on the tree branches participating vicariously in the happening and the journalist sending his messages in frantic excitement. Together they build up an unforgettable momentum. The immediate fall out of the Dandi March was the pricking of the world's conscience, the reluctant and half-hearted recognition on part of the British, arrests and violence on part of the police and then followed the Government of India Act, 1935. With the extracting of the salt, orchestrated in different parts of India and packets of the 'salt of freedom' being sold in the streets of Bombay, there was a feeling of both pride and involvement in various parts of the country.[1] The resonance of the moral purpose of the Dandi March can still be felt as is evident in its various official and personal enactments (BBC telecasts, reenactment in 1990 in Gujarat, and school children performing in their school functions). Raja Rao's *Kanthapura* (1938) transfers the event to a group of women satyagrahis' non-violent resistance to police atrocities as they march to Skeffington Coffee Estate and the toddy shops. It spelt out its moral idiom of courage and fearlessness, etching itself into collective memory.

The pro-Bhutto and the anti-Zia demonstrations in Pakistan in the 70s and 80s present a different scenario. Pakistan's young Republic (1957) has time and again been hijacked by dictators, and General Zia-ul-Haque's ten-year rule was one of the longest dictatorships of the country. It also happens to be the bloodiest. The events of this period have clearly wedged Pakistan into an international role which may be termed dubious by some standards. The time of history is parallel to the Russo-Afghan war, and to the last years of the USSR, it is also a period of the increase in the American pressures on Pakistan's policies. A strong sense of feudalism still persists and when combined with religious fervour, it begins to act as a deterrent to the formation of a democratic discourse. Thus there has been a fair amount of fluctuation in the assigned roles of the legislature and the judiciary. With frequent imposition of press and media censorship, curfews, tightening of the Hudood ordinance and bombings on processions, demonstrations have functioned differently. Crowds at political meetings, outside prisons and graveyards marked the protests against Zulfikar Bhutto's death sentence, and later what followed were the demonstrations of the Movement for the Restoration of Democracy (MRD). The Pakistan People's Party (PPP) has been a main player in many of them. Benazir Bhutto in her autobiography, *Daughter of the East,* offers a record of her father's prison experience, her own frequent house arrests, and later exile followed by a concerted effort abroad to win support. The autobiography brings us right up to 2007, covering a period of nearly three decades with demonstrations and protests marking the period. The account, however, is selective. It offers a single perspective, the bane of most autobiographies, and is concentrated on her growing up into a political role.

Benazir, and before her, her father's perception of the outside intervention especially during the Reagan years, right from creating unrest (85–86), birthing the Taliban (428–429), using Pakistan as a pawn in the Cold War and operating through Operation Wheel Jam conducted by the PNP (People's National Party), calling elections at will (269), right to Henry Kissinger's threat to Zulfikar Bhutto on his nuclear policy (86) which was carried out to its end. Yet, after Bhutto's execution, there were overtures from the PNP and collectively the two parties signed the MRD charter. The news when broadcast by the BBC 'electrified the length and breadth of Pakistan'. Benazir observes that it led the people to interpret it as a signal to launch a protest against the injustices of the Martial Law regime (167). There was a series of protests in 1981, followed by imprisonments, isolation and a continued persecution. During these years the foreign press and news media became a source of information for people both inside and outside Pakistan. The authenticity of some of the media shots has, however, been considered as constructed (272–273).

The other Bhutto, Fatima, Benazir's niece and Mir Murtaza's daughter, in her *Songs of Blood and Sword* (2010), fills up on her father's life, criticises her aunt for her autocratic decisions and accuses her of having had her brother (Mir Murtaza) eliminated (240, 289). Fatima Bhutto identifies four groups of resisters – the press, the lawyers, women and union workers, and political activists, the last including people like her father (199). At one point she compares the civil disobedience campaign of 1983 with Gandhi's movement and observes that the MRD drive was not entirely peaceful, and there was friction in the leadership itself (239) as well as within the Bhutto family.

Zia, though dead, had left behind political heirs in the most unlikely places. Fatima points out, how Benazir in order to get even with the MQM in her political battle, was prepared to 'fight dirty' and went on to adopt Zia-like techniques in the persecution agenda named Operation Clean-Up. The press played a significant, though a limited, role as it was muzzled. Nevertheless, the *Herald Magazine* carried a thirteen page report, filled with details of specific encounters, which Ghulam Hasnain and Hasan Zaidi had carefully examined. Their investigations tore apart the official version of events 'carefully and thoroughly' (Fatima Bhutto 372).[2]

The semblance of democracy fast deteriorated into a corrupt administration, leading to a final split of the father's legacy as the siblings faced each other in opposition (384–389). The nation's battle became a family feud, personal power being the main culprit. One needs to ask the question: can democratic forces survive in the face of feudal instincts and power greed? Or do they need a personal sense of commitment to the larger collectivity?

The third event I wish to explore are the Rath yatras, especially the Ram Rath Yatra of 1990, carefully staged and meticulously planned and carved out of a history of interplay between religion and politics. It was one of several successive ones. There had been a motorised VHP yatra in 1984 (Rao 25) and there have been many more since then, attempting to reduplicate the 1990 one but with limited success. Taking upon itself the familiar form of a pilgrimage, it effectively exploited religious symbols – dress, colour, format, temples, images and roles (such as a charioteer's), and tapping a subterranean stream in the Hindu consciousness, it embarked on a political battle, a quest for power. It was timed to yield results for the soon-to-take place elections. Advani's rhetoric and his record of this yatra in his autobiography, *My Country, My Life*, is revealing. The chapter is subtitled 'When India's Soul Spoke' (341) and there is an admission that Gandhi is one of the symbols he wished to exploit as well as that the objective is to explain the significance of the Ayodhya movement.

The Rath Yatra is not a self-contained symbol; it spills over into other formats of symbols, such as the ganga-jal campaign; it hijacked 'clean the Ganges' Operation. The brick-carrying jathas, the laying of the *shilayans*, just ten days before the 1989 Lok Sabha elections were due, all are events built around it, as were the televised versions of the two epics which were telecast in the years 1987–1990. Ramanand Sagar produced *Ramayana* from January 25, 1987 to July 31, 1988. It was slotted on Sunday mornings at 9:30 a.m. It is said to have drawn over 100 million viewers, and brought the entire nation to a stop. *India Today* described it as a phenomenal success and even trains and buses stopped running when the show was on. When the *Ramayana* concluded B.R. Chopra's *Mahabharata*[3] took its place (though in a different slot). The serialisation of these two epics, especially *Ramayana*, almost hypnotised the nation as well as its diaspora abroad. I had always noticed this connection in timing, but was unable to find a link until I read Advani's autobiography, wherein he admits that nearly a decade before this, as Minister of Information and Broadcasting in Morarji Desai's government, he had in 1977, in a gathering of film directors, producers and artistes, 'appealed to them to make movies on the great epics ...' (Advani 281). But a little later, he also mentions that they were aired only after 1990s (282) implying they were post Rath Yatra, but DD records state another story. Thus it is evident that the politically potential of the telecast has been used by the VHP/BJP combine to its advantage.

The fall out in terms of fracturising the nation, playing political musical chairs and reiteration of the same symbols during communal violence has been immense with a series of repercussions in different parts of the subcontinent, a long drawn-out legal process, the 1993 Bombay riots, and the riots in neighbouring Pakistan and Bangladesh and nearly a decade later the Gujarat riots, flaming hatred, encouraging the rise of militant groups and altogether making a mockery of the idea of a secular past. One of Advani's stated objectives was to redefine the word secular (373), ironically enough by creating a monolithic cultural nationhood, a *Hindurashtra*.

The fall out in terms of media has been even more disastrous. Loud and sensational news coverage by several news channels, replicas of religious symbols in the markets, transformation of personal greetings, mobile tunes geared to it on the one hand, and almost overpowering the imagination of the nation on the other.

There were, however, some sensitive films on these issues which represented the human condition like Mani Ratnam's *Bombay* (1995), Aparna Sen's *Mr and Mrs Iyer* (2002) on one hand, and the investigative documentaries of activists like Anand Patwardhan on the other. Of these *Ram Ke Naam*, a post 1990 Rath Yatra documentary investigated the whole scenario, including the disinterest of the common man, and was a dissident media voice amongst a chorus of the praise singers, and a later documentary, *Father, Son and Holy War* (1995) went on to interpret the rise of militant masculinity and hatred for the 'Other' as rooted in a sense of insecurity. *Ram Ke Naam* was telecast on Doordarshan in 1997 following a Supreme Court order and resulted in a heated debate in the Rajya Sabha (*Times of India,* 10 March 1997). Later there were some letters to the Editor which commended the telecasting. But these were all minority voices.

All these collective groups or crowds or, as in some case, mobs are not necessarily organised demonstrations but they are presentations of a visible collectivity, which can evoke either fear or admiration, and in some cases give rise to hysteria and self-immolation. Politics was a major player in all three under review, but in each case the underpinnings were different. In the first transfer of power to the people through non-violence was the main objective to be achieved by centre-staging the common Indian as the rightful beneficiary; the second focused on democracy, and to begin with had a national vision (Zulfikar Bhutto's period), resistant to outside intervention but later got embroiled in the game of self-seeking personal power; the third drew upon the late nineteenth century and the early years of the twentieth century, the rise of Hindu militancy and the Savarkar-Golwalkar inheritance. Gandhi had intervened to wean the nation away from it, but an apparent resistance to a single-party monopoly of power, resulted in reviving the Hindutva impulse and the rise of cultural nationalism.[4]

The semiotics of each event – Gandhi's lion-cloth, his body language, his pilgrim stick; Benazir's dress, covered head, and later, even a hijab, her use of Urdu; and Advani's dress, his religious rhetoric, the religious symbols of tilak, chariot and the like – each of these spells out their individual objectives. *India Today's* cover story commented on the symbol of the chariot. Hindutva supporters 'rang temple bells, beat thalis and shouted slogans' to welcome the rath ('L.K. Advani's rath yatra': internet source). Even the VHP leader Ashok Singhal is reported to have commented on Advani's motive for personal gains (http://www.zeenews. com/news562033.html).

One however, has to ask whether these semiotics are authentic or adopted merely in order to create an image? Whether the demonstrations are truly representative of the people's voice and will, or there is an underlying unacceptability of their protest ethics? Rebecca Jones in 'The Aesthetics of Protest' comments on the decline of faith in the representations offered by the media. Going back to John Dewey she points out, that despite media modernisation and expansion, the growing vacuity of democracy continues to be in danger. Impersonal technology instead of furthering communication is, in actuality, a hindrance. One could go further than this and call it a blinding force.

Each event discussed above mobilised support and caught media attention in a different way and the content, methodology, representation and media projection in each case has been sharply different. What we see in the period 1919–1930 is a direct involvement with people as a whole to raise the consciousness of the ordinary person. As Partha Chatterjee observes, 'Gandhism provided for the first time in Indian politics an ideological basis for including the whole people within the political nation' (Chatterjee 189). In 1992 what we have is a total reversal of this when religious boundaries adhere to different Gods and results in a reintroduction of blind faith and passive followers. Even the judiciary has been swayed by the general atmosphere (refer Irfan Habib's, 'These are fundamental matters for the SC to consider on Ayodha', *Times of India,* November 3, 2010, p. 10). Amitabh Bachchan in a Gujarat Tourism advertisement, telecast repetitively before the HC judgement on 30 October 2010 foregrounded the Somnath Temple, thus preparing a background of religiosity. How dumb can we get? How large is the shadow of fear?

Gandhi's emphasis on truth and inclusiveness was an evocation of the Bhakti spirit; the media representation was reflective rather than manufactured. It was an event between David and Goliath. The Pakistan demonstrations did display a positive impulse towards resistance to authoritarianism. In a modern-day democratic India, the freedom of dissent is there, yet dissent in itself is marginalised and invisible, for as mentioned earlier, capitalist-owned presses and paid channels cater to the advertiser's need. Noam Chomsky's concept of 'manufacturing consent', is visible in its full form.[5] There is a fairly intrusive web of astrological forecasts, auspicious timings, lucky stones and poojas to ward off evil, accompanied by several religious serials, especially reflecting supernaturalism, superstitions and the miraculous, that surround the political news and help create passive audiences. The questionings that occasionally find place, in the print media, or in works of art as in some films and literature, and autobiographies that supplement selective narration, are few and available only to the truly interested. Perceptive journalism also exists. It is true that literature too has an embedding of visual images, but only the discerning reader finds an etching in his mind, years after the reading. The electronic media has an immediacy, it generates an excitement, ignites at times a reciprocity and mostly always acquires followers[6] (unless we switch off the channel in sheer disgust). The questions we need to ask – is it neutral, does it present all perspectives, and how does it use language and image? Above all – is it truly informed or is it caught up in its own rhetoric and merely plays to the gallery? Despite power having a tendency to exclude, and despite its being vested in the elite (and the monied), the average score is below average and leaves much to be desired. Its impact on our present is unhealthy – and if we are turned into passive consumers, it is obvious enough that unknown forces are going to take over our minds and our lives.

Notes

1. Salt was extracted all along the sea coast and sold in the streets of Bombay as 'the freedom of salt'. Those who did not join in the making, joined the campaign by buying illegal salt. (See http://www.utexas.edu/cola/insts/southasia/files/pdf.

2. Fatima Bhutto gives an account of the report as well as the subsequent political fall out in terms of the administration's threats in fair amount of detail. See Fatima Bhutto 372–377.
3. See http://en.wikipedia.org/wiki/*Ramayan* (TV series). Last modified on 16 October, 2010 at 15.42. accessed 11 November 2010 at 13.30.
4. See J. Kuruvachira, *Politicisation of Hindu Religion in Postmodern India* (Jaipur: Rawat Publications, 2008) pp. 83–91. Kuruvachira traces Advani's base in the RSS and his identification with the ideologies propagated by its early leaders. Advani's *Prison Diary* has frequent references to his reading of Hitler's *Mein Kampf* (87).
5. See Edward S. Herman and Noam Chomsky. *Manufacturing Consent: The Political Economy of the Mass Media*. New York: Pantheon Books, 1988. Herman and Chomsky pointed out that corporate media was profit-driven and as such committed to the interests of dominant, elite groups, unwilling to criticise them. What was presented as news was in effect propaganda. internet ref.
6. Chomsky's concern for the deteriorating state of liberal democracy is a continuation of the fears which were earlier expressed by men like Adorno and Walter Benjamin and has been a persisting strain in his writings, as for instance in the essays included in *Powers and Prospects: Reflections on Human Nature and the Social Order.* (London: Pluto Press, 2007), especially the essay as 'Democracy and Markets in the New Worlds'. More recently in November 1, 2010, issue of *Outlook*, has an interview of Chomsky, where he comments on the intellectuals who are educated into a loyalist stand towards the state with the objective of 'controlling' thought. The Orwellian world of doublespeak and doublethink is never far. In fact it is real and visible.

11

The Fictional Form

From the Endings to the Beginnings (The Growth of the Realistic Novel)

Thou from the first
Wast present, and with mighty wings outspread
Dove-like satst brooding on the vast Abyss
And made it pregnant

(Milton, *Paradise Lost Bk 1, ll 19.22)*

The linear relationship between 'beginnings' and 'endings' is reversed in the title, primarily because I wish to see the connection between the two and the impact of the endings on the fictional form in the Indian novel. In 1870 or thereabouts Bankim Chandra Chatterjee wrote a fairly lengthy review article titled 'Bengali Literature' which reflects, amongst other things, on his own writing.[1] His observations throw light both on the socio-political environment as well as on the psychology of the intellectual of his times. There is a privileging of Bengali literature, because he is of the view that the quantum of the writing in Bengali easily exceeds those in other languages. It is common knowledge that several works from Bengali were translated into other languages in quick succession[2] and its impact or opposition to the development of form in other languages cannot be ignored. He wrote this essay when he had several novels behind him: *Rajmohan's Wife* (1864), *Durgeshnandini* (1865), *Kapala Kundala* (1866) and *Mrinalini* (1869), each one of them of a different kind, though three of these were located in the historical past. At about the same time Nanda Shankar Mehta's *Karen Ghelo,* a historical novel, had appeared in

1866, and Baba Padmananji's *Yamuna Paryatan* as early as 1857. Gauri Dutt's *Devrani Jethani Ki Kahani* (1870), a slim didactic pamphlet has also been viewed as a novel, though the place for the first novel in Hindi is now contested between *Bhagyavati* (1877) and *Priksha Guru* (1882). The first volume of Goverdhanram Tripathi's *Saraswati Chandra* appeared in 1887. When we turn to Urdu, Nazir Ahmad's novel *Mirat-ul-nissa* (translated in 1903 as *The Bride's Mirror*) appeared in 1869. Toru Dutt's novels had been written before 1877, though they were both, *Bianca* and *Journal de Mademoiselle d'Arvors,* published posthumously. The need to place these works in a horizontal parallelism has been felt because of the myriad forces which were impacting the writing of this period, some of which can be identified as education, translation, social concern, the presence of patronisation, development of languages and also the growing awareness of a national identity. It is not possible to look at these literary developments as a direct transmission from the west to the east. Sisir Kumar Das has subtitled his first volume of *The History of Indian Literature 1800–1910: Western Impact: Indian Response,*[3] clearly indicating the interaction but also simultaneously stressing that it was not passive. The element of the indigenous element is recognised though not necessarily elaborated upon. Keeping this background in mind, Bankim Chandra's essay, specially his views on contemporary writing, including that of his own, acquires additional significance. That the essay is written in English and was easily accessible across languages is also of significance.

There is an apparent tone of disappointment with the quality of writing as well as that of criticism. He laments the absence of 'anything like intelligent criticism' and is critical of the native writer's contempt for his own language. The writers can easily be categorised into two distinctive schools – those who belong to the Sanskrit school and those who are influenced by the west. Strangely enough, he goes on to observe, the latter have quality on their side (107). But the need for writing to be rooted in its own soil in order to be meaningfully creative, is also strongly felt. Further, style and ideas need to be more integrated than they were (at that time). This separation, the writer points out, is fatal to the idea of form and needs to be worked on in greater detail, as the two together shape form. Working through the work of a host of writers, he finally comes to his own and comments at length on *Kapala Kundala* which is very much like a gothic novel but in the Indian tradition. We have disguises, betrayals, conversions and intrigues. We also have tantric interventions, the demand for a victim to be sacrificed to the goddess Bhiwani, in fact all that can be identified as the staple matter of a tantric tale, including the supernatural, is present in it. Yet it is different. It seeks to subvert the mainstream Hindu tradition as well as the tantric hegemony. Naba Kumar is deeply in love with Kapala Kundala, but she is not fascinated by this male desire. The romantic enchantment is absent. Later, she keeps an appointment with a brahmin boy (who is none other than Luft-un-nissa, Naba Kumar's first wife, in male disguise). Bankim Chandra writes, 'No other Hindu wife would have kept the appointment but she did and not unnoticed' (123). There are several polarities which hold the structure together – the evil designs of Kapalika, the tantric, the reversal of his role of nurturer to executor, his powerlessness in the face of his professed power, and this is contrasted with Luft-un-nissa's good intentions. Kapala Kundala is placed at the centre of these opposing claims. Again, while Luft-un-nissa plans to work on Kapala's sense of gratitude to achieve her aim, Kapalika wants to arouse Naba Kumar's jealousy to achieve his. Finally there is the goddess Kali who is worshipped alike by Kapala – as Kali – and Kapalika as Bhiwani. This merger of the devotion of the victim and the prosecutor highlights another deviation. Kapala is finally not sacrificed, she defeats Kapilaka's desire by accidentally falling into the sea but voluntarily submitting to the flow of the current. Both the love stories end in disappointment. Luft-un-nissa fails to get her earlier wifehood, Naba Kumar his beloved. And so, Bankim writes, 'the story ends, much to the disappointment of most Bengali readers, who much prefer the orthodox ending where all live happily ever after' ('Bengali Literature' 123).

The fact that this analysis is offered by the writer himself reveals a high level of consciousness in the organisation of his material. One also needs to remember that all his four novels, up to this point, have tragic endings, a feature which 'made them moving and memorable' (Sisir Kumar Das, *Western Impact* 199). Bankim Chandra is obviously simultaneously trying to create a new form and a new kind of readership. The ending is the culmination of the earlier subversions. Why did Bankim Chandra deny the lovers fulfillment and a reunion? Why is Kapala so conscious of devotion to Kali and indifferent to Naba Kumar's devotion? What power or lack of power does the *tantrik* signify? These are important questions and compel the reader to connect the ending with the beginning.

The ending is, in part an adjustment to the demands of realism (which have been kept in abeyance for the major part of the novel), but in part it is also an assertion of human will and a subversion of the romantic tradition of Sanskrit drama which worked for a restoration after a period of trial, and which adhered to the notion of fulfillment as a reward for virtue and goodness. In contrast both the major epics, *Mahabharata* and *Ramayana,* do not project a happy ending. Similarly none of the *kissas*, whether of Heer-Ranjha, Sassi-Punnu, or Dhola-Maru work towards happy endings. They foreground the human condition marked by longing and unfulfillment. By using the unhappy ending, Bankim Chandra is also identifying the novel with the epic tradition. But this he does only as far as the ending is concerned. In other respects, related to characterisation, language, time and authorial framing, he departs from this tradition. I refer the reader to Bakhtin's essay 'Epic and Novel' wherein he traces the characteristics of the epic and locates it firmly in the national tradition. It is 'an utterly finished thing', in comparison with which the novel is as 'yet uncompleted' it is 'organically receptive to new forms of mute perception, that is, to reading', has maximal contact with the present and is located more in experience than in a national collective memory or image of the past. In many ways novelistic experiments are a constant re-evaluation of the past (13–17). By using an unhappy ending in the manner that he does in *Kapala Kundala*, Bankim Chandra delegates a degree of choice along with an element of responsibility to the character. One is responsible for the choices one makes. Luft-un-nissa, having first abandoned Naba Kumar, cannot be restored to her earlier position. Similarly, male desire is underprivileged. Simply by desiring Kapala Kundala, Naba Kumar cannot hope to gain her. The novel has two parallel discourses, one is romantic and the other realistic. When they stop running parallel, and intervene with each other, they upset each other's premises.

If we go back to Bankim Chandra's first novel, *Rajmohan's Wife* (1864) – his only one in English – we come across a similar ending of unfulfilled desire and disappointment. Matangini moves to her father's house as her husband, Rajmohan, is transported. And Mathur Ghose, who has lusted after other people's loves and property, hangs himself, leaving behind his wife Tara, 'to mourn in solitude'. It is interesting to see the manner in which the narrative progresses to such an end. Early in the novel, the reader is introduced to the unhappiness of the eighteen-year old Matangini, who is kept by her husband under close surveillance. The two are temperamentally worlds apart. Matangini's quiet submission is contrasted with Rajmohan's aggressive stance, her good with his evil. The initial episode when she is persuaded by Kanak to accompany her to the river to fetch water, is the first step to reach out to the outer world and a prelude to her midnight journey, which she later undertakes, to warn her brother-in-law about the planned dacoity on him. In both of these Kanak is with her. Matangini is conscious of the extraordinary step she is taking and the conflict in her mind between duty to her husband and duty to her sister's husband is realistically portrayed. She also has the difficult task of persuading Kanak's mother to allow Kanak to accompany her and all this without in the least betraying or implicating her husband. Matangini is fully conscious that her 'only resource lay in herself' (31). *Rajmohan's Wife,* despite this attempt at a realistic portrayal, is overcrowded with events, intrigues, hostilities, conspiracies and their reversals and conflicts as it moves towards its end at a rapid pace. This dominance of events is a trait which the realistic novel of this period shares with the romantic one, with one difference that the events in the realistic novel are instrumental in developing character and reflect moral choices.

Strange though it may seem, the realistic novel upholds moral uprightness and does not desist from expounding on the didactic element. In a way this is unreal, but paradoxically it also helps the realistic dimension which seeks to incorporate the 'ideal' code of moral behaviour. The distinction between sin and evil, between lust and its fulfillment is maintained. Indira is not raped (in Bankim Chandra's novel *Indira*), Matangini is not violated, only imprisoned and threatened (*Rajmohan's Wife*), Shanti (*Anand*

Math) is not sexually desired by the other *santans*. This is a common trend in most of the writing of this period. The virtuous woman, like Sita in the hands of Ravana, succeeds in protecting her virtue which acts like a wall between her and unsanctioned desire. Matangini, despite her love for Madhav, her brother-in-law, and the attraction she holds for Mathur, does not yield either to desire or to force.[4]

At this period of Indian literary history, several different forces which guided the theme and form of the novel, collided with each other. Certain novels were written to order, to fulfill a need felt by the government to understand India, and British officers extended their patronisation to these writers. These novels were written either as textbooks, as conduct books or as works which familiarised the foreigner with Indian culture. Nazir Ahmad's novel *Mirat-ul-Arus* (1869) was one such novel. G.E. Ward who translated the novel in 1903, wrote in the 'Translator's Note' that an earlier publication in 1899 in the Roman character was intended 'as a text-book for students of Hindustani'. He goes on to point out that it 'makes no claim to literary merit; but since so little is known in England about the social and domestic life of our fellow-subjects, an authentic picture of one phase of it' may hold interest for the British reader. Nazir Ahmad in his own preface apparently wrote the novel because he felt that 'purely religious subjects of study are not suited to the capacities of children', it depressed their spirits and 'checking their natural instincts blunted their intelligence' (2). Thus the work was an attempt to combine pleasure with learning. He takes the reader into the lives of two sisters who respond to their circumstances and handle them differently and we see Asghari managing the affairs of her husband's family with wisdom and restraint and thus commanding a deal of respect. What is important is the word 'authentic' in G.E. Ward's 'Note'. Nazir Ahmad allows the authorial presence to frame the narrative. There is an orality present in his style and he sums up his achievement in the thirtieth chapter when he says, 'We may call it a story for children, but in sooth it is a sermon for their elders. However, the novel does not end there. Asghari loses her children one after the other and receives a letter from her father advising her to reconcile herself to her loss'.[5]

Gauri Dutt's *Devrani Jethani Ki Kahani* (1870), a long story follows a similar pattern. In this case, the 'devrani', 'jethani' are only sisters-in-law and not sisters like Akbari and Asghari. *Devrani Jethani Ki Kahani* works through comparison, contrasts, jealousies and lauds the value of education and the development of character which ensues from it. Incidentally, such narratives begin to attach a lot of value to character formation, inner strength, will power and reduce the influence of destiny and environment alike. They also facilitate the movement outside domestic concerns to social concerns. The novels of the 1880s and 1890s are, all of a sudden, much longer, more rooted in socio-political concerns and have, in large measure, outgrown the purely romantic or gothic concerns. Bankim's later and Tagore's early novels, Hari Narayan Apte's work, Goverdhanram Tripathi's *Saraswati Chandra*, Ruswa's *Umrao Jan Ada* and Krupabai Satthainadhan's two novels belong to this period, Goverdhanram Tripathi was extremely conscious of the task of nation-building and determined to give up a thriving practice in order to do full-time writing. He turned to fiction primarily, as he specified in his Preface to the novel, because the Gujarati readers were 'for various reasons, difficult to reach through abstruse or discursive matter, and that illustrations of real or ideal life would be the best medium'. The character of Saraswati Chandra was a vision of his own desired ideals as he stated in his *Scrapbook* (Vol. 1):

> I have been training up, like tender plants, and to such mental and moral growth, as my circumstances allow, my children, my wife, my brother and my parents. I must do the same for my country. ... Saraswati Chandra does undertake at its own point, works without doubt and people feel the book. (31)

Though it is not possible to trace any single line of development, the presence of 'talsami' literature like the popular novels of Devaki Nandan Khatri cannot be ignored,[6] yet the unhappy or the tragic ending has been instrumental in making the claims of life felt, and providing a framework for the realistic approach. One of the reasons why the unhappy ending took over was the rootedness of the novel in experience. Autobiographical novels could not be fabricated; historical reality could not be falsified; social problems had no miraculous solutions. Further, conflictual situations, besides being psychologically real were also essential for narrative interest and character could only develop through challenge. Most of the novels of this period rely on dialogue and the spoken idiom. The orality of the native tradition is absorbed. Chandu Menon in his preface to *Indulekha* points out the impact of the oral tradition. He recounts how he used to orally translate English novels for his friends, to the extent that the taste thus acquired for 'listening to novels translated orally gradually developed into a passion' (x). Oral translation with its interventions, explanations and commentaries kept the text alive, which did not happen when it was a written translation, then it appeared just a 'string of words' (xi). Therefore he undertook the challenge of writing a novel in Malayam, apparently in the English fashion. But Menon went on to use the language which he would 'ordinarily speak' at home and brought in the spoken idiom thus adapting the western form to his own use. Realism for him implied a living language, location in the present and elimination of the supernatural. Contemporary politics is also reflected in *Indulekha*, but the novel stops short of an unhappy ending. It substitutes the miraculous with dreams and finally unites Indulekha with Madhavan.

Several of the novels which find a way out of an ending of unfulfillment do so by working towards a transcendental philosophy, religious mysticism or raising the suffering character to the level of sainthood. In Apte's *Mein*, (the title means 'me/I') the hero, an educationist, turned social reformer, acquires a moral stature which frees him from sorrow. In Satthianadhan's *Saguna* religious faith supercedes all sorrow, in Goverdhanram Tripathi's *Saraswati Chandra* the impact of the tragic end is reduced by the hero's rising above self-interest. *Sanyasa* or asceticism are not perceived as tragic. Contrast the ending of *Saguna* with another novel, Mirza Hadi Ruswa's *Umrao Jan Ada*, which is a first person narration cast in the form of a memory novel, a recollection in retrospect. It is a narrative of unfulfilled dreams, desires and possibilities. Women – whether in *Kapala Kundala, Mein, Kamala* or *Umrao Jan Ada* – all move in this direction. Even as writers such as Tagore and Premchand move in the same direction, in *Choker Bali* (1903) and *Sewa Sadan* (1918), they fail to find any way for women to be happy, primarily on account of the constrictive social practices and customs.

The endings are obviously connected with the beginnings, they follow a logical development. *Rajmohan's Wife* begins with Matangini's transgression of the boundaries laid down for her, *Kapala Kundala* is framed in the past, taking the reader back by two and a half centuries, *Umrao Jan Ada* begins with a response to an admirer's query. It opens with an epigraph posing a choice between the personal and the universal (*aap beeti* or *jagbeeti*) and goes on to address the listener, 'Listen then, Mirza Sahib! What is it that you want to know, what is there in the tale of an unfortunate being like me that interests you?' (Hindi edition 9, translation mine). The narrator then goes on to describe the background, the abduction which, by suddenly shifting her life from her family's protection and the preparations for her wedding, changes the direction of her future life.

Both the novels of Krupabai Satthianadhan begin very differently thus clearly marking the difference despite their similarities. *Kamala: The Story of a Hindu Life* is narrated from the outside and locates Kamala's life in the socio-cultural context. This setting determines the authorial point of view. The opening sentence is, 'India may not be a perfect paradise, yet there are spots of surpassing beauty and grandeur'. It is against this background, and in this setting that Kamala, the daughter of an old Brahmin recluse, makes an appearance. Class, caste and location are all firmly defined, in the midst of which the lonely child awaits her father's return. *Saguna* originally subtitled 'A Story of Native Christian Life' is intended to be a contrast to *Kamala*. Chandani Lokuge by changing the subtitle to the 'First Autobiographical Novel in English by an Indian Woman' dislocates it from this parallelism and places it directly in the western market by stressing gender, language, form and nationality, thereby bypassing the intention of the author. The two novels are both woman-centred and stress the socio-religious context which affects a woman's life. The story of *Saguna* falls into two clear-cut divisions, the story of Radha, the mother, and the second the story of the daughter. This division is marked only by a narrative shift in the fifth chapter. From the literary point of view, the authorial interventions, both in narration and in projecting a point of view, may strike a discordant note but the description of the household scenes, the woman to woman relationships, the conflicts caused by lack of freedom evoke a certain emotional response in the reader.

The point, I think, is sufficiently clear. The framing is structured by the beginnings in each case, time, memory or present, by the narrative voice and a subtitle (when there is one), socio-religious frameworks and the first act which may establish a contact with the outer world. Plausibility, character development and action are then determined by the time, location and tone, and work towards an ending which, though not predetermined as inevitable, is predetermined by the narratorial logic and the demands of the new social situation. The writer is responsive (unless he is engaged in writing escapist literature) to the ferment of ideas of his contemporary life.

Form cannot be imposed on nothingness; it merely shapes the material which is already there. The antonym to form is not necessarily formlessness but it could be chaos; form by imposing a shape, even when it is fluid, becomes part of the meaning. It has a number of constituents – story, events, temporality, imagination, language, values, purpose – but none of them is in itself form. Structure is also to be distinguished from form. It is instrumental in realising form and is the relationship between the different elements; it is the strategy through which meaning is created through arrangement, sequence, imagery, reference, myth and allusion, it is the framework which by stressing the 'present' also evokes the 'absent', but it is not form. Form is the overall shape which structure is instrumental in creating. Or is it the other way around? The vision of the form precedes structure and structure supports this vision?

Both form and structure are governed by generic affiliations which determine the framing. In large measure they are culture bound and emanate from the philosophical and narrative traditions of the society. If this were not so, the distinctive traditions one can trace in England and America, France and Russia would not be there. Translations, influences, ideas travel but the roots are in the socio-cultural environment. The novel, more than any other literary form, reflects an immediacy of response. One begins from the wrong end if one works from the outside to the inside. It has to be the other way around. At some point the writer's own vision has to respond to the outside world. Translations, exposure, readings may evoke responses, shape differences, stimulate thinking, send one into the opposite direction but do not automatically lead to imitation.

Official patronisation did cut across languages but very often, a counter discourse exists, if not in the text then around the text, therefore it is not possible to separate the writing in other Indian languages from the writing in English. Bankim Chandra's historical novels do differ from the work of writers like R.C. Dutt and Sardar Joginder Singh who wrote about historical characters, highlighted heroism and boosted up the idea of national glory. They both wrote in English. Bankim Chandra, on the other hand wrote for the purposes of analysis, introspection and a reconstruction of the past. He does not take up characters from history. More often than not, they are imagined ones. He wrote in Bengali. Sisir Kumar Das, commenting upon Bankim Chandra's historical novels, writes:

> Bhudeb Mukhopadhyay and later Bankim Chandra, though apparently closer to the indigenous tradition in their love of the dramatic and exotic elements, really identified themselves with the European novel form: Bankim's choice of history was regulated by his admiration for Scott, but his use of history was different from that of the British novelist. The anachronisms in Bankim are his deliberate choice. ... They are not just exciting stories for brief enjoyment but moving human documents. (200–201)

He goes on to comment on *Karen Ghelo* (Nanda Shankar Mehta's novel in Gujarati) and stresses the regional quality of these novels. But Mehta's work, in Das's view, shares some features with the *adbhuta katha*. Thus there was no getting away from local forces, the demands of the social situation, the question of readership and the aesthetics of *rasa*. It is interesting to note that the history plays of this period were more influenced by Shakespeare's tragedies rather than his history plays (Sisir Kumar

Das 284). Was the tragic ending an expression of the nation's frustration at the consciousness of its subordination?

Indian writers of this period seriously debated the issues of influence and form. We find this in Chandu Menon's 'Preface' as well as in the essays of Bankim Chandra. Evidence of this lurks in the writings of others. The novel as history was discussed by writers like Rabindranath Tagore, Vrindavanlal Varma and Hazari Prasad Dwivedi[7] amongst others, writings which compel us to look at fictional forms not merely as byproducts of influence, but as a response to societal needs, a rootedness in tradition, and an interplay between the real, the imagined and the desired.

An important category which many an Indian writer had to contend with was the category of 'truth'. Truth was not mere fact, it went beyond that, and there could be a discrepancy between the observable or projected 'fact' and 'truth'. Truth was compatible with imagination. A second factor which needs attention is the relationship between legend and history, or myth and history. How far is myth a part of history? With the Indian tradition rooted in the *Mahabharata* and the *Ramayana* the two freely crossing over from one to the other (myth and history), another factor which needs attention is the process of transforming the particular into the universal. How is this to be done: through imagination or through factual narration? The literary representation lifts the personal to the level of the universal by expanding itself to include the societal framework. No tale of an individual is entirely only of that individual: it is inhabited by others. Native traditions like the *akhyan* tradition, the *adbhuta katha,* the *purana,* the *janamsakhi, tota-maina kahani* surface over and over again. But the realistic novel, using them as a springboard, outgrows them. It formulates itself on the conflict between the individual and external forces, the relationship is no longer passive; individual will, choice, responsibility and accountability all are centre stage. The social and moral frameworks are interrogated, action is often transgressive and subversive. The element of orality is incorporated with great ease in the writing in most of the Indian languages, moving away from the rhetoric and grandeur of the epic poetic tradition. This is not so perceptible in the writing in English.

Having travelled this distance, let me ask the final question: is the form of the Renaissance novel an imported one or an indigenous one – native or non-native? I have argued that in the main it is a native one though no generalisations are possible. I have moved horizontally between languages and sub-genres in order to trace their commonalties as well as their differences. The moment we remove our focus from the west-governed normative patterns we find the growth and development of the inherited forms. The nature of both aesthetics and imagination is governed by cultural and philosophical contexts. The gradual submergence of the didactic factor and the surfacing of 'non sermon-like' narrative is influenced by the growing readership, national concerns and the intellectual's conscious need to relate. Acts of subversion do not violate a moral vision, they are legitimised in the interests of a larger vision. Bankim Chandra's unhappy ending in *Kapala Kundala* (as in many other novels), is meant to shock the reader into the reality of failure; Umrao Jan's life, narrated objectively and often unconsciously, subdues the didactic, critiques societal structures and by standing dispassionately outside self-pity, maintains an aesthetic distance (which is not always visible in *Kamala* and *Saguna*). This reversal of the happy ending is a significant marking of the new late nineteenth century form.

Notes

1. One of the books he lists there has been published in 1870. Thus it is fair to assume that it is written approximately at about that time. And he does not refer to any of his novels published after 1869.
2. Refer Acharya Ramchandra Shukla's *Hindi Sahitya Ka Itihaas*. Varanasi: Nagaripracharani Sabha (1976), 1997 p. 272.
3. I would like to identify this as the Renaissance period. Though many critics extend it to 1930 or even later but that would ignore other literary shifts.
4. A similar situation exists in Bhai Vir Singh's novels, *Sundari* and *Satwant Kaur*. But it undergoes a change in novels like *Umrao Jan Ada* (1899) where the young girl is abducted and sold and in some of Tagore's novels where the younger sister replaces her older sister in her brother-in-law's affection and enters the household as a second

wife (as for instance in Tagore's *Do Behne*). But by and large the code of purity within domesticity is preserved in the Indian novel.

5. One needs to look at this kind of writing more closely: is it devoid of literary merit or of social utility? Did this kind of writing contribute or not to the development of the fictional form? It is not possible to dismiss its popularity lightly. *Mirat-ul-Arus* sold over 100,000 copies within a few years of its publication in 1869. Such novels brought in the element of graphic description of social life and offered practical advice. They made an entry into protected areas, propagated the values of education and combined amusement with learning. They also sought to develop values of independent thinking and choice. *Mirat-ul-Arus* was prefaced by two recommendations, one by Kempson, the Director of Instruction, North Western Provinces and the other by Sir William Muir, the Lieutenant Government of the North Western Provinces. Kempson compared its prose with the 'recently published letters' of Ghalib and traced its lineage to *Alif Lailah* and *Boston-e-Khiyal*. Sir William Muir recommended it for its reliance on experience and clarity of language (200–203) Patronisation often took the form of literary prizes and monetary benefits. And Nazir Ahmad, a government employee, benefitted in several ways. The work, despite its didactic element, has a realistic base and is subversive in its intent of allowing Asghari a degree of freedom which undermines 'unquestioning subordination to her male elder' (Frances Pritchett Afterword, 215).
6. Acharya Ram Chandra Shukla in his *Hindi Sahitya Ka Itihaas* considers Devaki Nandan Khatri to be the first original writer in Hindi and his great popularity was due not only to his ingenuity in plot constructions but also his language which was very much a mixture of Hindi and Urdu and had a broad colloquial base. Many people learned Hindi in order to read his novels and he had a host of imitators (272–273).
7. Refer the essays of Rabindra Nath Tagore and several other writers in the volume *Itihaskik Upanyas*. Ed. by Govindji published in Meerut. n.d.

Note: *Devrani Jethani Ki Kahani, Priksha Guru*, etc., were read at the India Office Library, London.

12

Contestatory Relations

Sobti's *Shabdon Ke Aalok Mein* and *Sobti-Vaid Samvaad*

> *Ek ster pe rachna aur rachnakar ke sambandh bakaida pratidwandi ke taveron ki tarah teekhe hote hain. Yeh raagatmak dwandho ki hadh tak gahre bhi hoten hai.*
>
> (Sobti, *Shabdon ke Aalok Mein* 181)
>
> (At one level, the relationship between creation and its creator is invariably sharp like the antagonistic posture of rivals. At the same time it is deep to the measure of a harmonious conflict).

The nature of creativity, its linguistic base, the writer-critic relationship and the controlled playfulness of mixed genre formation are my main concerns when approaching these two texts by Sobti. Creativity for a writer constructs itself on the 'word'. All other concerns – experience, imagination, self and the world – either converge towards it or emanate from it. Therefore Sobti's use of language is primary to her own vision of writing. The use of language can either be expressive, where language is used for effective articulation, or it may be extractive, where every word is made to yield its meaning and the process of this extraction involves a grappling with its core. Language does not only express, it also moulds ideas: in itself writing is a dialogic process and not a filter. Her two recent non-fictional works, *Shabdon ke Aalok Mein* (2005) and *Sobti-Vaid Samvaad: Writing and Writer* (2007 with Krishna Baldev Vaid), are about the process of writing and simultaneously they challenge conventional genre formations. The first announces its multiple thrust in the blurb, acknowledging that it has brought together varied forms as a means of communication; the second places the dialogue between two well known writers as a means of reflecting on the chronicles of time through their memories, visions and perceptions. They are unusual in their intent: the focus in each is multi-functional and the movement centrifugal.

Shabdon ke Aalok Mein is part memoir, part letters, interviews, articles, imagined and dramatically constructed self-critiques, confessions, veiled glimpses of the personal self and a continued discussion on the nature of writing. Sobti discusses, in this work, her position on feminism, on language and most prominently the nature of literary evaluation. The *Sobti-Vaid Samvaad* is a dialogue between Krishna Sobti and Krishna Baldev Vaid, but it has its shades of an oppositional argument. A joint communiqué about the nature of writing, each writer acts as the mirror for the other, and as a result, compelling both a statement as well as a judgement from the other. They disagree, debate and express divergent opinions and move from memory and history to linguistic constructs, nature of simplicity, the necessary 'distortion' in realism and throw light on the nature of representation as distinct from mere narration. The discussions in the two overlap but the authorial control is more assertive in the *Samvaad*. *Shabdon ke Aalok Mein* with its single author centre is less inhibited in its sense of freedom and is marked by a degree of willfulness, a giving in to the impulse of the moment whether it is to get wet in the rain or sit down in the middle of the lawn to have a cup of tea. The two together are enough to push the reader to a closer examination of the relationship of a writer to her writing and her need for the 'other', the oppositional self.

Sobti in the dock

The following extract is a translation of a dramatic trial from *Shabdon ke Aalok Mein*:

> Guilty?
> With a nod of the head – Yes, Sir.

Guilty?
With a bowed head – Yes, Sir.

You, who are such a loudmouth, how come suddenly so docile? You who are so fierce even in your writing. You are beguiling us!

No sir, the truth is that I am greatly oppressed by my shortcomings, weaknesses and limitations. I am aware of them. That's why–

So all that has been said in the review seems to be valid to you?
Yes, Sir.

All that was hinted at the writer – you comprehend it?
Yes, Sir.

Those faults that were detected in your craftsmanship, in your language, did you understand that as well?
[...]

Whatever little has been said in praise of your writing, did you understand why it was so?
Yes.

What was the reason?
Kappad-chhan, the straining through a cloth.

What do you mean?
All that is wasteful is strained in the three drafts.
[...]

You are known for being an old hand at trouble making, you have the audacity to argue!

(*Shabdon ke Aalok Mein* 342–343)

The above extract, offers a very interesting self-examination by the writer. She spells out the criticism which has welcomed the arrival of every new work of hers and singles out *Zindaginama* for special mention. The main charge against the writer is her departure from standard Hindi. The language she uses is adulterated with folk languages, dialects, localised idiom and regional inflections and on these grounds the writer is dismissed as an uncultured person, untrained in literary practice. This accusation is the final straw and it cuts through the submissive stance of the accused. The concluding paragraph of this piece reads as follows:

> Nagari [Devnagari] is not anyone's paternal property. Its glow has nothing to do with its being a language of power. It is not the language merely of authority or of the priests. Hindi is not an old garb of Sanskrit. It is, in its own right, a living language – the language of the rich and the poor, the farmers, the workers, the disadvantaged.
>
> (*Shabdon* 345)

This dramatisation of the criticism levied at her on account of the variations and range of the language, uses a male persona, perhaps in the interests of gender neutrality. It alternates between self-reflection and self-assertion. The language is double-voiced, the tone a 'tongue-in-cheek' but the purpose is serious. Sobti, admittedly, has been a controversial writer, at times on account of her themes but mostly on account of her linguistic deviations from normative patterns. There are two ways of looking at it. Her critics look at it from the purist angle and insist that Hindi is the language of the Hindi-speaking heartland. But what they see as an infiltration of other speech forms and linguistic registers is exactly what her admirers admire her for. Hindi has expanded and evolved in her hands as she has stretched it to accommodate the multiple voices in which it is spoken. As K.B. Vaid has observed, Sobti has never so far repeated herself. For every novel she has sharpened her tools accordingly to meet its requirements. *Zindaginama* and *Dilo-danish* both cover almost the same period but as the locations, class and power structures are different the language of *Zindaginama* is of a small hierarchical, feudalistic community and has a larger share of the spoken idiom even as it distinguishes between public and private space, family and community get-togethers and between the language of the learned and the workers while *Dilo-danish* locates itself in the environment of Chandni Chowk and Jama Masjid in the opening decades of the twentieth century and uses Urdu of that period.

Dilo-danish also makes a distinction between the language spoken in the two households of Kripanarayan and this distinction begins with the names. His wife is Kutumbpyari (beloved of the family) while the mistress is Mehak (fragrance). Sobti does not hesitate to move out of literary Hindi. Kripanarayan's last will – '*Lal Behi Ke Aakhri Panne Se*' (From the last page of the red ledger) is a superb example of sophisticated urban Hindustani (*Dilo-danish* 191–197). The strengths of her prose are in its flexibility and range; it vibrates with the vigour of the peasants, the sophistication of aristocracy and restraint in expressions of love. Again, it is the folk language heavily laden with proverbs and idioms peculiar to those lifestyles which enriches her prose.

Sobti has also been attacked on grounds of the boldness of her language (as well as of her theme) in *Mitro Marjani*. Published as early as 1966, the novel invited criticism on two grounds – the strong, bold language and the articulation of female sexuality. A similar charge was also levelled at *Yaaron ke Yaar*. In her interview with Anamika, Sobti states that abusive epithets have their own power as they express the incompatibilities and hostilities present in society (*Shabdon* 313). Both accusations were levelled at her primarily because she is a woman. Very few critics saw in this the reach of the writer who was able to transcend the limits of gender and capture the essence of reality.

Sobti apparently has no claim to the lineage of Bhartendu Harishchandra, who was a purist in language, but she has, as she has herself pointed out, very respectable antecedents in writers like Chandradhar Sharma Guleri (of *Usne Kaha Tha* fame), and Phaneshwar Nath Renu (the writer of *Maila Anchal*), who did not hesitate to move outside standard Hindi. Guleri went on to substitute *kudmai* for *sagai*, *ladi* for *dulhan* and so on in order to capture the local colour.[1] Writing is not author controlled and in the novelistic discourse, it has to inhabit a variety of sub-discourses. A point extremely significant is that Sobti has not used the first person narration in anyone of her fictional works. One can see the continuity of style in both *Shabdon ke Aalok Mein* and *Sobti-Vaid Samvaad*. One can also identify repetitive patterns in her essays but not so the novels where the going across to the particular period in history, linguistic register, class, religion and gender comprehensively creates a world. This going across is not merely an act of identification, or empathy or of reaching out but something more than that. It is an attempt to extract something from a relationship with a stranger. It involves a whole process of getting into the mindset of the people, their circumstantial compulsions, lineages, linguistic knowledge and historical realities. The author begins from the opposite end and works her way towards this stranger. Speech is intimately connected with one's whole being: it is not merely a communication. In the interview given to Anamika, Sobti comments upon the simultaneity of belonging and not-belonging, the stepping in and out of oneself and working towards an unfamiliarity not only of the 'other' but also of one's own self. The absence of the writer from the text (*Shabdon* 9), the distancing from one's self and one's experience (*Samvaad* 46), are the processes that free the writer to relate to others, both writers and readers, horizontally. A writer is rooted in an intellectual community from which be draws both his freedom and objectivity creating conditions when one can take a stand against one's own self and support the other (*Shabdon* 179). Qualities like realism and simplicity both depend on the kind of language one uses – as does authenticity. First person narration or a dominant authorial voice as a *sutradhar* goes only half way to the other. It internalises the dialogue but does not internalise the dialogic process – that is the dialogue often emerges from the imagination of the author not from the author's struggle with the newness of the other, with what is alien to the author.

The process of dialogisation

Sobti-Vaid Samvaad is framed as a dialogue between two writers, near contemporaries and near neighbours. They both hail from Punjab. Sobti was born in Gujarat (in West Punjab) and Vaid in a township near Rawalpindi. Both have witnessed the same political upheaval and have written about it in their fiction. Further they both write in Hindi. As they discuss the creative process, they continuously shift ground. It is part autobiography, a move into the writerly self, an account of their writings, moments of self-critiquing and self-reflection, debates related to the role of the critic and criticism and validity and nature of experimentation. Sobti's adoption of Hashmat, a male persona, for her writing of and about her contemporaries in *Ham Hashmat* is one significant moment of discovery as well as of transformation.[2] Not only did her handwriting change but her style and the nature of assertion also did. It became a comfortable niche in the male world and allowed her a double vision.

The *Sobti-Vaid Samvaad* and Sobti's use of language in her fiction are examples of heteroglossia, which is used to challenge generic definitions. The first to be done away is the unity of the language and the conventional confines of the form. The Bakhtinian division of poetic discourse and novelistic discourse becomes relevant in this case. Whenever Sobti resorts to verse in any of her works – fiction or non-fiction – it is either a policy statement or a neutral fact. It remains isolated in itself even as it captures and restates the underlying narrative approach as in *Zindaginama* or as it is used in *Shabdon ke Aalok Mein*.[3] In fictional discourse heteroglossia is 'consciously opposed' to the literary language as in the parodic inbuilt performance of the *mirasi* at the wedding of the Shah's daughter in *Zindaginama*. There are several such embedded stories, episodes, retellings and enactments that take us to the past as in the Chaju Bhagat-Mian Mir episode. These work within double or triple narrative frames and freely move between different linguistic registers.[4]

Bakhtin in his essay 'Discourse in the Novel' elaborates upon the dialogic process:

> But no living word relates to its object in a *singular* way: between the word and the object, between the word and the speaking subject, there exists an elastic environment of other, alien words about the same object, the same theme, and this is an environment that it is often difficult to penetrate. It is precisely in the process of living interaction with this specific environment that the word may be individualized and given stylistic shape.
>
> [...]
>
> The word, directed towards its object enters a dialogically agitated and tension-filled environment of alien words, value

judgments and accents, weaves in and out of complex interrelationships, merges with some, recoils from others, intersects with a third group: and all this way crucially shape discourse [...]

(276)

Bakhtin ascribes an agency to the word, it is an actor in a complex world, it conceptualises its object and interacts with other words and also possesses verbal intentions. It needs to break through its own meaning and define anew its own 'semantic and stylistic contours' (277).[5] It is this contestatory nature of the interaction and of opposition, which is of importance to Sobti. She extends this to the form as well as her 'writerly' self. Sobti's work is a challenge to the translator primarily because of the deep-rooted relationship between choice of word and meaning. Every word has been extracted out of its origins, after a hostile confrontation with it and then replanted along with the whole weight of its roots. The reader and the translator are pushed into entering a similar struggle.[6] Sobti's relationship with language compels one to resort to similes – it is not like skin on the flesh of ideas, it refuses to sit comfortably, yet it is not distant, it is a relationship of closeness, but a closeness won after dispute, questioning, knowing the other, multiple interactions through which the hidden or forgotten layers of meaning are discovered, geographical areas and ages are entered, orality is brought in, and then, the writer comfortable with the resulting closeness, is inseparable from it.

The writer and her 'Other'

The constant pressing of language against meaning marks also Sobti's thought processes. The *Sobti-Vaid Samvaad* is a cheerful going over to the other camp, in order to strike boldly. At times it is no longer merely a dialogue or even a debate. The interrogation, the laying bare of the mind of the other sporadically becomes an inquisition. But the writer's 'other' is not merely the 'reader'. It exists at several other levels – the material which resists organisation, the critic who turns himself into an observer, the milieu which pushes you out and that part of the self which fails to merge or cohere. But the 'otherness', resistance or failure to cohere are, for Sobti, essential to the writer's self. Perhaps they are essential to all creative processes – even the critic's reading of the writer's work. 'Otherness' implies a refusal to surrender to the text and reverses the hermeneutic process. Instead of going across to the other's position it involves a constant resistance. One needs to look more closely at gains of this persistent 'otherness' which forces the reader to simulate the writer's struggle.

Acknowledging the need for a rigorous critical evaluation, both Sobti and Vaid comment upon its importance for the creative process. This critical evaluation – which goes beyond reviews or mere hostility – has not really been forthcoming. In *Sobti-Vaid Samvaad* they together go through the work of major critics and comment upon the roads not taken (*Samvaad* 122–132) and earlier Sobti had discussed it with Niranjan Dev Sharma, the Hindi critic (*Shabdon* 316–321). The kind of oppositional stance she got from Jaidev (*Shabdon* 210–218) is the kind of questioning that the writer looks for. But the real 'other' is still contained within the writer's self. Sobti says of herself *'Ek to mein dheet hun, dusre mujhme lachak hai'* [One, I am stubborn and secondly, I am flexible (*Shabdon* 79)].

Jeevan yadi ek rough draft hota – the writer in the world

When Anamika posed the question to Sobti 'If life had been a rough draft …' Sobti purposefully directed her response to the possibility of a blueprint, once again an oppositional stand (*Shabdon* 184–185). If life had been a rough draft, then the natural question is what would have emerged in the revised version? What are the things that Sobti may have liked to do differently, handle differently or write differently? Why did Sobti, who normally pushes her work through three drafts, choose to respond in this fashion? Despite her letters to Sarvar, despite the occasional confessional stance, Sobti's personal self is never revealed. The public figure of assertion, of a wall of resistance, of a woman able to meet men on their own ground, not only in the social world of interaction but also as a writer, in the selection of themes and use of language, is dominant. Time and again, Sobti has been asked about her position on feminism. And repeatedly she has asserted her right to belong to a wider world in terms of gender without letting go of her right to be a woman. The creation of Hashmat is demonstrative of the fact of this freedom. Consistently she has resented being framed in a limited gender context (*Shabdon* 185–191), or being judged against the popular perception of feminist writing. Literary critics and historians are clearly to be blamed for this, the first for expecting a certain kind of writing and the second for segregating it and having failed to evolve more comprehensive and inclusive evaluative norms. In *Sobti-Vaid Samvaad*, the two writers discuss this issue at length. Vaid, in a somewhat patronising manner, expresses appreciation of Sobti, Mahasweta Devi and Qurrutulain Hyder's work to which Sobti's response is characteristically sharp. In the gender debate, men have written extensively about and on women, and now when women have begun to delineate their own image and critique masculinity and its limitations, they are being pushed back. Now that a woman writer has begun to look at herself as an independent construct and incorporate her views of masculinity in her writing her intentions have become suspect. Sobti strongly resents that critical evaluation be framed by gender constructs placed within a hierarchical positioning or masculine patronage (*Samvaad* 148–150). Towards this end sexuality does not have to be denied or suppressed, or the sexual desire marginalised (*Samvaad* 154–160). The relationship with the gendered self is not one of confinement, and that with the gendered 'other' needs to be on an equal footing. The lack of consciousness about gender is not a denial of it.

Whatever little that is known of Sobti's personal life bears testimony to this. Her independence, extensive travels, a sense of camaraderie, lack of inhibition, giving way to impulse and often affronting opposition with an astonishing amount of assertion – are all traits that define her. In fact she constantly steps out of stereotypes and normative patterns with the result that she has produced work which refuses to be contained within standard definitions. Have there been any losses on the way? Anamika's suggestive question about the rough draft is what would then have been the final draft? Losses in term of romance? There is a very powerful relationship between Kashi Shah and Rabiyaan worked out at length included in *Shabdon ke Aalok Mein* but not part of *Zindaginama*. It reworks the theme of eternal, undying love in the mainstream tradition of legendary romances like Sassi-Punnu, Heer-Ranjha or Laila-Majnoon and frames it in an extramarital but an irresistible relationship that ends in death for the lovers ['*Uttarardh*' (Epilogue) *Shabdon* 238–274]. Sobti introduces it with the comment that it had no place in the novel. She wrote it spontaneously in a moment of inspiration without any indecisiveness or hesitation. She presents it with the idea that it should say something both to the reader and the writer (*Shabdon* 237).

What does this extract convey? Closely followed by *Dilo-danish*, again a story about a love relationship not contained within normative patriarchal institutions but still patriarchally controlled, the piece does say a great deal. Lalli Shah and his uncle are far more sympathetic towards Rabiyaan than Mehak's own children in *Dilo-danish*. Kashi Shah's relationship is only marginally exploitative in the sense that he casts his mantle on Rabiyaan on his deathbed while Kripanarayan's is possessive, extending to the denial of even the remnants of dignity and the rights of motherhood. Are these love relationships playing on the same theme to work out the various emotional angles? The 'Epilogue' to *Zindaginama* and the thematic centre of *Dilo-danish* juxtapose romantic love within patriarchal institutions. In this extramarital relationship, a woman's desire and a man's ego both look for expression and fulfillment. They question both: the accepted models of behaviour as well as the expectations of the self in a world not quite one's own.

The weaving together of various narrative forms in *Zindaginama* is carried forward to *Shabdon ke Aalok Mein.* As it progresses from a letter to an interview, to a talk delivered, to a moment experienced, research undertaken for purposes of historical documentation, the narrative moves in and out of a variety of forms, shades of reaction and locales, putting together a whole lot of fragments that bind together in a meaningful relationship. The critic has to enter this labyrinth to discover the connecting routes. Sobti's constant need for the listener, for the other, is also a reality of an independent life where one is slow to yield one's space while still wanting a sounding board. The stimulation comes from the ricocheting effect of the self as it knocks against the 'other', whether it be person, word or creation. It is in this ricocheting that imagination and experience come together. This too is a kind of dialogisation. Experience which is rooted in a person's life, circumstances and environment is yet separate from the person's identity as it comes into existence through interaction, reading, observation and memory. It is always difficult to pin down its definiteness. Any attempt to express it in words uses both a conscious acceptance of it and an internalised version of it before it can flow into a larger world view (*Samvaad* 59–60). For Sobti the creative process does not work merely on lateral lines; it is a process of extraction, marked by the adoption of a contestatory pose, pushing against the margins, with a miner's determination: a constant struggle with 'self' and the 'other'.

Notes

1. See *Sobti-Vaid Samvaad* 75. Sobti asks the question: Why did Guleri decide to do so: would it have been possible to raise the story to the level of a classic without this? (This is a free translation of Sobti's observations).
2. Ibid., 47–50. Sobti found in this persona a completely new self – not an imposition but an aspect of herself. It was also a way of discovering how much of an 'I' is contained in the self. She did not experience any contradictory impulse, on the other hand her handwriting as Hashmat was also different from her writing as Sobti. In 'Discourse in the Novel', (*The Dialogic Imagination*) Bakhtin observes that the poetic discourse is 'one unitary and in disputable discourse' (286). Unity, both of language and the poet's individuality are 'indispensable prerequisites' (264). The language of the poet 'is *his* language, he is utterly immersed in it, inseparable from it ...' (285).
3. The reader is referred to the use of poems by the author in *Zindaginama* (prefatory poem, 9–16) and *Shabdon ke Aalok Mein* 30–31, 52–53.
4. Both the episodes mentioned here are from *Zindaginama*, For the mirasi performance refer 314–318 – and the Chajju Bhagat episode. 372–374. For English translations of these passages refer *Reading*

Partition/Living Partition. Ed. Jasbir Jain (Jaipur: Rawat Publications), 2006.

5. Also see 279. Bakhtin writes: 'The word is born in a dialogue as a living rejoinder within it; the word is shaped in dialogic interaction with an alien word that is already in the object. A word forms a concept of its own object in a dialogic way'.
6. Tharu and Lalitha in their Preface to *Women Writing in India: 600 BC to the Present* (OUP, 1991) write: 'Unfortunately we have had to leave some important selections out because the translations "failed". For volume 2, we wanted to include the work of Krishna Sobti [...] but she writes in a dialect translators felt would be difficult to render into standard English and uses an earthy, lewd diction' (Vol. 1, Preface, xxii). The use of words like 'standard English' is questionable, and the statement ignores both the variety and richness of Sobti's language by dismissing it as 'dialects' and 'lewd'. It becomes in the end a limited view of the relationship between language and form and places Sobti within a conventional notion of gender-defined respectability which in its very grain is against the spirit of feminism.

13

Purdah, Patriarchy and the Tropical Sun

Womanhood in India*

There is a mystique attached to the word 'purdah' and its multiple aspects, meanings and practices. Attitudes towards it fluctuate, not only in accordance with the rise and fall of fundamentalisms and ethnicities but also through the different purposes it fulfils in language. It is part of many an idiom and indicates emotions ranging from belonging, privacy to coyness. It also has a whole range of synonyms and metaphors attached to it. *Ghunghat* (a veil pulled over the face), *odhni* (a head scarf which is used for the *ghunghat*), *chunri, chadar* (sheet, mantle, cloak) are only some of them. And from being a mere part of a dress it has the capacity to signify a relationship between the self and the other. As part of a dress, its manner of use is often indicative not only of the religion one follows but also one's caste, class and perhaps region. The real significance of purdah lies not in these external signifiers, but in its impact as a social construct. It impacts both men and women alike and defines the notion of both masculinity and femininity.[1] It impacts even those of us who have always believed that we are outside its influence. In a larger sense it sustains the idea of patriarchy. Primarily it is about space – about segregation and division – and signifies a conjunction of power and space. In its implied meanings it goes much beyond the covered face and the hidden

---

* First published in *The Veil*. Ed. Jennifer Heath. Berkeley: University of California Press, 2008.

body to encompass notions of respectability and virtue, class and caste, protection and exposure.

When I ask myself what does the word 'purdah' mean to *me*: daughter of a Sikh household, married into a conservative Jain family (both outside Hinduism), an educated professional who has travelled extensively, I get conflicting responses. At the outset I am outside it and have been able to negotiate the boundaries of my physical and emotional spaces fairly well. But a deeper reflection shows it has affected my code of behaviour and my sense of moral values. True, purdah was much more real for my grandmother and, to some extent, my mother. Both my grandmothers always wore full-sleeved and loose baggy shirts that fully hid the contours of the body. They moved around with their heads covered, especially in male presence. My mother often recalled her journeys in the horse carriage (tonga) with a chadar stretched across the rear to protect the women from the bazaar gaze. This kind of purdah was seen as a social necessity and sought to protect the women from the public gaze. Marriage revealed to me another aspect, that of discrimination between daughters and daughters-in-law. My husband's mother insisted that daughters-in-law should not sit on the front seat of a horse-carriage or wear salwar-kameez. Marriage brought additional responsibilities that affected the code of behaviour. It was easy enough to laugh at these restrictions and tolerate them, as our visits home were of a short duration. None of these really meant anything in the social circle we belonged to. But the linkage with social roles was underlined in more than one way. It implied prohibition, exclusion and hierarchy.

Ordering of space into the private and the public brings in the notion of ownership and belonging. It has implications for socio-cultural as well as intellectual mobility. For a moment, if we place purdah in the centre, it is possible to see the different controlling mechanisms it lets loose. It controls a woman's mobility, her morality, her sexuality as well as her intellectual freedom. Purdah, in some form or the other, is a trait shared by almost all societies, west or east. It is the difference in economic and political histories that marks the difference in external manifestations. In India itself, the manner in which it may be practiced by the same caste and economic group, may differ with the difference in location (whether rural or urban, open countryside or crowded cityscape), class (aristocracy, peasantry, working class), status (wife, courtesan or mistress) and power (rich or poor). At times of cultural encounters, whenever there is a threat to cultural survival, the hardening of attitudes often takes place and a revivalist, protectionist approach is adopted. Similarly colonial India rushed into restrictive practices where purdah was concerned for reasons of protecting its cultural identity and preventing British intrusions into the personal sphere.[2]

The practice of purdah has a long history in India and during the course of time several myths have accumulated around it. These have usually been passed on by word of mouth, through oral traditions and through interpolations in written texts. At times this may have happened through translation, and at times through political manipulation. Of these there are four such myths that I propose to discuss: (i) purdah has come to India with the Muslims and Hindu purdah owes its origins to the defense against Muslim invaders; (ii) that Lakshmana drew a circle defining the limits of Sita's confines at the time when she was left alone in the forest (in the *Ramayana*); (iii) that purdah is identifiable primarily with sexual segregation in social space and defined by the dress code; (iv) and it is always negative and oppressive. There would be many more but these should suffice. They are interwoven and overlapping and at times contradictory. As for instance the first and the second say very different things and while the first emphasises the religious opposition, the third makes a subtle distinction (an unwarranted one) between moral sphere and dress code, between protection and denial of freedom. The Hindu mind wills itself to believe it as necessary and different.

Purdah in its sense of patriarchal control is native to the Hindu. *The Laws of Manu (Manavdharma Smriti)* subordinates woman to man whether a father, husband or son and deprives her of a free agency. The very fact that a woman's *dharma* (her sense of duty), her *stree-dharma* is defined through her obedience to her husband, denies her free access to the outside world. Other defining constructs like *sati* (one who is pure), and *pativrata* (committed to the husband), also place a woman within limited loyalties and freedom. The *Ramayana* is one of the two Indian epics that have defined Indian society. While the later *Mahabharata* is a non-conformist epic, the *Ramayana* is a conformist one and depicts the character of an ideal son and king. Rama is referred to as *maryada purshottam,* the best of men, in his adherence to normative traditions. It has survived as a living tradition, written or reinterpreted by successive generations across the length and breadth of not only India but the whole of South Asia. Its concepts have become part of everyday language and of the collective unconscious. It has lived through different mediums – recitals, *kathas* (tales), Ram-lilas (annual enactments) normally in October every year – the two festivals Dussehra and Diwali relate to the story of the *Ramayana* – ballets, movies and tele-serials. It has also inhabited the political imagination. Gandhi in his search for an ideal society projected the concept of Ram Rajya. Fundamentalists and protestors alike have used this story. In the 80s a tele-serial which trapped the country's imagination leading to trains being halted at the time of its telecasting, was Ramanand Sagar's *Ramayana*. The political agitation surrounding Babri Masjid and the construction of a temple for Ram-lalla refers to the Rama of this epic. Deepa Mehta's film *Fire* uses *Ramayana* as a background narrative for purposes of showcasing gender oppression.

The *Ramayana*, it is obvious, is a living reality for the Hindu mind in personal and political terms. Thus the contradiction between purdah being a result of invasions and the myth of the *Lakshmana-rekha* needs to be examined more critically. There is no denying the fact that every threat, no matter from where; every war no matter in which country or age, has led to the protection of women as they constitute a vulnerable group. Honour and progeny are linked with them. Attacks by some caste groups also result in this kind of protection. The British presence was instrumental in the hardening of gender-based space divisions. As for the *Lakshmana-rekha* neither Valmiki's *Ramayana* (700–500 BC) nor Kamban's (900–1200 AD) or Tulsidas' *Ramcharitmanas* (16th century) make a mention of this. *Ramcharitmanas* belongs to the Bhakti period and is written in *Avadhbhasha*, a language of the people. It is the one most popularly recited in the Hindi-speaking heartland of India.

Lakshmana-rekha is the demarcation line or circle that Lakshmana is supposed to have drawn when compelled by Sita to go to Rama's rescue. The popular legend goes that because Sita crossed this boundary and stepped outside this protective region, she was consequently abducted by Ravana, the demon king who was lusting after her. This abduction scene is the central episode leading to war, to Ravana's defeat, Sita's return and her *agnipriksha*, the trial of chastity by fire. A Hindu woman's life, whether she likes it or not, every now and then comes up against 'lakshmana-rekha' and 'agnipriksha'. In Valmiki's *Ramayana*, Lakshmana leaves Sita to the care of the forest deities (274), in *Kamba Ramayana* he leaves her to her *dharma*, her sense of inner control and to the overlordship of Jatayu, the eagle (141), in *Ramcharitmanas*, once again she is given to the care of the deities of the forest and the four directions of the sky, that is the world of nature. In *Kamba Ramayana* Ravana enters the leaf-cottage, disguised as an ascetic. The step by step progression is through desire and the yielding to this temptation. Rama thwarts Surapankha's (Ravana's sister) advances and resists her attempts to seduce him. Sita desires to possess the golden deer in whose pursuit first Rama and then Lakshman have to go. On the face of it this is not very different from Eve's yielding to Satan's persuasion, but differences soon creep in. Sita's resistance renders her a victim of oppression of both her abductor and her husband. The trial by fire signifies both oppression and purification.

The *Ramayana* story in its multiple readings, reinterpretations and retellings defines first the limits of legitimate sexuality and then the violation of these limits. The controlling figure remains male: definitions and purificatory rites are male prescriptions. These two episodes – the mythical (passed on through oral tradition) *Lakshmana-rekha* and *agnipriksha* define Indian womanhood within Hinduism and form a part of the socialisation process and work at both conscious and unconscious level. The Muslim invaders brought tailoring to India, not purdah, which happens to be a home-grown product symbolising the relationship between self and the other.

During the British period purdah was reinfcrced in two different ways. The first of these was through legislation and the codification of half-forgotten cultural memories and beliefs. In its attempt to introduce a written code for legal interpretation in the courts of law, the British government turned to *Manusmriti*[3] for the purposes of defining Hindu 'personal law' (as supplementary to the general law). *Manusmriti* prescribed a strict code of control over women and evoked an outdated gender behaviour. The second move was from the Indians themselves who increasingly began to perceive women as custodians of culture. This led to a division into public and private space, the first being the outside world of political life and the second of domesticity and women. Purdah as segregation began to appear as the last bastion of a cultural defence against both modernisation and westernisation.

This segregation of space is depicted in fiction as well as in autobiographies, as often leading to a comedy of errors, fatal accidents or taking a tragic turn due to mistaken identities on account of the bride's *ghunghat*. The *ghunghat* in itself calls forth romantic associations of mystery and desire, of hide and seek in the game of love. Many a folk song is centred on this. In Punjabi there is many a song which expresses the mischief and the playfulness behind the *ghunghat*. A young man in search of a bride expresses the desire to marry a girl who would wink at him through the *ghunghat* (*Aasan kudi O laini jihri khund vichon akh maren*). In another folk song the daughter-in-law-father-in-law relationship is talked about when the young bride observes purdah from her father-in-law but leaves the side with the hair-clip open to his view (*suhre koluun khund kad-di, nanga rakhdi clipwala pasa*). There is no end to the large number of songs and ghazals that build romance around purdah/*ghunghat* as it symbolises the desire for the unknown 'other'. There is pain and suffering, restrained love, and imagined beauty. The framed relationship between men and women, father-in-law and daughter-in-law is often the mainstay of a family. In a very powerful feminist novel *Mitro Marjani* (*Damn You, Mitro*), the daughter-in-law lets her *dupatta* (scarf) slide off her head as a gesture subversive of his authority.

These worldly material aspects of purdah are matched by its spiritual intensity in Bhakti poetry[4] and in Sufi verses. Meerabai's religious hymns refer to the *ghunghat* as the veil between god and his devotee. It is only the devotion, concentration and meditation of the devotee that can help him cross the distance to god. The devotee has to bring about the required change within his heart, to remove the veil – *ghunghat ke pat khol, tohe piya milen ge,* (Transcend the veil and ye shall find god). Sufism again expresses similar emotions. We find references to the *ghunghat* (the veil) in the verses of Amir Khusrau and of Bulle-Shah.[5]

One of the Hindi words for revelation is 'darshan'. During certain hours, a curtain is drawn across the idol in a temple. At the time of worship, this curtain is lifted and the worshippers can have a direct view of the idol. The word also carries within it the right to accord an audience. The impact of both Sufism and the Bhakti movement can be seen in the rise of Sikhism, a faith that provides space for a woman to relate directly to god (and not through her husband), and does not perceive her as subservient to man. It does not also exclude her from priestly tasks on the grounds of bodily impurity.[6]

Spatial divisions are reflected in the purdah-observing households. It is not only the Muslim households who had their zenana and mardana, Hindu households, especially in Bengal and Rajasthan, also had separate living spaces. As Malvika Karlekar observes, the *antahpura* (the inner quarters), distinguished itself from outer spaces, it went on to define a separate sphere of function and influence (Karlekar 48). Rama Mehta's *Inside the Haveli,* a semi-autobiographical fictional narrative, describes a similar division of space in the havelis of Rajasthan. Set in the princely state of Udaipur, it focuses on the three-hundred year old haveli, the ancestral home of Geeta's husband. The first chapter of *Inside the Haveli,* with its dominantly a socio-anthropological tone, is a description of the physical and social environs and the protected and secluded inner courtyards. One would assume that this seclusion would allow more privacy but the chapter ends with the observation, 'There are no secrets, there could be none in the haveli' (6). Even the communities (heterotopias) that are created in the women's world abound in eavesdroppers, messengers, observers and manipulators. Working through the mind of the young city-bred girl Geeta, who has come to the haveli as a new bride, the novel proceeds to examine the affects that purdah has on the body, the mind and on relationships. Husbands and wives do not meet during the day, there is no normal social life that includes mixed gatherings; cajoling, confidence-sharing and persuasions, all are carried out through servants and have their moments of frustration and suppression. A double discourse runs right through the narrative. The upper layer is one of a gradual growing into the purdah tradition and of accepting its priorities of family and tradition over individual aspirations. This endorses and attempts to capture traditional values. But then there is a parallel discourse which expresses the frustrations of suppression and resentment against the compulsions of tradition. Geeta extends her world by starting an informal class for the children of the servants. This has both positive and negative aspects. While it opens out her world as well as that of the children, it also disrupts existing feudalistic structures. Again the excessive decorum and restraint in the behavioural code amongst women of equal status is a dampener for all emotional expression and spontaneous impulses. The loyal haveli servants, no matter how well treated, are like bonded slaves. The flow is against democratic set-ups and encourages reticence, restraint and secrets; in the haveli no one expressed their feelings (Mehta 32–33). Behind the latticed windows, the women are like caged birds that have no control over their lives, their aspirations and relationships.

Seclusion and feminine resentment to it is found in a large number of novels across languages, religions, regions and generations. Attia Husain's *Sunlight on a Broken Column*[7] takes up the story of a Muslim taluqdar family in Lucknow, locating this autobiographical work in the forties, Ashapurna Devi, in *Suvarnlata,*[8] projects this theme through the nine-year-old child bride's growing up in a middle class Bengali joint family in the twenties and thirties, and M.K. Indira recalls a real life story of Phaniyamma, a great grandaunt who widowed as a child lived to the age of 112, in the Kannada work *Phaniyamma*. Many of these works, as is obvious from the above three, are fictionalised accounts of personal experiences and recount the frustrations and struggles of women as they are sacrificed to family and tradition.

The practice of purdah has its origins in an overriding social concern with a woman's purity – no matter whether child, married or widowed. Purity is a multi-layered concept and includes non-violation of the body, moral purity, and sexual abstinence and is used to prioritise body over mind. It is seen as necessary to lineage protection and also surfaces as an economic necessity as in *Phaniyamma*. The concept of 'madi' is propagated to bind women to menial tasks. The sanctification of the kitchen area, the idea of pollution through touch, the need to have frequent baths, and consequently often work in a wet sari, are all fallouts of this concern with purity. The idea is to protect a woman's sexuality, which is perceived as a threat to masculine supremacy. Male ownership offers protection and respectability: public women like courtesans, mistresses, devadasis fall outside the notion of respectability and the *bhadar-mahila*, the genteel, respectable woman. The joint family extracts its own pound of flesh. The sexuality of a woman is perceived as a 'potentially pernicious influence' with the dominant fear that a woman may cause her husband to neglect his duty (Kakar 1978: 63). And within the family, the husband's elder brother and father are perceived as possible victims of her seduction (Minturn 76), hence the need to segregate her.

The question naturally arises what about purdah today, does it still exist with the increase in education, use of technology, the architectural shifts in design and the disintegration or near extinction of the joint family? Despite the shifts in fashion, the excessive body exposure, couples living together in metropolitan towns, purdah continues to exist in other ways. It persists in the mindset, both male and female but proportionally more in the male. It still allows for easy divisions between the respectable and the not respectable. It is evident in the violence against women, in the gender-based moral values voiced publicly. It is supported by religious fundamentalists and, amusingly enough, it has come back as a protection against the increased heat of the tropical sun with the fall in the ozone levels and skin-burns becoming more widespread. Young women with their faces covered with only their eyes visible can be seen in India, riding scooters, driving cars, going for a job, activities that require them to be outdoors.

Incidentally it also offers anonymity and protection from eve-teasing or sexual harassment. Ranging from the mundane to the spiritual, from the personal to the social, purdah continues to occupy an ambivalent space, difficult to accept in its totality, equally difficult to reject it completely. In its oppressive aspects and the bodily and mental restrictions it imposes, the exclusion it defines, it is a reprehensible social practice. But in its meanings of social grace and decorum of behaviour (where the burqa or the *ghunghat* are not relevant), it continues to be a desirable part of social life.

Notes

1. Women needed to be chaperoned, moved around in salon chairs and were generally the protected gender as depicted in late eighteenth century British novels like those of Fanny Burney. Their roles were limited to domestic life. In the nineteenth century, Victorian England had both its camouflaging robes and its moral prudery. Tod in his *Annals of Rajasthan* time and again, draws attention to the common element between Indian life styles and western constructs where women were concerned. The differences whatsoever were of degree and details and not of kind. Again, if one reads the *Ramayana* as a tale of desire, temptation, resistance, trial and exile the Biblical story of Eve's seduction by Satan and the consequent exile would form an interesting comparison. The transgression of a taboo leads to the exile of Adam and Eve. In the *Ramayana*, at the very outset, there is Kaikeyi's (the stepmother's) longing for power that leads to Rama's exile. But later the narrative becomes a psycho-drama with contrary desires resulting in the conflictual situation.
2. Barbara Daly Metcalf in her Introduction to *Perfecting Women*, commenting upon this writes, 'the Indian woman was to be the bastion against all that was corrupt in the west'.
3. *Manusmriti* also known as *Manavdharma Sastra* was one of the earliest texts to be translated into English (1794). In the Introduction to *The Laws of Manu* (Translated by Wendy Doniger O'Flaherty and Brian K. Smith, New Delhi: Penguin, 1991), the translators write, 'Under the British, the text become instrumental in the construction of a complex system of jurisprudence in which 'general law' was supplemented by 'personal law' determined by one's religious affiliation' (ix). Pandita Ramabai in *The High Caste*

Hindu Woman (1888), set herself the task of taking it up clause by clause and interrogating it.

4. The Bhakti movement was a religious movement spread over several centuries (roughly from 8th to 18th), which sought for a direct relationship with god, sidelining the Brahmin control. Several of the *bhaktas* (devotees) belonged to marginalised groups and included people who often did not have direct access to temples and other centres of worship on grounds of caste restrictions. The movement spread all over India and allowed a social mobility not possible in upper class society. Sufism is a parallel movement having its offshoots from Islam. There were several women bhaktas, of them Meera and Bahinabai are two well-known ones. Meera (1498–1565) was married to the king of Mewar and a devotee of Lord Krishna. Constant harassment by her husband's family drove her from home to Dwarka where she became an itinerant singer. Meera's life can be read in different ways and her worship of Krishna can also be seen as an alternative to marriage or resentment against male impotency or a need for greater freedom than a woman's life permitted.
5. Bulle Shah (1680–1757), was born in Punjab in the family of Syed Shah Muhummad and was well-versed in Arabic and Persian. His verses are still very popular across religions. In these verses, the devotee is female who seeks to please god, her lover. His 'kafis' speak of submergence, frenzied emotions and a game of hide and seek, a search for identity in God and of union with him. He uses god-names like 'Shyam' (identified with Krishna) with ease. In many of his verses he reprimands god for hiding himself (why do you peep from behind the veil?), and of total abandonment and surrender in front of the lover, discarding all inhibitions. (*Bulle-Shah* Urdu-Hindi bilingual edition, Eds. Harbhajan Singh and Shoeb Nadvi, New Delhi: Hind Pocket Books, 2006; 152; 136).
6. See J.S. Grewal's *Guru Nanak and Patriarchy* (1993), pp. 6–9, pp. 16–18.
7. The divisions of space clearly demarcated roles even in Muslim families. Attia Hosain opens *Sunlight on the Broken Column* (1961, New Delhi: Arnold Heinemann, 1979), with the lines. 'The day my aunt Abida moved from the zenana into the guest-room off the corridor that led to the men's wing of the house, within call of her father's room, we knew that Baba Jan had not much longer to live' (14). Abida's physical move into the front room, marks the shift of authority in the household and her stepping into a male role.

8. See Ashapurna Devi's *Suvarnlata.* In this novel the confines of space and relationships, of imposed sexual attentions of the husband, the restrictions on Suvarnlata's reading and discussions, the constraints on her creativity, are all very subtly portrayed through her growing up from a child-bride into adulthood. All along she desires some degree of freedom, dignity and privacy, and all are denied her. And when finally she succeeds in getting a book of her own published through a relative, the family's mockery pushes her to make a bonfire of the five hundred copies.

14

Refracted Nationhoods, Redacted Loyalties

Culture-Language Connections/Disconnections

The last three decades or more have evidenced an upsurge of the writing in English across nation-spaces – the writing of the diaspora, of Asians and Africans at home, Iranians and Egyptians seeking a place in a language other than that of their culture. A phenomenon, in itself, it is an accommodation of the strange into the familiar, or the familiar into the strange, depending on which side of the fence one is located – language or culture. Naturally, the fall out is of immense significance, for it indicates a shifting of positions and priorities, a decentring of western ideas and ideology and a leading to multifocality. This move away from Eurocentrism signifies a surfacing of the erstwhile subordinated 'others' – Forster's punkahwallah, or Fugard's houseboy – into recognisable human beings. And this compulsion to mould language to accommodate cultures hitherto dismissed as 'dead' or worthless has expanded the field of both aesthetics and sociological researches.

But can we afford to look at the writing as text and not relate it the production and the consumption economy of globalisation, the first casualty of which is the small producer? Again, what value ethnicity, if it is framed as the 'ethnic', the anthropologists' treasure? In this case, the first casualty is the nation space. For this writing, even as it simultaneously moves both in centrifugal and centripetal directions, is looking for an anchor. It is engaged in a constant dialogue between the forces of globalisation and localisation, and in the process, either loses on the immediacy or becomes culturally dense. One needs to be wary of generalisations for such a vast body and variety of work. They never are fully applicable, yet there is some truth in each one of them.

More often than not, 1980 is the year chosen as a marker. Perhaps because it celebrates large-scale migrations from the erstwhile colonies to western centres of power. For us, in India, it takes us back to Rushdie's *Midnight's Children* (1980), when he wrote English with a tongue-in-cheek attitude. Anita Desai reviewing the book, praised it for the courage with which he punctured the formal correctness and coldness of the English language. The same year Ngugi Wa Thiong'O moved away from English to write his first novel in his native GiKuyu, *Detained: A Writer's Prison Diary*, marking the intimate relationship between language and culture. In the Preface to *Decolonizing the Mind* (1986), he wrote, 'In the eighteenth and nineteenth centuries Europe stole art treasures from Africa to decorate their houses and museums, in the twentieth century Europe is stealing the treasures of the mind to enrich their languages and cultures. Africa needs back its economy, its culture, its languages and all its patriotic writers' (xii). In the decade preceding that, the long-drawn American presence in Vietnam had finally ended and the British were, in the 80s, going through their final romantic fling with the Raj. The experimentation of the 50s-70s was tapering off. The rising chorus of literary voices in English, however, has another dimension. In fact it is split in two, divided right across. One wonders whether this trend is neo-colonial or post-imperialist? It cannot be treated purely as a literary event. One needs to look more closely at the links of the post-1980s writing with high capitalism, and its value or otherwise as part of a resistance movement, visibility of ethnic issues and a shaping of new cultural forces, in bringing to the surface hidden histories and struggles, unexplored systems of knowledge and unfamiliar social systems and narratologies.

Ben Okri begins his 1992 novel, *The Famished Road* thus:

> In the beginning there was a river. The river became a road and the road branched out to the whole world. And because the road was once a river it was always hungry.
>
> In that land of beginning spirits mingled with the unborn. … We knew no boundaries …
>
> We feared the heartlessness of human beings, all of whom are born blind, few of whom ever learn to see. (3)

The story of Azaro, a spirit child, it begins with all the essence of orality and its slow meandering continuous flow, demanding not only a new language but also a new aesthetics.

The post-1980s writing, over all else, has problematised location – location of the author, the location of his/her imagined worlds, as well as the location of the reader. It has gone on to change the nature of the text. Let me juxtapose two different positions – one traditional, the other postmodern – expressed nearly ten years apart. In 1983 in an essay in the eighth volume of the New Pelican Guide to English Literature titled *The Present,* John Holloway recognises the presence of V.S. Naipaul, Chinua Achebe and Wole Soyinka, but observes they can 'in no way be seen as part of the literary scene of the United Kingdom' (Holloway 124). And Toni Morrison in her 1992 William E. Massey Lecture talks about the act of reading as a writer which implies the ability to imagine the other, to 'enter what one is estranged from' (4), to link 'utterance with the writerly act of imagining' (16). She writes, in order to discover the meaning behind the hidden layers, 'I stopped reading as a reader and began to read as a writer' (15), a process one can define as writerly reading, the way to see the invisible in the text as it projects parallel 'others' to relate to the meaning caught between the narrative disjunctions as the presence of the blacks in the writings of the nineteenth century white writers. Morrison thus goes beyond Ronald Barthes's distinction between readerly writing and writerly writing. Barthes's focus is on the act of writing, while Morrison evokes the participation of the reader as a co-creator of the text.

The two thinkers who preceded this upsurge and have perhaps contributed to it most significantly are Foucault, with his engagement with space and the concept of heteretopias, and

Bakhtin with his emphasis on dialogism and heteroglossia. Struggling against personal and political adversities, Bakhtin's work runs parallel to the language revolution in the west, but he turned to ideas usually ignored by others. Michael Holquist in his introduction to *The Dialogic Imagination,* writes – 'It is as if he has set out to carnivalize . . . the normal periods and figures we use to define the relay of culture' (xvii). In 'Discourse in the Novel', Bakhtin writes about the constantly changing relationship between a 'fixed' system of language and the various specificities, deviations and the constantly growing burden of the word introduced into this fixed system. The meaning reveals itself in the 'socially heteroglot multiplicity' of its names, definitions and value judgements – it is in dialogic interaction with the alien word and just as in a living conversation, a word is oriented towards a future answer-word, it also provokes an answer (278–281). This requires a responsive understanding – something visible in Morrison's writerly reading. At many levels it means coming to terms with alienness. Traces of the Bakhtinian concern with the dynamic, fluid and meaning-loaded nature of 'utterance' are perceptible in Homi Bhabha's emphasis on enunciation. More than hybridity, it is the act of enunciation that marks the post-80s literature. It moves across genres, much more freely than dialogicism. I quote from Rienzi Cruse – a Sri-Lankan Canadian's poem 'Roots':

> A Portuguese captain holds
> The soft brown hand of my Sinhala mother
> It's the year 1515 A.D.
>
> When two civilizations kissed and merged,
> And I, burgher of that hot embrace,
> Write a poem of history
> As it were only the romance
> Of a lonely soldier on a crowded beach
> In Southern Ceylon.

(qtd. by Arunprabha Mukherjee 139)

Space, as Edward Soja, has pointed out, has been driven to the margins by an over-emphasis on time, durée and history. Foucault restored the balance by exploring closed and open spaces, prisons and heterotopias. What happens when one is under observation, or dislocated, or in strange environs or in public spaces like a stage, a political arena, a hospital or a nunnery? What happens – as feminist writers/theorists have asked – when the body is used as an oppositional force? Imperial concerns with space were of conquest and adventure. Even as they marked loneliness and enclosures, they were of power – the power of race and a civilisation which rode rough over all else. (Russian writers do not fall into this category, but their work was not written in English).

The story of T.E. Lawrence (film made in 1962. Dir. David Lean, based on Lawrence's autobiography *Seven Pillars of Wisdom*), is imagined against the background of the expansive desert. Contrast this with Michael Ondaatje use of space in *The English Patient.* Of the many spaces, two stand out, one the villa, once a nunnery, now an improvised hospital which houses the unrecognisable English patient and other the Libyan desert where, during the war, his plane had crashed. This desert is a burial ground of love and loved ones and the wreck of the plane; the accident which takes place there is both a termination and a beginning, reducing space to the hospital bed. The villa has been declared an unsafe building but is occupied by these self-turned exiles who have found their way there. The patient is actually a Hungarian spy. Others are: his twenty-three year old Canadian nurse, escaping from her own personal past, Caraviggio, an Italian friend, and Kirpal Singh, an Indian sapper. The patient has long confessional sessions with Caraviggio, as he goes over the past. One can see that like the shifting waves of the desert sand in Libya resulting in new formations, time can obliterate the past and memory reconstruct it differently; one can also feel the dialogicity of the confessions, no matter how silently they are received. The self is in dialogue with itself. The wreck of the plane and its lone survivor would have seemed so tiny in the vast desert. Where is the sense of space of *Lawrence of Arabia*? Instead, it is the infinity of the sky and the littleness of man which strikes one. What really holds the centre is not the patient struggling to establish contact with reality, but Kirpal Singh, with his healthy able-bodied presence. He becomes a catalytic agent between history and geography. The relationship between Kip and Hana allows the body to successfully negotiate the problematics of race. For the timebeing, in this cordoned-off area, space, race and politics become irrelevant. Interestingly enough, the English presence is muted, pushed behind the stage. The real 'English' patient, James Clifton is only a name and exists only temporarily under a mistaken identity. Lord Suffolk, Miss Morden and Kipling with his novel *Kim* are now figments of memory. There is a reversal of roles. Together, these mixed inhabitants of the villa, pour over maps – as migrancy, exile and uprootedness take possession. They describe themselves as international bastards – born in one place and choosing to live somewhere else (176, 251).

An altogether different use of space is made in Nayantara Sahgal's *The Mistaken Identity*. Like the English patient, Bhushan – a prince, is also taken to be someone else, and put into a prison cell with nine other people of different religions, ideologies, class and caste, representing almost the whole range of the Indian scene. This prison cell expands itself through the ongoing squabbles, discussions, dialogues, the court trial, debates on strategy, quibbling over definitions and the occasional contact with the outside world. History is compressed into the present moment acquiring symbolic representation for the reader to explore and venture out. A triple dialectic between 'history, geography and modernity' (Soja 11–12) is clearly under way as the present locale of the prison cell, and sense of history spreading horizontally in time, taking place in other spaces, such as Turkey, United States, Egypt and Russia, come together and the nation is constructed – its refractions placed together – working out their differences.

Sahgal and Ondaatje both work out their locations differently – one works with the process of denationalising, putting aliens together, who go back to their origins via self-introspection and an encounter with the other; the other works with a defined space within a nation and brings together the divergent forces. Do their concerns differ because of the different histories they take up – one the aftermath of the Second World War, the Holocaust, and Hiroshima and Nagasaki, and the other the thirties, the Gandhian phase of Indian history?

Both history and location also work very differently in Caryl Phillips, *Crossing the River* (1993). Phillips born in British Guyana was shifted to England while still a few months old baby. His work belies Holloway's dismissal of Asian and African writers as not of the literary scene of the United Kingdom. His settings use metaphors of space in novel after novel. In *The Nature of Blood* (1997) it is a refugee camp of holocaust victims, but in *Crossing the River* he straddles across both space and time, prioritises wildernesses, moves across different linguistic registers, and delves into the underside of the history of slave markets, the fractured lives of the slaves, contrasted with the lives of those who buy, sell and own them and the missionary intrusions topsy-turvying their world view, making it difficult for them to belong anywhere. The narrative has a prologue and four sections. Beginning in the mid-eighteenth century, it moves on to Liberia in the nineteenth century, the forested hostile wilderness where a former slave is sent to engage in missionary work. He feels abandoned, writes 'home' to his former master for help but receiving no response, gradually deteriorates and dies. The next one is the Civil War in USA and an old woman slave on her way to freedom and hope of a better life, dying on the snow-engulfed land. The third takes us back to the eighteenth century, connects with the Prologue, and locates itself in a slave-ship on the pages of the Captain's diary. The final brings us to the Second World War and after, where a black American soldier and an English woman try to build a relationship. This is a very bald summary but I could not resist including this novel in my discussion because it violates the principles of realism, constructs plot and character both in time and space and disrupts historical continuities in order to trace the history of a race – the dislocated, disoriented, subjugated body and the freedom-aspiring mind of a slave. It critiques the whole of western civilisation along with its sense of adventure, conquest of territory, development, modernity riding high on the difference of colour. *Crossing the River* unveils what civilisation has made of man – even the white master suffers. It is a disturbing novel. It is meant to disturb. It summons the reader to what Toni Morrison has described 'writerly reading', and entering 'what one is estranged from' (Morrison 3–4). As individual memory and historical memory travel back and forth – the words of the father who of necessity had sold them echo, reminding us of the beginning: ... 'my own children. My Nash. My Martha. My Travis. Their lives fractured. Sinking hopeful roots into difficult soil .... There is no return' (Phillips 1–2). Another example of the evocation of memory through metaphors of space is the word 'Kala

Pani' by writers with a history of ancestors who were indentured labour – the *Jahazibhai*. Ramabai Espinet in *The Swinging Bridge* has used it as an anchoring refrain, to identify a point of origin, to hold together a twice-hyphenated identity.

The post-1980s novel is constantly engaged in rectifying the omissions and silences of history and rebuilding the image of the 'other', dismantling the stereotypes, the subjugated, parodied reflection of the imperial novel. We find this in novel after novel from different locations and origins – diaspora or otherwise – in history, in language, race and religion, whether it be Amitav Ghosh concern with knowledge systems, false boundaries and peripheral existence or Khaled Hosseini with probings of his conscience and the mess Russia and US have made of Afghanistan. Even the novel *Shantaram* (2003), written by a fugitive from law Gregory David Roberts, an escaped prisoner, joins them to reveal not only the underside of history but also the making and working of the underworld. Constantly, the once ignored people, whom history has bypassed, get up to remind the power holders and wielders of their own legitimacy in the making of history and often enough of the nation – be it Allan Sealy with his *Trotter-Nama* (1988) or Rohinton Mistry with the powerful images of all the various Indian gods representative of all the religions of India painted on the compound wall in *Such a Long Journey*, to prevent passers by from urinating there (*Such a Long Journey*, 1991: 184). A juxtaposition of body, faith and nation all together with their cracks, fissures and refractions. Sealy not only remaps the nation's history but also creates a new narrative method – the *nama* which consists of a variety of styles ranging from self-praise to parody. The protagonist, Justin Trotter, is modelled after Claude Martin, the founder of the La Martiniere Schools in Calcutta and Lucknow. Shyamala Narayan comments upon Sealy's use of English as we would use 'any other Indian language'. These are the new redactions. Lost documents – letters, diaries, newspaper articles – are found, as for instance in Sahgal's *Rich Like Us*, Phillips's *Crossing the River*, Espinet's *The Swinging Bridge* and Ghosh's *The Hungry Tide* to name only a few, to fill up not on individual lives but on historical representation, to shift the character's and the reader's perspective and question all that has come to us by way of 'knowing' and 'knowledge'.

Before I conclude, I want to address two more issues, which constantly nag my mind. One, is English language writing adequately representative? And two, has the definition of a classic changed? Highly debatable and perhaps without any definitive answer, they still demand our attention. When I searched my mind for authentic narratives from women – they were, in India, mostly translated ones; the same was true of the writing of the tribals, the dalits and other marginalised communities, of folk songs, revised/reinterpreted fairy tales and a host of other kinds of writing. This fact is closely connected with language, its relationship to experience as well as the definition of a classic. English, even as it is the language of education, of communication, science and technology; even as it has opened out to accommodate other cultures, the native cultural concepts still resist absorption. Language captures experience through its nuances – it is both the creator and the creation of a lived reality, and English language writing does not fulfill all the needs of the new realities.

Any working or a tentative answer to the definition of a classic, needs to consider the new literatures and the constantly growing reading strategies. We have moved through oppositional ways of reading and evaluating literature, have debated the aesthetics of protest, have quarrelled over acceptance of experiential writing and the rawness of anguish and have looked for texts which stand the test of time. Now that protest has been validated we are compelled to rethink. A classic, to my mind, is that which captures reality and experience, creates a powerful, unforgettable image or set of images, evokes response and disturbs the reader to relocate himself or herself in history and politics, relationships and culture. It ruffles one through and through. Poetry has always been read through images, now we also read the novel through images for the image is simultaneously fluid and defined, it relates to the context as well as steps outside it, it communicates through suggestion and uses language to extend it. There could be a hundred thousand ways of defining a classic or of reading literature – I leave it to you to fill the gaps.

15

Postcolonial Constructs – Exit?*

Postcolonialism, with or without the hyphen, is a word that has been bandied about by theorists, artists and writers for more than three decades. Rarely does its use imply the same meaning. Nationalities, subnationalities, regional concerns and languages intervene to give it new or different meanings. In India, its acceptance was reluctant and inevitably forked. There were those of us who celebrated the term as a break from the past and as a process of legitimising the aesthetics of 'protest' and those who resented the tag colonialism in its new birth. Certainly, it did open up space in academics for the Third World voice. And in Canada and the States, also grudgingly in Britain, it offered a comfortable niche for employment for specialists in third world literatures.

I could go on enumerating the history of postcolonialism's progress from a convenient term, a term of liberation, to that of becoming a full-fledged industry. Any random bibliographical search will testify to the truth of my statement. Anthologies, full-length books, summing up of theories and debates now reduced to territorial wars. The debates and the disagreements are a natural fall out of the whole approach which is split right in the centre and is as hegemonic and proprietal as imperialism.

Is postcolonialism a theory or a methodology? What are its aesthetics? Does it work primarily through resistance and reversal

---

* Public Lecture delivered at Vishwabharati, Shantiniketan, 12 January 2011.

or does it open out/or build upon epistemological and psychological theories? Is it a political ideology or the recovery of lost histories? In its myriad manifestations it has touched on all of the above. Bill Ashcroft thinks of it as a methodology; Aijaz Ahmad traces within it and highlights the need for an ideological presence; Edward Said, as he uncovered the underside of the Orientalist phenomenon, went on to examine the nature of representation and the construction of the 'Other'.

It is evident that the constructs of postcolonialism are varied, with roots in different histories, disciplines and movements, spread over a huge portion of this world, and with the power to rebound on the western world which, over a period of six hundred years or more, went on to use psychology, medical science, anthropology and several other knowledge systems in order to establish its hold over the rest of the world, building its authority on the principle of difference. Naturally when the nature of this 'difference' is explored, one comes across a whole range of issues which are located in specific concerns and add to the multiplicity of the discourse. A related question which surfaces is the importance of this difference and how it can be prevented from degenerating into mere essentialism; and how, at the same time, can it refuse to be subsumed into a homogenised category of the 'Other', a stage which stalls both visibility and production of knowledge.

On the face of it, there may be no apparent reason to attempt an 'exit' from a theory/methodology/or discourse of this nature – and when one considers the possibility and projects the necessity of making a break with it, there need be sufficient grounds for it. I have several, questionable, debatable but deeply felt reasons over a fairly long period of time. I am using this opportunity to place before you my responses. Has postcolonialism really freed us from the shackles of the past or has it succeeded instead to root us even more firmly in the colonial past, by making it a consistent reference point and guiding our addressivity to it? Our addressivity – both as theorists and writers – continues to be towards the west, a fact which is reinforced through the use of such phrases as 'writing back', 'reversal' and 'resistance' and now more recently 'empire calling'. Not only do these terms determine the addressivity, they also automatically limit our explorations of the subject or the epistemologies we may like to explore. Further there appears to me no pride or dignity in the use of the terms generated by this discourse – words which carry with them the colonial baggage of marginality and subordination, irrespective of the dictionary meanings, and get planted firmly in our imaginaries. As for instance the word 'vernacular' has a heavy colonial baggage and when we use the term in India, in juxtaposition to 'English', we are establishing a hierarchy within a geographical territory and transferring it to a wider audience, an act which reinforces the past, rather than reverse it. Postcolonial critics ranging from Gayatri Spivak to Feroza Jussawala and Amit Chaudhuri, use the term unhesitatingly and indiscriminatingly.

Again, the word 'subaltern', extremely handy as a noun or an adjective, is an all embracing term for margins in varying contexts – class, gender and history. Why are descriptive words loaded so much in favour of power and authority? Subaltern studies, in its birth, heralded an area which could be used to explore unrecorded histories and expose the subterranean levels of ideology and movements, but its continued use works against all notions of equality and is conducive to hierarchical approaches. Here I draw attention to Gayatri Spivak's introductory prefaces to her translations of Mahasweta Devi's stories, a practice which she defends as necessary in order to get through to the west (Translater's Preface xxi–xxvi).

Postcolonial theory is far too homogenous despite its internal differences. Almost everything can be put into this huge basket – even the writing emerging from the erstwhile imperial centres. Yet, it is strange, that in the academia this writing is placed on the margin of mainstream courses – a place at the peripheries of white academy, marked for the immigrant literatures of a huge chunk of the world. Despite its large and multiple holdings, it continues to be invisible. The 1995 *Cambridge History of Literary Criticism* does not even make a mention of it. Moreover it encourages easy misrepresentations. As Edward Brathwaite has observed, complex cultural and national histories are steamrolled into one and literary beginnings are mislocated. Literary expression in the Caribbean was born out of the experiences of slavery and African history and was not a case of writing back to the Empire.

I do not have to repeat what Arif Dirlik wrote linking the rise of postcolonialism with global capitalism, or the more grounded views of practitioners like Arun Prabha Mukherjee but would like to draw your attention to Aijaz Ahmad's scathing criticism in *In Theory*, of the direction which postcolonial theory has taken. He critiques it mainly on the grounds of its monolingualism, a practice which excludes multi-lingual traditions and perceives third world literary texts in terms 'always of their determination by the colonial encounter'. The very terms of this discourse repress alternative starting points, which maybe rooted in culture, class or gender (92). The single language representation is one which is truncated and partial and any theory 'based upon what is currently available in languages of metropolitan countries becomes an alarming undertaking' (98).

Visibility of the diaspora or of the writing in English at the cost of all else is a huge cost to pay and mortgages all our intellectual pursuits to that enterprise. Arun Prabha Mukherjee in her two works on postcolonialism has drawn attention to the need for oppositional aesthetics as well as translated texts along with the difficulties of carrying culture across on the back of an alien language. For her the fact of being translated, of being 'borne across the world' (Rushdie 1991: 220) overlaps with the hyphen. *Oppositional Aesthetics* carries the subtitle *Readings from a Hyphenated Space* and together the two project a problematical area and an identity perpetually placed in precarious balance, probing cultural histories and memories, and eternally placed in opposition to the imposition of hegemonic structures. The diasporic self becomes a resisting self, but on what authority remains an unanswered question. Mukherjee insists that the articulation of cultural difference attempts to change the direction of western interpretation as it works for projecting the excluded other into history. Bhabha is in agreement with this when he too states that such a theoretical enterprise, 'simultaneously seeks to subvert and replace' (Bhabha 22). Bhabha's concept of hybridity can be extended to both theory and discourse. It moves in multiple directions as it encompasses within it the act of writing as well as the actual social reality which is always in a state of flux and necessitates a constant dialogue between individuals, cultures, time past and time present. Working with this, Bhabha problematises ambivalences and interstitial spaces. None of these are free of complications or stalemates. Stereotypes fix identities and are no less dangerous than the universalism which laced the civilisatonal discourse. Additionally they wrap up all histories of colonialism into a time capsule and a single vision. Moreover, Bhabha's concept of hybridity ignores the whole history of genetic engineering carried on in the racial context. The attempt to induct the suppressed and subjugated knowledge systems into the dominant discourse often ends up as exoticisation or window-dressing. It does not subvert the dominant authority instead it reinforces the colonial concepts related to backwardness. The way we think of ourselves, as Ahmad has observed, is governed by the west. (44)

At the heart of the whole project is anger, and perhaps also a deep sense of failure. Both negative emotions in themselves and those which have prematurely terminated the process of decolonisation in its initial stages. There is hardly any collaborative effort visible at bringing together the knowledge being generated by other disciplines or even the creativity of the writers writing in Indian languages other than English, writers like U.R. Ananthamurthy and Nirmal Verma. In fact little attention is paid to what even the writers writing in English have to say. Both Nayantara Sahgal and Amitav Ghosh, representatives of different generations, have projected new ways of thinking and conceptualising, and have attempted to create epistemological frameworks. It makes sense to work with other theoretical frameworks rather than postcolonialism. It is here I would like to introduce the concept of schizophrenia, which continues to be a part of both national and postcolonial discourse. Nayantara Sahgal, in a perceptive essay titled 'The Schizophrenic Imagination', referred to it as the divide between the outer world of colonial power and the inner world of culture she has developed it more fully in her later work – especially the historical novels. In *Lesser Breeds* (2003), when she has Nurullah follow Bhai's advice to look for alternative forms of knowledge and alternative histories, Sahgal works with it not only in the field of epistemology but also in the making of the self. Shan, the young child whose education he has been trusted with, is able to overcome this schism of her childhood world, to grow up and take her place as an integrated person confident of her convictions and values. Sahgal points towards the possibility of the two halves coming together.

This schizophrenia has also been expressed by writers as different as R.K. Narayan in *The English Teacher* (1945), and Amitav Ghosh in *The Circle of Reason* (1986) and *The Calcutta Chromosome* (1996). These writers focus on the making of the self as it confronts its two separate worlds and tries to make sense out of them. The site here is not the dominant discourse but the presence of the dominant discourse within one and on inward self-reflection which leads to its subversion either through practice, ideology or politics. Gandhi is a major exemplar of this process. In *My Experiments with Truth* he describes both the outward and inward journeys, each necessary for the transformation and restoration of balance in his thought. Reading the autobiography and going over the various shifts in his headgear, dress code and name one is able to sense how M.K. Gandhi became first Mohandas, then Gandhibhai, before becoming a mahatma. Gandhi's *Hind Swaraj* is a work which discusses alternative culture, value systems, history and modernity, and in direct contrast to the Fanonian thesis, proceeds to work out processes of self-formation. History, Gandhi observes, is one-sided and the other side needs to be written. Robert Young in his *White Mythologies: Writing History and the West* (1990), takes up this point in his chapter 'Disorienting Orientalism', though his inspiration lies in African resistance movements. Human intervention both in the making of history and in the making of theory needs to be discussed at some length. In fact, the theoretical positions are not necessarily explanatory, they are often conscious attempts to intervene in the flow of history.

Another matter of deep concern is the absence of Gandhi or only a marginal presence in the theory of postcoloniality, a point I have raised elsewhere in fair amount of detail (Refer 'Untapped Seam' in the present volume). Even Tagore is absent from this discourse. His fiction and non-fiction both are rich source materials of debates and discourses on cultural encounters, shifts and meanings both of culture and civilisation. *Home and the World* discusses modernity, critiques violence and reflects on the nature of revolution; *Gora* projects a view of nationalism. At some point we need to discuss them with reference to our present-day realities. Most of our attempts at indigenous theory have not been able to sustain themselves for long. They are either too heavily ideological or parochial and monolingual. They are unable either to locate themselves or find any substantial philosophical support. Disciplines such as the philosophy, psychology and history need to support theory. Gurbhagat Singh advocates a differential criticography which seeks to interpret the ontology of each *bhasa* literature as a product and negation of its own genetic geo-culture (93). Singh's theory rejects the imagined unity projected by Gandhi and Nehru and expressed through the institutionalised slogan of 'unity in diversity'; instead he projects a confederative one. Towards this end he gives the example of *Adi Granth* and its composition which established the right of the language traditions to intervene in a major way. It freely moved across languages – Persian, Sanskrit, Hindavi, Braj Bhasha and a sprinkling of words from Arabic, Marathi and other Indian language. Homogeneity privileges power, polarities lead to subordination and inequality in terms but plurality enables exchange and interaction. Any move of a migrant ontology leaves behind a residue. As one travels from one part of India to another, from one language to another, residual elements are traceable even though socio-economic histories differ. Singh's assertion is that it is exactly in this polyphonic discourse, in the crossing of borders and boundaries that the possibility of a new interpretative discourse dies, for despite all these differences there is an identifiable degree of commonality in history, in the sense of time, in kinship patterns and in the relationship to land. To this, I may add the value of Agyeya's scholarly interventions in his non-fiction and his critical essays, several of which seek to reclaim history and philosophy, and the indigenous positions contained within them. He also chooses to expand upon the concept of memory. He observes that all perceptions of reality also work through memory. And the limits of memory – like those of language – become the limits of one's identity. When the postcolonial theorist does not go further back in time than the encounter with the west, she fails to perceive earlier colonisations, or the joint products of those encounters in language and culture, the presence of Persian in the Guru Granth Sahib, the convergence of movements such as Sufism and the Bhakti, or the presence of resistance in Basavanna. These are all important locations of theory and for theory. And locations alike of ideas and of people are of immense significance as any disjunction brings about a sense of insecurity and bewilderment, and perhaps also a certain degree of self-reflection. Gandhi's journeys outward were paralleled by similar inwardly directed journeys. All journeys are not physical journeys – they are often reflective or metaphorical ones, journeys that recapitulate the past or open out cultural spaces. These acquire the power to subvert the tyranny of space and place tradition within the continuum of time.

I want briefly to move into the 30s, a period which witnessed the growth – more accurately the recognition – of an indigenous tradition of humanism putting aside both the white man's burden and the corresponding *mai-baap* servility. The white man's humanism was exclusive: it divided human beings into 'men' and 'natives' or 'men' and 'negroes'. It was based on separation between culture and civilisation, and on distinctions of colour and race. In opposition to this both Gandhi and Tagore revived a humanistic tradition based upon ethics of belief, faith and on compassion. Even for writers of marked leftist leanings like Mulk Raj Anand, human conditions demanded 'the mirror of creative emotion to reflect them'. In *Apology for Heroism*, Anand confesses the futility of his earlier pursuit and the false emphasis on the brahmanical tradition. It was the human being, with all his failings and weaknesses, who mattered. Anand's humanism demands a confrontation with the self – a confrontation based upon humility. It does not base itself on any purist concepts but goes on to effect a conjunction of different cultures. Neither a condescension, nor an ideology, it is based on the recognition of dignity. Anand recalls how his mother placed the Hindu idols 'side by side with a crucifix', 'a picture of the Aga Khan, and of Guru Nanak'. In a dialogic passage between his conscience and his worldly self he projects his questioning of religious Absolutism and of the self seen as separated from the Divine.

For Anand, humanism cannot be reconciled with the notion of any individual salvation or an exclusivist religion – it was vested in a social reality and gave birth or at least worked for a new idea of selfhood. One must admit that for him, more than spirituality, it was a sense of social involvement which determined our sense of the human.

I have travelled far from my critiquing of postcolonialism – but to my mind, my links are quite clear. In addition to the limited and oppressive vocabulary of postcoloniality, its constant squabbling for a little more cultural space and resistance to an other-culture interpretation – my reference here is to the Gayatri Spivak–Benita Parry–Julia Kristeva's responses to each others' criticism. (Spivak, 'Three Women's Texts and a Critique of Imperialism' and Parry, 'Problems in Current Theories of Colonial Discourse') Kristeva's *About Chinese Women* aroused Spivak's particular antagonism. She is critical of her First World approach, and places her work in the tradition of appropriation. To these I add a fourth name, that of Erin O'Conner who attacks Spivak for her audacity of encroaching into the field of Victorian Studies and accuses her of doing so on skimpy evidence, and as an outsider. O'Conner uses the words 'hostile takeover', which encourages territorial thinking. This is an accusation that many of us could fling back at a western reader. O'Conner's argument is in terms of Us and Them.

Postcolonialism has shifted the ground of postcolonial resistance from aesthetics and an evolutionary strategy to an empire-directed one; it is dominantly diasporic, and has little to do with those who never came into contact with the west, people who have lived in other dimensions. (Ananthamurthy's 'The Search for an Identity: A Kannada Writer's View'). There is an additional risk of a new canon being constructed not out of our frames of requirement or our realities but guided by the needs of cultural projection of the diaspora intellectual. Translations with long glossaries, aimed at the western classrooms and highlighting of issues of interest to them, yielding to market forces are some of the fallouts of this misguided notion of representation and these in their turn prevent a genuine interaction and evaluation of the classics of our languages.

One of the unstated objectives of postcolonial studies was to legitimatise a new aesthetics. But has it done so? On the other hand, at a recent International Conference, I found an American scholar shifting the whole debate to Comparative aesthetics. And it came to rest on open text and closed text, open meaning that which was accessible to the west and had shed all cultural complexities and closed implied a cultural density. There was no reference to readerly or writerly, or writerly reading (Barthes and Morrison), instead it was focused on being comprehensible to the west, requiring the postcolonial novel to bend backwards to fit into the mantra of globalisation. No doubt, I exaggerate but I felt angry at the total indifference to aesthetics and to the writer's relationship to writing and to home concerns/cultures. Today, we still find experiential aesthetics on the margins. I would be interested to know how language departments use postcolonial methodologies.

The signals are in plenty. Postcolonialism has lived out its life. Are we not yet ready to step out of it? And look out for new directions, redefine our research priorities and locate ourselves, more meaningfully, in all that is around us?

16

How Strangeness Takes Possession

The Ongoing Negotiation Between the Familiar and the Unfamiliar *

An occasion like this when an honour is being conferred on a writer demands a retrospect, the need to travel the same ground the writer has travelled, to place the different frames side by side, to work through the pattern through which the writer has evolved, to look for departures, experimentations, repetitions, continuities and view their interconnections as they create a cumulative meaning. Each successive work alters the earlier placement; each new strategy sends the reader back to look for an earlier trace. The autonomy of an individual text is misplaced; the text co-relates to contemporariness, locates itself in a continuity and flows out into a contingent world.

Today, as a reader, I too need to rework my own critical alignment with Anita Desai's work. For the reader, like the writer, travels and returns after several journeys in other directions. For us, as near contemporaries, the journeys have been somewhat parallel in time though different in manner and pursuit. It was when Desai was engaged in writing her sixth novel, *Clear Light of Day,* that we first met. And this novel in itself makes a very good entry point into

* Presented at the Felicitation Ceremony held at Sahitya Akademi, New Delhi, on the occasion of Anita Desai's induction as Fellow of the Akademi, 30 November 2007. First published in *Indian Literature*, Vol. 244, March–April 2008.

Desai's work. It belongs to a kind of writing, I choose to call the sibling novel. To date Desai has three of these – *Voices in the City* (1965), *Clear Light of Day* (1980) and *Fasting, Feasting* (1999). These may also be seen as the novels of the plains, a landing place after the heightened intensity of the loner novels, such as *Cry, the Peacock* (1963), *Fire on the Mountain* (1977) and *Baumgartner's Bombay* (1989). There is also a third category, the novels of travelling the past, novels of journeys that trace an earlier route. To this belong *Journey to Ithaca* (1995) and *The Zigzag Way* (2004). In some measure *Where Shall We Go This Summer* (1975) also fits in here. *In Custody* (1984) stands apart, all by itself as it is a work about the nature of art and continuity, about an artist and his devotee.

The sibling novels occur at almost regular intervals and appear to fulfill a need to put the pieces of a jigsaw puzzle together, to look at their jagged edges and to wonder how they came out of the same family, similar childhoods and experiences. The jagged pieces that are sharp and vulnerable in the loner novels come back in these to fill each other's gaps. The four siblings in each novel follow different routes, chase different dreams and work out their lives differently. *Clear Light of Day* is the most positive of them and is also more firmly anchored in the socio-historical reality. These three novels form a continuity and work out the transformations of the characters. It is as if the writer is imagining in how many different ways these lives could have been lived – leading into newer routes – the roads taken and not taken as they work out their resentments, feelings of guilt and confront their failures.

The concerns of these novels spill over into her other works: childhood fears and memories, dreams, fascination with poetry and music, need for freedom, working out escape routes and anchoring onto other human beings who, even if they are peripheral and vulnerable, constitute figures of solid support to a child's mind. Family structures are opened out and exposed for what they are – domineering, controlling and exploitative – yet not without a supportive mechanism. The peripheries step in to sustain the crumbling edifice. Memory is contemporaneously located even though perspectives are different. These novels are also a kind of a workshop for Desai's sharpening of her narratological approaches.

Desai's novels do not work with the conventional polarities or oppositional structures, but they do work with parallel worlds as interior worlds are lived in exterior space. This is visible in several of her novels wherever there is a non-acceptability of the outer reality – whether it is Maya (*Cry, the Peacock*), Monisha (*Voices in the City*) or Nanda Kaul (*Fire on the Mountain*). The gap between the external reality and the individual's perception of it, or relationship to it emphasises the instability of the 'real' and leads to a continued ambivalence or multivalence. In fact, except for *Cry, the Peacock,* and in some measure *The Zigzag Way*, the narratives unfold themselves either through parallel voices like Raka's (*Mountain*) and Lotte's (*Baumgartner's Bombay*) or through multiple narrators who decentre the narrative, establish a contrapuntality and allow variations of the same theme to emerge.

Anita Desai is one of the most worked-on Indian writers both at home and abroad, a fact which places her work at the intersection of cultural perspectives and readings. This calls for a closer look at the authorial role in the making of the text – the images, the language, the recurrence of narrative junctures, and to free her work from the obsessive psycho-analytical analysis. Desai's work resists such easy or a single lens categorisation. With this in mind, I wish to draw attention to those aspects of her work which have not attracted similar attention: her creative use of realism as she has gone on to employ it very differently from her predecessors of the early years of the twentieth century, her modernist leanings, which again are unobtrusive yet significant and her appropriation of the unfamiliar. These three are interconnected and overlap and together they constitute her narrative approach. Measured in conventional terms there is nothing that is akin to the methodology of realism in Desai's work. The interior mindscapes dominate – but one needs to recall that they are located within detailed and minute descriptions of the external world and the setting is meticulously put together with fine brush strokes. One would think a zoologist or a horticulturist is at work as lizards, snakes, rats are described and the flora and fauna of different regions come alive. The descriptions also bring in a certain degree of objectivity and perform a dual function. On the one hand a concrete, real setting is created facilitating the entry of the reader into the world of the novel and on the other it detracts from the human subject and goes on to create an almost scientific base for the emotional self-indulgence of the character.

Desai's descriptive passages – whether it is the storm scene in *Cry, the Peacock* or in *Fire on the Mountain* – are heavily sensory and even sensual, and overladen with narrative significance. Maya recounts, 'I exulted, and raised my arms to return its impassioned embrace. If the closed windows protected me from its whiplash and scorpion-sting, it still allowed me the sensation of standing waist-deep ... in the centre of a churning broil' (188). In *Fire on the Mountain*, there is greater restraint but Raka too sits on the knoll, hugging her knees, 'watching the long-tailed rose ringed parakeets that clung to the cones ... as the wind knocked into them and tore away the cones, tossing them down the hill' and Nanda Kaul finds that the wind whips at her sari 'cracking the silk folds' (81). Verbs like whip, crackle, retreat, drum bring the sounds alive.

The subnarrators and substories add to the realistic anchoring and counter memories allow the reader to distinguish the hallucinated and imagined realities from the actual happenings as they occur. Counterviews intervene with linearity. This is a method which is employed with fresh variations in novel after novel. Events are unfolded not merely through flashbacks – actually there are hardly any – but through parallel narrations, counter narrations or through back tracking, travelling the ground travelled earlier in memory, or travelling the ground travelled by someone else as in the case of Sophie who duplicates Laila's journey (*Journey to Ithaca*) or Eric who pursues the track his grandfather had taken (*The Zigzag Way*). The socio-historical anchoring is another aspect of realism, which is different from the purpose driven or ideologically committed realism. It becomes a narrative strategy for framing subjectivity. This is especially strong in *Clear Light of Day* and *Baumgartner's Bombay*. In the second of these two novels, Baumgartner's boyhood memories, the time spent in the internment camp, the years in Calcutta and now the streets of Bombay provide anchoring points to the almost surrealistic setting of his flat crowded with the presence of stray, orphaned, wounded cats, very much like his own abandoned self. Baumgartner is a victim, an exile, a fugitive all in one. The postcards received from his mother with the impersonal number J673/1 stamped on them are a recurring feature in the narrative, punctuating it and calling attention to the war-torn world as well as the absent mother (see 1–2, 164, 215, 229–30). They also provide a frame both for the novel and Baumgartner's life. He is loner – 'he would not live in a pack, he did not need the pack' (150). The narrative, through the German hippie Kurt, travels the length and breadth of a geographical territory right from Tibet, Nepal to Goa and Lucknow.

Desai's modernism is visible not merely in her narratology, the ambivalent endings, the engagement with urbanscapes but also in her portrayal of loneliness, aloneness and solitude. Some of her subjects are lonely, some prefer to be by themselves, others withdraw from the outer world like Matteo and Nirode and still others are dropouts – and they prefer invisibility. In the course of these portrayals both the feminine and the masculine come in for redefinitions. Nanda Kaul through hindsight attempts to revise the whole notion of wifehood and motherhood, Bim sidesteps them, others try to keep their inner beings intact, still others like Amla and Aunt Lila debate womanly roles. Several male characters in Desai's novels refuse to live according to the conventional idea of masculinity – Nirode, Arjun, Baumgartner and even Paul, Eric's father in *The Zigzag Way*.

The Zigzag Way builds up history and narrative structure through the use of epigraphs. In many ways, even as it uses Desai's favourite trope of travel both metaphorically and physically, the novel is very different from her earlier novels. It is different in subject matter, choice of location and in its treatment. Somehow loneliness and failure do not warp the soul. It is a two-directional journey – Eric moves backward to trace his grandfather's life, to find his grandmother's grave, to connect with his ancestors, to live through the past in order to discover who he is. He moves forward towards self-realisation and independence from the dominating female figures in his life – his mother and his two girl-friends. It is also a journey of another kind both for Desai and for Eric; it is a move towards appropriating strangeness: the immigrant's journey to connect with the immediate environs. Eric, in his journey to the mines, stays at an inn where Andre and his wife Paola act as commentators on Dona Vera and the many chapters in her life – European, Mexican, Huichol – and the idea is that in order to begin anew, one has to leave the past behind. 'On one level or another, it is what we do' (102). Paola further explains how they came to be there – 'because there was so much space, and it was free' (104). As one travels, one settles down, one learns to belong – by learning languages, getting involved with histories, working through geographical terrains and celebrating rituals, in short creating new landscapes of the mind. Ironically enough, the celebration of rituals connects with the past. Eric joins the Mexicans as they celebrate the ritual homage to their dead – so they could 'experience the time of their ancestor and understand where they came from and who they were' (155), he follows them in search of his grandmother's grave with a bunch of flowers in his hands. And then he sees what can be described as a vision. A young woman descends the hills and asks him whether he is Paul – 'No', Eric replies – 'I am not. Paul is my father, I'm Eric, his son'. She talks about Cornwall, about the graves of the outsiders, asks about Davey (her husband) and then disappears. Eric is unable to follow her but the light is brighter, the day dawns calling the living back to their world (176–179). A little bit of mystery, a haunting atmosphere, a validation for the continuity of life – even as directions change and new spaces are inhabited. In fact, even as Desai has analysed the role of mothers, worked through the perception of children in almost all her work, *The Zigzag Way* happens to be the first novel in which childbirth actually takes place in a foreign land during a period of flight, and new life emerges.

Joseph Conrad once wrote: 'A work that aspires, however humbly, to the condition of art should carry its justification in every line'. And the images that are created, should be clearly visible, as they rise before us even when we close our eyes (Preface to *The Nigger of Narcissus*). Desai's contribution lies primarily in filling up the gap between feeling and communication, between thought and language, in employing language to cover extra-linguistic dimensions, depending on other arts like painting to create images, and evolving strategies to confront the conflictual life of the mind. The human mind is what she turns round and round with all its baggage of guilt, nostalgia, dreams and hallucination to expose every angle, every crevice and simultaneously unfold its mystery as well as let it persist. Her fiction, anchored in social constructs, sets out to create a different spatio-temporal reality and then sets it free from a narrow anchoring in any specific time or culture. Strangeness takes possession, to be appropriated and owned, to be related to and communicated across cultures and literary traditions.

17

Contrapuntal Narratives

Shifting Paradigms in Comparative Literature*

The debates that have been going on regarding the health and future possibilities of Comparative Literature make it necessary to look at the issues from the perspective of the South. I welcome the opportunity to do so from my location in a multi-lingual culture. Mainly marked by the conservative spirit and overtly concerned with its insecurities, the discipline has not allowed itself to expand. In India – and this may be applicable to several other parts of Asia – Comparative Literature has retained its exclusiveness. Jadavpur is the oldest centre. In the last three decades some other centres have come up either devoted to Dravidian or Sanskrit aesthetics in the field of comparative literature or merely clubbed with English and Other European languages. Yet, in departments of English, we have been engaged in teaching British, American, Commonwealth literatures and Indian Classics in Translation side by side, doing a kind of comparative literature.

It is evident that disciplines as defined traditionally no longer hold sway and the serious scholar is selectively breaking bounds in order to explore other worlds. Most of what is happening has come about because of the need to respond to changed political centres. This response is not necessarily a desire to be accepted or

---

* Presented at a Plenary Session at the XIX International Comparative Literature Congress, Seoul, Korea, 2010 and published in an abridged form in *Literary Research*, Vol. 27, Summer 2011.

to be part of the larger world. It is often an act motivated by a resistance to hegemonic centres and is a consciously entered into space. Such moves are somewhat limited due to lack of theoretical formulations and also by an over-dependence on English and translated texts. Many of us, in the last few decades, have also been sidetracking into Indian language literatures, especially languages we are competent enough to read and interpret in the original, forming new links with our own histories, literatures and traditions. In the process, the relationship with other literatures is constantly being worked out afresh.

When I look back, I ask myself, did we ever consciously decide to do so? No, this happened simultaneously in different places. We have had bilingual and trilingual writers right through the nineteenth and twentieth centuries; many teachers of English are highly regarded poets and novelists in their own languages. Now, the transition has taken place in the field of theory and criticism – a move which even as it negotiates Sanskrit aesthetics and western frameworks, is also consciously moving towards redefinitions. It signifies a larger protest against hegemonic structures whether of theory, language, perspective or location and is marked by a need to find recognition for oral traditions, performative art and indigenous theoretical formulations. In fact, all that does not find place at the 'centre'.

Thus this conscious move to expand the frontiers of comparative literature is both a felt need and a political necessity. We are possessed by a desire to rehabilitate our pasts, to relate to each other horizontally across the surface of our continents, rather than through a centrally governed distribution network. Geographical locations divide us not spatially but through power structures which connect through hierarchies rather than equality.[1] In psychological terms, comparisons are odious, but strangely enough when we compare cultures and literatures, the comparison adds value. What do we look for when we compare – sameness or difference? Meeting point or otherness? And how do we work – through juxtapositions, pluralities, histories or simultaneities? How do we dismantle hierarchies to make room for difference? These and questions such as these confront us when we seek to enter this field.

I borrow the concept contrapuntal from Edward Said's use first in *Culture and Imperialism* and then from its surfacing in his writings published posthumously in *On Late Style: Music and Literature Against the Grain* (New York: Pantheon, 2006), a work where Said offers definitive theorisations of contrapuntalism as method and as both a historical and a deeply historical position (Feldman, Review 1). Said first used it as a reading strategy but apparently the method is also firmly rooted in the act of writing, especially in the kind of writing which brought together the conflictual relationship between his intellectual and his political selves. In Said's case, as he seems to suggest, it was born out of exile, in Adorno's out of the trauma of dislocation, where participation, witnessing, critiquing and opposition worked in criss-crossed relationships. The new shifts in comparative literature similarly reflect multiple dislocations and incorporate several rebellions both in literary and political terms, shifts which call for a new approach.

Contrapuntalism as a method extends to both the art of writing and the ways of interpreting. Incidentally it applies equally to the spilling of the text into the world of reality. Every text, in itself, is a fragment of a larger pattern. It makes several kinds of different journeys both inside and outside the text, and works with attitudes and experiences which are oppositional and chaotic and refuse to be controlled. The concept of contrapuntal has its origins in music and is a relationship between melody and harmony as oppositional tones surface, each working toward accentuation or reconciliation. The move is neither parallel, nor necessarily sequential but a kind of constant pressure pushing against the narrative level. In the literary act the suppressed silences, conflicts, presences, absences, crosscurrents and undercurrents that disrupt become significant indicators. Contrapuntality pulls the other in as a co-traveller. In Indian music the relationship between raga and tala maybe seen as a near parallel, but as Indian music does not work through counterpoint, it goes on to provide a lot of space for improvisation and allows the raga to stretch itself in innumerable ways.[2] But not competent enough to comment in terms of musicology, I shall be content to base my arguments on literary narratives.

If definitions are to be constructed through difference then perhaps we need to look at Bakhtin's dialogicity which concentrates primarily on language and its multiple contexts, locations, objectives and interplay as it encompasses the movements of history and social expanse. The dialogic interaction between words and their use is simultaneously a means of decentring and centring the text. The heteroglossia of the text is matched by its heterogenous movements. Contrapuntalism, in contrast, begins with a conscious or an unconscious absorption of atmospheric forces to be reworked in the act of writing through the interplay between the writer, his known world and his subconscious world as personal responses, situations of history and political positions clash. Bubbles of pressure points surface both within and outside the text, especially in its addressivity to its heterogenous readers.

The existing dominant positions/approaches in comparative literature are limiting as they have failed to frontally address its attitudinal hierarchy both in terms of aesthetics and of location. This hierarchy is reflected in the postcolonial discourse, which now in its turn, is being viewed as a threat to the methodology of comparative literature. The theorisation in both gets caught in the norm of classical aesthetics. I recall that in the post-1950s protest writing was viewed as non-literary and non-aesthetic. Postcolonialism then came up as an alternative measuring tape, to be gradually homogenised and interpreted through texts in English or in translation, to become the monopoly of the diaspora of various hues,[3] with languages of the erstwhile colonial people remaining outside this fold. Then an attempt was made to include them through translations apparently directed at creating a postcolonial canon. The centre of power in all this, continues to remain the same: in terms of theory, recognition and cross-distribution of texts.

As recently as 2006 Susan Bassnett, in her essay 'Reflections on Comparative Literature in the Twenty-First Century', has gone on to state that for, 'Spivak and southern hemisphere scholars, the crucial issues of comparative literature are indeed *politicised*. In contrast, however, I believe that the crucial issues for European scholars are as much aesthetic as political' (emphasis mine, 4–5). Bassnett's statement displays a lack of humility, which I believe, any serious reader must possess while approaching a text, and is almost a necessary precondition when we initially approach a different culture. There is also in such a statement a reflection of the belief in a 'singular' and perhaps a non-evolving aesthetics, in fact a rejection of all that is 'different' and thus peripheral. There is no way literature is not political, else *The Tempest* and *The Heart of Darkness* would not fit in so snugly with contemporary theoretical discourses. Often our recognition of its values, especially as texts have an afterlife and are contrapuntal, is even more political than the writing itself. Location of political power creates a visibility, but the different locations of the writer and of the reader create a counter-discourse. I have been using the word 'location' in more than one sense. It goes beyond the mere sense of physical location – locations are multiple, layered, ideological, conflictual and also subject to fluctuation and change. But they are of significance in the relationship they evoke between the text, its readers and critics. At one point they directly relate to the evaluation of the aesthetic value of the text.

I would not go all the way with Susan Bassnett's advocacy of the use of translated texts, despite its obvious advantages. True, we are free to enter cultural areas without going through the acquisition of the language/languages and it facilitates movement across the literatures of the world. But the method is fraught with risks. Translations, as both Edward Said and U.R. Ananthamurthy have demonstrated in different contexts[4], can be manipulative. They impose secondary 'fabricated' frames onto the original, thus creating other levels of discourse. Gillian Wright, in her translation of Rahi Masoom Raza's *Aadha Gaon* (*Half-a-Village*), has left out chunks of the original, in the process omitting a significant sub-text.[5] At times, the translator's focus shifts from the text to the addressivity to the non-culture reader, and it tends to gloss over the finer shades of meaning. And at others, the translator has perhaps never really succeeded in entering the world of the text. In this context, Arun Mukherjee in *Oppositional Aesthetics*[6] has pointed out the limitations of cross-cultural translations, especially as the act involves a relationship between the ethos of two different cultures. It requires a complexity of literary and extra-literary activities to come into play – understanding, interpretation, going across, familiarity, addressing linguistic gaps as well as the problematics of readership. The level of integrity one asks of a translator is very high. Is there a philosophical commitment to conveying the 'otherness' and relating the cultural specificities, topical references and local histories? Is there an understanding of cultural codes? In another context, Mukherjee also used the term 'cultural density' to describe the residual which inhabits translated writing.[7] Languages carry with them a whole cultural ethos with its traditions, histories, unverbalised nuances and contradictions. For the third world, the resistance to translation is fraught by another fear: the construction of an artificial canon being made out of the translated texts. This fear has surfaced mainly because texts are being translated to fill up the necessary sociological slots in postcolonial studies and as such they are singled out on counts of availability, theme and market demands and tend to bypass the literariness. We need to be wary of such moves. Moreover, translations often present truncated worlds, removed as they are from much of the writer's work, non-fiction, reviews and debates. The absence of this surrounding material limits a genuine comparative aesthetic evaluation.

True, many of us have grown up on translations of European literatures, perhaps facing the same limitations. But, it is equally true that the shared theology of several European cultures and the third world's knowledge of European histories allow us a certain familiarity. The same cannot be said of the west where we are concerned or about us in the context of cultures closer home. We have been compelled by the fact of colonisation to learn about imperial cultures first through imposed education systems and now through other monopolies. But our cultures have largely been a matter of archaeological, anthropological or political interest. Even today the inauthentic writer of the diaspora can get away by exoticising singled out segments of culture. As for our neighbours whose borders we can touch, of their histories we know very little – as for instance the Japanese occupation of China or of Korea, or their movements of survival, that this year is the 60th anniversary of the commencement of the war in Korea, or the 30th of the Kwangju Uprising. (Though we all remember Tiananmen Square because the ideological resistance it put up was of significance to western policies). I confess that despite my desire to read Asian literatures, not much is available all around me. Even our travels, at times, do not yield enough. And obviously, as I do not know these languages, I will fall back on translations. Justifying Susan Bassnett's stand. But then one comes up against other requirements in order to support these translations, such as dictionaries and encyclopedias of customs, rituals, terms, myths with their regional variations and oral literatures of which we hardly have any in the Asian context. This is a task awaiting comparative literature centres which, in a country like India, literally means an entry into multiple languages and their worlds.

Having expressed my concerns for the growing monolingual base for comparative literature, I would like to dwell on the phenomenon of transformation which a shift in cultural origins demands. Kazuo Ishiguro's short narrative 'Nocturnes' serves, for me, a double purpose. It illustrates contrapuntality and it comments directly on the complete make-over required by host cultures and globalisation. One of a series of five stories, all of which are related to music, 'Nocturnes' is about Steve, a saxophone player who is not handsome in the accepted sense, and thus is persuaded to undergo cosmetic surgery to transform his looks. The characters of this story are a carryover from another story in the volume, 'Crooner', where the narrator is a guitar player. Steve, in 'Nocturnes', lives in a small rented apartment with cardboard walls and in order to practice his music has to shut himself up in a padded cubicle so that the sound does not carry across. This self-imposed isolation stresses his marriage and his wife leaves him. But she persuades her rich lover to finance Steve's cosmetic surgery, who is finally pressurised by his agent into accepting this offer. In the luxury hotel where he is awaiting the removal of his bandages and the return of flexibility to his facial muscles, he meets another patient, a minor star, who makes him aware of the compromises which the visibility of talent requires. This transformation, which is projected as a necessary condition of acceptability into a homogenised world is also an act of transforming his perceptions of himself and his art. It amounts to what Arvindpal Singh describes as 'an act of assimilation' which refutes the possibility of exchange without loss and is a common phenomenon besetting migrant population.

Despite the counterpoints that the five stories work out for each other, and in addition to Kaziguro's shift of locale to Europe, the musical instruments and the human voices – singer, guitar player, sax player, cellist – all project both consonance and dissonance and work through different auditory sounds. The story also presents a counterpoint to all other metamorphoses – literary and mythical. What immediately concerns me here is Kafka's short narrative 'Metamorphosis' (1915), Kafka's hero wills this self-alienation and works his way to social and family rejection, in search of freedom and his own core self. It is altogether a different matter whether his 'will' is free or not, conscious or not. 'Metamorphosis' turns the Nietzschean 'will to power' on its head and can be read in multiple ways, but my purpose is served by drawing attention to this comparison. 'Nocturnes' is a counter-discourse and the conflict is in Steve's mind, his self-worth and its non-acceptance by the world. At another level, the story invites reference to Walter Benjamin's essay, 'The Work of Art in The Age of Mechanical Production' (1936). Only, in this case, the human being is also at the mercy of an external force. What happens to both originality and authenticity in such cases? And to what extent is Steve's relationship to his art and his self-image going to be affected by this re-modelling?

Comparative literature is not about erasing differences but of understanding and investigating their worth. If a text like 'Nocturnes' is to be taken up, a comparative exercise would have to extend beyond the comparisons in literary tradition and the debates in theoretical and psychological fields; in order to be meaningful it may have to wander further abroad to work with biography, history of dislocation, nostalgia and music; it would need to work with the notions and concepts of ambition and of fame. 'Nocturnes' is located in several discourses as the pressure points surface all over and need to be worked out. One of the categories it questions, is the whole notion of authenticity. If originality is the essence as Benjamin has said, then the original here has been over-written in every way. Again where do we look for in search of authenticity – the writer, his writing, his multiple relocations, Steve and his sense of self, his music, his relationships or the reception and aesthetic evaluation of the story, where? How do we test it and against what norms? 'Authenticity', as a term, has been variously defined. Trilling's work was an important contribution to this discourse, though now we hardly mention him. But one important fact he mentions is of value to our contemporary writing. Trilling brings out its connections with violence. As he traces the Greek ancestry of the word he points out that *authenteo* means 'to have full power over, also to commit a murder. *Authentes*: not only a master or a doer, but also a perpetrator, a murderer, even a self-murderer, a suicide'. He goes on the comment on the violence reflected in the creative will, 'how ruthless an act was required to assert autonomy in a culture schooled in duty and obedience to peremptory and absolute law, and how extreme an exercise of personal will was needed to overcome the sentiment of non-being' (Trilling 131–132). The process of birth – whether physical, emotional or national – is possessed by violence, and this violence, representing alike the sacred and the profane, is present in almost all acts of expression as they question, oppose or resist.

Another significant point, which Trilling makes, is the location of modernism in an environmental disassociation with the idea of the organic (127–128). It automatically privileges difference, fragmentariness, breakaway segments and attacks the notion of a dominant sameness. By relating authenticity to literature, Trilling lifts it out of a purely philosophical or an existential discourse. But in the act of reading, the 'authentic' is often attached to the reader's response and knowledge of the culture he is encountering. Thus aesthetic judgement invariably seems to be moving out of the text to other texts. Marshall Berman defines it as expressive of a radical rejection of things as they are and considers the desire for it as the 'most politically explosive of human impulses' (qtd. by Martin Jay 12). Critical of the near-hegemonic use made of the word 'authenticity', Adorno observed that it rested on a dubious ideal of self-possession and integrity (Martin Jay 17). Given these shifting views, often contradictory to each other, the category of authenticity is tossed about between Self and God. Why then, one may well ask is the third world aesthetics, along with its dominant experiential aesthetics devalued and negated? Is it not possible for politics and aesthetics to inhabit the same world? The creative act absorbs multiple elements, traditions and philosophies. And it little behoves us to dismiss it on grounds of difference.

Contemporary writing, especially the one emerging from hitherto invisible centres, whether in English and French, or non-European languages, is moving out in different directions. Several of these writers have been made by hostile environments, whether they be colonial or totalitarian, many of them have lost their original selves either through the imposition of a colonial education system, ideological pressures or through dislocation and assimilation. This writing connects up with Edward Said's concept of contrapuntality, even as it approaches the Derridean idea of the supplement. Comparativists need to move across without yielding to the temptation of tailoring difference for reasons of comprehension or acceptability, and without anchoring themselves in a single aesthetic norm; they need to recognise and relate to the difference. In some measure, premature comparisons suppress the emergence of the original. The failure to recognise the emergence of experiential aesthetics and to redefine such concepts as beauty and ugliness are barriers in literary appreciation and assessment. When a dalit writer, describes her childhood and her washing of lice-infested clothes on the banks of a river, or the strings of animal flesh being hung up to dry in the small hutment, or the liberating experience she has when possessed by the spirit of a goddess, authenticity and aesthetics are both in place. Neither sophistication, nor a consciousness of the other, nor even a stylisation of language has come between her experience and its expression (except the act of recollection). These literatures do not yet belong to either classical or postcolonial literature (which more than signifying a historical fact, is now a position which homogenises and builds clusters). These texts are not preoccupied by any sense of addressivity to the 'other', and least of all to the west. Yet they refuse to remain confined to a single discourse for as they express the facts of their existence, they enter into a discourse with the different worlds inside and outside the text, drawing the reader in.

Contrasted to Ishiguro's *Nocturnes*, the work of writers like Chimamanda Adichie, Kamila Shamsie or Michael Ondaatje occupies itself with different histories, acts of violence and human relationships. These writings go beyond the local to encompass other histories and acts of violence. We have modern classics in Hindi, Urdu, Kannada and other languages, several now available in translations, which meet all rigorous aesthetic standards and refuse to be dismissed as 'writers of the Southern hemisphere' interested in politics. I will not go into examples of authenticity or of contrapuntalism in them except for a couple of examples from contemporary writing.

Chimamanda Adichie's novel *Half of a Yellow Sun* is about the Biafra civil war. It has a British character – Richard – an outsider, who later marries one of the twin sisters. He is engaged in writing a novel titled *The World Was Silent When We Died*. There are nine short fragments, indicative of Richard's intention to write 'after the war, a narrative of Biafra's difficult victory, an indictment of the world', marking a shift in his affiliation (374). The two sisters – Kainene and Olama – are twins, but very different in appearance. And their life courses are also different as they live through their personal and political conflicts, moving between the need to remember and the need to forget. Adichie writes about the indifference and the brutality which had entered the souls of those who wielded authority, and about the corresponding shrinkage of space for human values. In an interview, Adichie described her novel as a 'tribute to love, the unreasonable resilient thing that holds … and makes us human'. She also dwells on the decentring of the narrative and writing about people 'driven by impulses that they may not consciously be aware of; without subjecting them to an analysis'. She has, for the purpose of the narrative, disrupted linearity, chronology and locations, but has not strayed away from the factual core. Moving thus between remembering and forgetting, between the real and the imagined, her primary concern throughout was in presenting the 'emotional truth' of history (Interview 2). Not only is the category of reality being tested as a literary method but simultaneously individualism as formed by the ego is pushed aside and a larger collective sense of belonging is foregrounded. In its own way it addresses the very challenges which are perceived as threats to the field of comparative literature by projecting not only a critique of past histories but also turning around perceptions of reality through its multiple narrators and by working out an aesthetic integral to its origins.

The category of 'emotional truth' is in line with the concepts of 'emotional history' and the 'historical unconscious'. Through them literature takes upon itself the task of entering into the silences of memory. An Indian historian Rajat Kanta Ray has attempted to trace the emotional history of nineteenth century Bengal, through a trajectory of gender, class and social shifts, working with literary texts. Distinguishing it from intellectual histories or histories of ideas, Ray believes that emotional history is broader than psycho-history because it 'focuses on private sphere across periods of time'. There is a constant interplay between the reality principle and the pleasure principle as each affects and explains the other (Ray Preface vii and 318). Emotional experiences are governed as much by the unconscious as by the conscious collective mind. Reviewing historical events across a stretch of time, one begins to ask why do people behave in a particular manner at a particular time, even though located in different places? Why is there an orchestrated or even linearly continued move across time and space? The category of the historical unconscious as it works through the history of a people needs to be explored in its psycho-social origins. Does it, in anyway, approximate Fredric Jameson's 'political unconscious', especially with reference to political revolutions and resistance movements in the context of the histories of the silent collectivities? Working with novels in Bengali, Malayalam and Hindi about different kinds of resistance and questioning of history, I was overwhelmed by a sense of the unconscious connectivity of these questionings.

Silences need to surface as well as to be heard, just as borders need to be crossed. They form a counterpoint to the existing discourses and divisions. Jung Chang in her autobiographical three-generation work *Wild Swans* writes how her mother when she came to England was unable to engage with the world outside. Her restlessness was caused by her desire to talk. And then she 'talked everyday for months about herself, her mother, her childhood, the ideals of beauty, the value of love and devalue of personal choice, wars, invasions, revolutions, repressions – all of them. By the time she left Britain, she had done sixty hours of recordings' (xxii). Memory and history work from two different points, looking for junctions; they are directed not only towards the past but also prepare one for the future. Memories, especially when they are of repression and suffering, are difficult to face; one wants to forget them. When her mother talked about the past she also showed her how to face it as well as the future. *Wild Swans* evokes comparisons with other three-generation novels and autobiographical histories of self-discovery, rehabilitation and revolutions. Why do such writings need to work through lineages, pasts and continuities? Sally Morgan's *My Place*, Khaled Hosseini's *The Kite Runner*, Ashapurna Devi's trilogy, Sorayya Khan's *Noor* and a host of other autobiographical as well as fictional works move across time and space interrogating their own multiple journeys to and fro. Subcontinental writing has produced several novels of truncated and grafted families signifying both loss and gain, rejection and acceptance (such as *Broken Verses, Noor, Meatless Days, Family Matters*). The Korean writer Ch'oe Yun describes her novella 'There a Petal Falls Silently', a work which I look forward to reading, as a story about a situation that 'couldn't be gotten past without being written about'. The creative writer, she observes in her article, 'The Dilemma of Writing about Reality', was faced with the problem as how to 'conceive a way of writing fiction which could recollect (narrate) a form of time which was unendurable except through oblivion'.

The mystery of narration is such that language tries to capture the silences of absence and of memories, which long to be buried, and which through the non-rationality of suffering and endurance reach the human core in the reader, sharing and unveiling the past. And literature is all about sharing. There is a young teenager in Orhan Pamuk's *Snow* (2004), who has always dreamt of the day when he would have a chance to share his ideas with the world (282). It is this kind of sharing which needs to go across to the other, move horizontally and vertically, across time and space. Why is comparative literature hesitant to move into these areas of old traditions and their unfamiliar aesthetics, which are outside classical studies or European frameworks? There is a reluctance to engage with collective and individual revolutions and the recurring motifs of resistance which have a continued lineage in our histories, and these are pushed into the field of postcolonialism. Most contemporary writing reflects a return to history, except that when the erstwhile margins turn to history their focus is different from the west's pre-occupation with history.

The contemporary novel's concern with history reflects a major shift in the historical novel, which is being subjected to reinterpretations from hitherto ignored perspectives. The location of the writer in terms of nation, home and power is of immense significance. An additional perspective on the writing of history surfaces, when the diaspora turns to it. Why is it drawn to the process and how does it address it are issues which demand further probing. Comparativists need to work with these taxonomies and the shifts and experiments in literary genres and to search for the differences that lead to them reclaiming a great deal, which has inadvertently been pushed into postcolonial studies.

Contrapuntality as a way of writing is a constant endeavour to grasp contradictory emotions, histories and aspirations – in fact to bring order in presentation to the creative surging of chaos. I return to Pamuk's novel *Snow* for two reasons. First, it is a novel in translation – from Turkish – and second, it is in many ways a border novel as the writer as well as the narrator move between Frankfurt and Kars. Like many another cross-over novels, it is about a creative writer and the phenomenon of blocked creativity as it engages with the process of the inner and the outer world yielding to each other. Wrapped in the continuing snowfall, Kars evokes responses to the visual image and sensuous feel of the snowflakes. The momentum of constant change, the mixed predictability and unpredictably of the outside, the frozen surfaces and the melting of the flakes, their constant brushing against the human body – are all images of transmutation into different forms, conveying a fluidity and an impermanence. Pamuk in his own records, 'From the Snow in Kars Notebooks' (February 24, 2002) has written of his need for the 'ever-falling snow to cut the city of the book. If from the rest of Turkey' (*Other Colours*, 273), (like Camus's *Plague*). Strangely enough, it is the evocation of loneliness and melancholy that insulates him against the rest of the world. Elsewhere he describes Kars as a spiritual experience.

Snow carries within it a multi-pronged symbolism of colour, form, sensation and a constant metamorphosis, creating an equivalent for the poet's mental and emotional states.[8] In the narration it acts both as an organising principle and one which frames the fears of enclosure, darkness and imprisonment. In effect, the choice between the two – the outside and the inside – is difficult. Both are places of being at the mercy of others – yet so different. There is a constant sense of tension between the two, as it is between creativity and non-creativity, between belonging and exile, between Frankfurt and Kars.

More than halfway through the novel (267), there is a hexagon representing a snowflake and the complexity of the creative act. The first reference is made to it much earlier (216). From one line logic runs through to the other side encompassing stars, snow, chess, the suffering of the helpless; the second strand is of memory which likewise cuts through Ka, who is at the intersection of these lines and goes on to the other side carrying with it dreams, places where God is absent, revolution and the end of the world, beyond which obviously there can be no memory. The third and final strand is of imagination, which too like the other two has conflicting and contradictory inputs – suicide and power, desire for happiness and the home of heaven, and

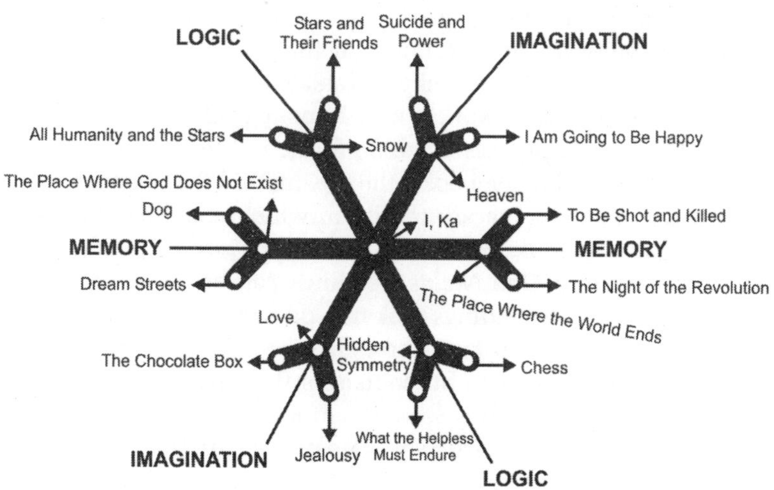

emotions like love and jealousy. These conflicting inputs in each strand and their common assault on Ka's mind and memory are in themselves a powerful illustration of contrapuntalism. Memory and imagination are polar opposites, but both together clash with logic. Logic which tries to decipher, explain and organise them is confronted alike by the fact of human suffering, which really has no logic and cannot be rationally explained. Other inputs like chess, representing a game of anticipation, timely action, and the ability to outwit your opponent, and the dark hole represented by the absence of God, leash the mental and the spiritual vacuum together. Yet they all feed each other. Later, when Ka's friend finds the Notebook and reads it, two different time-spaces are connected through the act of reading. The primary time is the time of writing in Kars, the second act is the act of reading by a different person, after the death of the poet, in Frankfurt where he had lived for the last four years. This act of reading is doubled as the reader becomes a second reader, looking over the friend's shoulder. The hexagon rises up as an experience which destroys all kinds of singular worlds, an experience which is full of contradictions presents rival claims on our responses and is simultaneously fragmented and coherent. Incidentally, the hexagon also comments on the multiple themes of the novel.

How does one read *Snow*? As a novel about creativity or about a revolution? Or as a novel in the tradition of writing of uncertainty such as Dostoevsky's, Kafka's and Camus's work? It can also be read as a work about human resilience. The 'I' is perpetually in the process of being formed. Life is contained in different places – the notebooks, the dreams and the poems. There is, however, another literary tradition, which conjoins with this sombre world. Pamuk traces this back to his several readings of the *Thousand and One Nights*, readings carried on at different stages of his life. His readings took him on a journey encountering the miraculous and working through love and hate towards an understanding of the deep humanism of the tales. The *Thousand and One Nights* has stories where men learn to retain their faith even in their ongoing struggle against despair; they possess a 'secret internal geometry' as the reader is brought face to face with mortality. The novel is strewn with the telling of stories in the face of death. Literatures travel from one culture to another with their themes, forms, atmosphere and symbols. Pamuk points out that the *Thousand and One Nights* boasts of a mixed heritage from India, Iran and the Arab world and in its turn has found its way to Cervantes, Coleridge, De Quincey and Poe (*Other Colours,* 120). But this travelling has largely been downplayed and perceived as part of the imperial gains.

The performative element and the carnivalesque when they inhabit a literary narrative, as in several novels of Dickens and Hardy, project another kind of narrative edge. Performance assumes the presence of the listener/observer. Oral traditions have several performative forms where impersonations are carried on openly; in fact, they constitute the main strand of the narrative and disrupt its dominant discourses. Pamuk also has a play performance *My Fatherland and My Scarf,* to which he devotes two chapters in order to comment on the veil as a symbol of Islamic nationalism. The novel had begun with the spate of suicides being committed on the issue of the veil, an issue that encompasses a whole lot of questions – tradition and modernity, religion and identity, and the looming shadow of the 'clash of civilizations' over freedom, peace and love.

Classical aesthetics including the Indian *rasa* theory that is aesthetic pleasure, is viewed in itself as a total indivisible experience. We tend to forget that Bharat Muni put forward the theory in its primary application to the performative act. Today classical theory has become exclusive as it has failed to stretch itself to meet new art forms emerging from the hitherto silent cultures, also at times, it is rooted in an elitist/classical language. Most of the problems of comparative literature and the hierarchies within it arise from this inability to recognise the new idiom. A whole new area is open to the discipline once its practitioners are bold enough to democratise it. My argument is in favour of this democratisation and the need to recognise that art cannot but be political and yet it does not cease to be art. The contrapuntal narrative of literature is birthing the new waiting to be legitimised and accepted.

Notes

1. I have several experiences which I could connect with this – such as the emerging concept of 'cosmopoetics', which has been practised by African and Asian writers for more than half-a-century, or the clustering of the discourse of forgiveness amongst clusters of cultures which again, are divisionary and discriminatory. My reference here is to the work by Jacques Derrida and Paul Ricouer on forgiveness and hospitality. The discourse of forgiveness in international politics has also been debated in philosophy and law. It encompasses historical and political happenings and the wrongs done through racism and imperialism. But primarily the focus has remains on the holocaust and apartheid, though public apologies are often forthcoming for past acts of commission or omission on part of current rulers. The two philosophers who have dominantly examined it closely are Paul Ricoeur, a Protestant, and Jacques Derrida a Jew. While Ricoeur examines the moral responsibility of guilt and forgiveness and the legal aspects especially the *Truth and Reconciliation Committee* set up by Nelson Mandela, Derrida works with the Abrahamic tradition – the cultures which share the Old Testament. This exclusiveness totally bypasses Eastern cultures like Buddhism, Hinduism Confucianism or Sikhism or even the tribal world, thus ignoring a huge chunk of reality. Further he locates hospitality in the Messianic tradition, generalising about its absence in Eastern cultures. This discourse is one-sided as it also fails to look at the wrongs committed by the imperialists, not only by violent acts like large-scale massacres or scorch-earth policies but also the more long-term and sinister wrongs it has done by pushing several countries like India, Vietnam, Korea into ideological and religious divisions. It also fails to address the problem of guilt or its location in what Russia and America have made of Afghanistan.
2. *Raga* is a melodic mode which despite its strictly defined form and rules for elaboration, has 'an infinite capacity for improvisation'. *Ragas* have traditionally been assigned to different deities and moods. Different colours as well as gender have also traditionally been assigned to them. But Indian music's interaction with Muslim cultures allowed it to evolve in other directions. *Tala* is the fixed base which repeats itself regularly, and works in accordance with the same number of beats. But the arrangement can be changed and experimented with and can be 'made quite complicated in its elaboration by mixing varieties of *matras* or *chamdas* or *jatis*. It is through the experimentation with tala and raga that the contra-

puntal comes into play. An individual artist can work in various way with the raga and stretch it in several ways. I draw my references primarily from M.R. Gautam's *The Musical Heritage of India* (New Delhi: Munshiram Manoharlal Publishers Pvt. Ltd., 2001).

3. Postcolonialism has served as a convenient term for clubbing together the literatures of the erstwhile colonies and accommodating them under one nomenclature. It is often referred to as the theory of migrancy and has been used to accommodate the World intellectual in the academia. Critics like Arun Mukherjee have often enough expressed their resentment of the monolithic structure of these courses.
4. Edward Said's *Orientalism* (1978). and U.R. Ananthamurthy in his essay 'What does translation mean in India?' (in *U.R. Ananthmurthy Omnibus*. Ed. N. Manu Chakravarthy, Gurgaon: Arvind Kumar Publishers, 2007: 395–398). Also see Bhabha's *The Location of Culture* and his reference to Alexander Duff's use of the term 'second birth' an easy substitute for twice-born, for religious conversion to Christianity. (Chapter titled 'Sly Civility' in *The Location of Culture*. London: Routledge, 1994: 101).
5. Gillian Wright has omitted some important passages, including one on the Muslim participation in the First War of Independence, 1857 in the As the novel is about the position of the Muslim who has not moved out of India after the partition of the country, the loyalty demonstrated to the national cause is of great significance. By leaving it out, the meaning of the novel has been curtailed in its expression.
6. For details see the essay 'On Reading Renu: Text/Language/Culture/Translation' in Arun Mukherjee, *Oppositional Aesthetics* (Toronto: Tsar, 1994). 56–66.
7. Arun Mukherjee refers to the residual 'cultural density' which still remains for the non-culture reader in her Introduction to *Her Mother's. Ashes*. Ed. Nurjehan Aziz (Toronto: Tsar, 1994).
8. Pamuk has Ka read *The Encyclopedia of Life*. On p. 324 of the volume from PE to TA there is the following entry:

   SNOW. The solid form taken by water when falling, crossing, or rising through the atmosphere. Beautiful crystal starlets, usually forming a hexagon. Each crystal snowflake forms its own unique hexagon. Since ancient times mankind has been awed and mystified by the secrets of snow. In 1555, when a priest named Olaus Magnus in Uppsala, Sweden, discovered that each snowflake, as indicated in the diagram, had six corners ... (219)

18

From Encounters to Introspection

Negotiating Cultural Pasts*

The Commonwealth of Nations in its present form is a post-WWII phenomenon and symbolises the coming together of divergent cultures across oppositional histories. The past – cultural as well as historical – is constantly in need of reflection and re-vision. The differences of geographical and historical locations of the writers have thrown up an interesting interplay of forces which do not move either linearly or in relationship to contemporary politics; instead they move close towards an interior landscape to come to grips with past events that cast long shadows.

Sometime in the mid-eighties, just when the erstwhile empire was wallowing in Raj nostalgia, a new kind of inward-directed literature came up countering the remake of *A Passage to India*, and *The Jewel in the Crown* (both in 1984).[1] Writers on both sides of the power politics were engaged in filling up the gaps, and in 'remapping' reality in more than one way. Both Soyinka and Derek Walcott have pointed out at different times about the need for an ethical 'remapping' (Soyinka 143) and have regretted that history, strewn with the 'ego of race', is 'a kind of literature without morality' (Walcott 1974: 371).[2] Literature, through an inward

---

* Presented at the Commonwealth Seminar, Sahitya Akademi, New Delhi, October 2010 and first published in *Indian Literature*, No. 260, November–December 2010, 134–141.

glance, engages in an attempt to enable a transcendence of pasts that oppress and require self-reflection. But the acts of transcendence, of necessity, follow a different course.

In India we have, as early as 1953, in Dharamvir Bharti's *Andha Yug* – a play based on the Kurukshetra war – a critical look at the political scenario and several of Nayantara Sahgal's novels right from the early seventies to the mid-eighties are an in-depth scanning of India and its contradictions, as she explores the morality of a society that could push a woman to her death as 'sati', and finds a similar brutality in the ethical compromises which men make in search of power in *Rich Like Us*. But in Sahgal's work all along there has been a strong element of hope, of the possibility of a fairy tale world coming true as Bhushan in *The Mistaken Identity* lives in a prison cell with other prisoners representing different ideologies, languages, religions and regions and where dreams are meant to be pursued, where a rani can elope with a Muslim lover and the prince can marry the daughter of his mother's lover, where flowers can be grown even if the water has to be ferried from a great distance.

Similarly in the years 1968–1975, Paul Scott's Raj Quartet also was an introspective look when the Bibighar Garden episode is analysed in the context of power and colonialism, an episode which projects Hari as a better man than Merrick, an approach which overcame the ego of race. And Sahgal's fairy tale environment finds a parallel in the novels of Graham Swift. Swift's 1983 novel *Waterland* shares its historical impulse with the nineteenth century and is a novel concerned with Englishness and national identity. It is, in more than one sense, an island novel interwoven with Kingsleyian innocence and fabulation, fantasisation and supernaturalism of *The Water Babies*. It is a land of rivers – the Ouse, the Welland, the Cam, Bedford and New Bedford, and the river Leem. Two of the characters Fred Parr and Dick Crick literally live out T.S. Eliot's 'Death by Water' (Section 4 of *The Wasteland*.) by finding a temporary burial there. Hermoine Lee observes in an early review that the novel is a mapping of a new Wessex. The central narrator, Tom Crick, is a history teacher but he has long ceased to tell histories, he tells stories – half-truth, half-yarns – leading his students to say that he has gone 'bananas'.

There is a going back to the French Revolution, the Rights of Man, and the Fall of the Bastille, and even further to the seventh century and all the wars thereafter – a kind of a post-mortem conducted on the past, its gaps and failures wrapped up in a fairy tale frame of 'Once upon a time', 'Far away from the wide wide world'. The novel is strewn with reference to stories such as Red Riding Hood and Hansel and Gretel working out the basic human predicaments of loss, loneliness, desire and fear.[3] Swift's exploration of the collective past is an inward-looking narration which develops in *Out of the World* (1988) as well as in *Ever After* (1992) and *Last Orders* (1996).

In *Out of the World,* the central character, Harry, who happens to be a photographer, describes England's map which looks 'like a little hunched-up old lady at the seaside, her back towards the rest of Europe, dipping her toe into the Atlantic Ocean and pulling up her skirt round her shriveled body .... once a big, plump, bossy Empress .... England is small ...' (191–192). Working out this self-reflexivity in novel after novel Swift is a fair representative of the main trend of native-born British fiction. This writing has entered into a dialogue with the nineteenth century, the high-point of the imperial era, and there is a recurring engagement with Darwinism, a closer look at Victorian moral prudery and a move towards plural perspectives, ambiguity and fabulation. The engagement with Darwin is also present in Swift's 1992 novel *Ever After,* where the whole question of 'survival of the fittest' is debated. In fact, there is a question mark after it. Do the 'fit' really survive? And is survival at *any cost* worth it? The search for an answer leads to an analysis for the roots of brutality which paves the way to power, and which incidentally also results in a slow maturation. The dead narrator in *Ever After* opens his discourse with the living by pointing out that 'If natural selection had had its nasty way, we should have been wiped out long ago a fragile, etiolated experiment ...' (2). Wading through past lives and Shakespeare's *Hamlet, Antony and Cleopatra* and the rest, through a collision of the personal, the political and history in the making, the narrator returns to Darwin: 'What can Darwin tell me that is new? That nothing in this world is fixed, that everything is mutable? But poets have been saying it for centuries' (235).[4]

These are macabre fairy tales. Swift refers to it as 'inverse colonialism' (*Ever After*, 62) where a constant mutation is going on of earlier narrative forms, fairy tales without a happy ending. In consonance with this introspective analysis of history and the macabre endings of fairy tales, Julian Barnes, locates his novel *History of the World in 10½ Chapters* (1990), right at the beginning, in the Flood and Noah's Ark. Ever since then history is a long list of disasters, of brutality, of indifference towards and a ruthless trampling on others, working towards their extinction. The principle of selection was enforced strictly giving the go-by to several species (13), in fact a wholesale extermination. Barnes moves to the wars of religion, equally irrational, to colonialism, to dissidents and cannibalism, exposing the history of civilisation as one long march of cruelty selfishness and barbarism. His narrators and perspectives constantly shift and his illustrative intertextuality moves through various forms of art.

Memory, in these engagements with the past, is not historical or real – it involves a shift of perspective and a degree of mythification.[5] True to his calling, Tom Crick, the history teacher in *Waterland,* tells his pupils 'we are one-tenth living tissue, nine-tenth water, life is one-tenth Here and Now nine-tenths a history lesson' (*Waterland* 61). Historical truth has escaped history, it lies in the yarns. By changing the reference points and narrative forms, the expectations of the reader are constantly being pushed into other frames.

Closer home, in Sahgal's *Lesser Breeds* (2003), the fantasisation of *Mistaken Identity* (1989), is transformed into a real life-size fairy tale -- Gandhi's faith in non-violence and the whole movement anchored in it (184). The novel moves between personal and political histories and the weaving together a pattern of non-belief and faith. Nurullah, a young lecturer, a bastard born of a rape constitutes the questioning mind, the non-believer who gets involved in this search for alternatives to existing structures of power and knowledge. Entrusted with the task of over-seeing the education of Shan, the eight-year-old daughter of Bhai, he is constantly told to look for alternative ways of 'seeing', of turning known and narrated histories round, to fill in the gaps in knowledge and to overturn the master narratives (see 15, 23, 42,

80, 97, 117). It is this which leads him to realise the mystical power of the central fairy tale. Later in the novel, we come across another young person, a translator who works in the family publishing house of Mr Jenner. This woman, Leda, is Edward Knox's sister, who during his visit to India is able to see the Indian point of view sympathetically. Leda is a collector of fairy tales. Whatever she reads, she looks for the underlying semblance. Fairy tales are not always fair and comfortable, often they end by punishing the oppressed and rewarding the powerful (184–185, 221). But they are necessary for they carry hidden meanings and nurture the values that sustain human essence. They nourished bold dreams of possible change. Another observer/interrogator in the novel is Pete Ryder, a researcher trying to interpret the movement. With reference to a letter by Lord Linlithgow, Pete wonders whether there was a deliberate effort on part of the British to underplay non-violence for, 'Why would they make a dangerous new weapon public knowledge?' (216).

The capacity to dream, to experience wide-eyed belief in the mystery of fairy tales, is essential for personal realisation and assertion. Giriraj Kishore's novel based on Gandhi's life in South Africa *Pahla Girmitya* (*The First Contractee*, 1999) reinforces this. The opening line of the novel is 'Goron ke sapne the' ('The white men had dreams' 19). In the third chapter emerges a counter-statement in the opening line: '*Sapne Mohandas ke bhi the*' ('Even Mohandas had dreams' 52). And consequently strategies had to be evolved for their realisation.

The connection between dreams, determination and power is obvious; it is a different matter that it may be ethical or not. Two novels, both published in 2009 bring up this aspect forcefully. The first is Keki Daruwalla's *For Pepper and Christ* (New Delhi: Viking,), and the other is Hilary Mantel's *Wolf Hall* (London: Fourth Estate), both are located in near contemporary histories. While Daruwalla steps into the making of dreams, the sense of adventure and the accompanying religious discipline with all its restrictions as well as the naïve innocence laced with surface materialism of the home society (in India), Mantel dwells on the conflict between the Church and the state and its roots in personal desire. Incidentally, both are masculine novels primarily because the world at this point of time, was constructed by male power. In both novels, dominant religions are being subjected to alteration. In Daruwalla's novel the authorities, in their search for new markets, carry out a strict surveillance over the common man (even without the technological help now increasingly available) and the world that emerges is a claustrophobic one despite the physical movement involved in travel. A sense of persecution hampers both artistic freedom and sensibility. The responsibility of yielding to the materialist seduction presented by these invading communities, at some point, lies with the host country itself, which in this case happens to be India.

Mantel's novel is not concerned with empire-building, instead it is much more interested in cutting-off connections with outside power structures. Cardinal Wolsey is aware that Henry plans to degrade him in order to assert his freedom against the authority of the Pope (167). But this assertion is made on the sacrifice of many heads as well as of morality. It is achieved through willful reinterpretation and is anchored more in the flesh than in the spirit. What price freedom? One may as well ask – what price faith and religion? Are there different streams of hypocrisy assigned to each category? Elizabeth's birth is accompanied by controversies of inheritance, of visions, forecasts of doom, of a handful of other claimants, legitimate and not so illegitimate. The atmosphere is rife with flattery and betrayal, and with murder and sacrifice. Darwin's game of survival is being played all along. History is being made in purgatory, and very often, in the present tense. The novel ends with Thomas More at the block, his lips moving in silent prayer.

The relationship between history and literature is being played out in multiple ways, but the concern with mindscapes and landscapes is dominant. The flow of history is caught between individual and collective memories, between temporality and spatiality. If one were to refer to the two categories of memory which Paul de Man uses – *Gedächtnis*, specifying temporality and *Errinnerung* indicating the myths, folk culture and racial memories, it is obvious that in these writings about history, history is being re-written. It is being subjected to introspective analysis, rendering the epithet of 'postcolonial' redundant. It is personal, often autobiographical, and concerned not only with the past and the present but also the future – the aftermath of what becomes history. Enough evidence is available in the work of a host of Commonwealth writers like Sara Suleri, Kamala Shamshie, Gita Hariharan, Chimamanda Adichie and Sally Morgan. No matter whether one moves backwards or forwards, the shape of both writing and history has altered as it flows concurrently with the present and between fairy tales and Darwinism, in its attempt to understand both.

Notes

1. David Lean turned Forster's 1924 novel into a framed master-slave narrative, highlighting power on the one hand and pageantry on the other in 1984. And a novel of the Raj Quartet, *The Jewel in the Crown* was also converted into a tele-serial in 1984.
2. Refer Wole Soyinka's *The Open Sore of a Continent* and Derek Walcott's 'The Muse of History' (*The Postcolonial Studies Reader.* Eds. Ashcroft et al.)
3. Refer Bruno Bettleheim's *Uses of Enchantment* and Tolkien's essay 'On Fairy Tales.
4. Derek Walcott in 'The Muse of History', observes how myths constitute distant memory, 'The farther the facts, the more history petrifies into myths' (370–371).
5. Paul de Man refers to two kinds of memory: The first *Gedächtnis* reflects the memory which recollects, thinks and remembers, and the second *Errinnerung* is interiorised memory, often lying dormant. The relationship between the two could be dialectical or one of rupture and disjunction. See Derrida, *Memoires for Paul de Man*. Translated by Cecile Lindsay, Jonathan Culler and Eduardo Cadava (New York: Columbia Univ Press, 1986). Derrida refers to Man's 'Sign and Symbol in Hegel's Aesthetics', 51.

Bibliography

Achebe, Chinua. *Home and Exile.* New York: Anchor Books, 2000.

Adichie, Chimamanda Ngozi. *Half of a Yellow Sun* (2006). New Delhi: Harper Perennial, 2007.

Adorno, Theodore W. *Minima Moralia: Reflections From Damaged Life.* Internet reference http://en.wikipedia.org/wiki/minima-moralia. downloaded 13 February, 2010.

——. *The Culture Industry: Selected Essays on Mass Culture.* Edited with an Introduction by J.M. Bernstein. London: Routledge, 1991.

Advani, L.K. *My Country, My Life.* New Delhi: Rupa & Co. (2008) 2010.

Ahearn, Ed. and Arnold Weinstein. 'The Function of Criticism at the Present Time: The Promise of Comparative Literature' *Comparative Literature in the Time of Multiculturalism* Ed. Charles Bernheimer. Baltimore: The Johns Hopkins University Press, 1995. 77–85.

Ahmad, Aijaz. *In Theory.* Delhi: OUP, 1992.

Ahmad, Nazir. *Mirat-ul-Arus* (1869) translated into English as *The Bride's Mirror* by G.E. Ward, 1903. Ed. used New Delhi: Permanent Black, 2001.

Akhtar, Jaan Nisar. ed. *Hindustan Hamara* in 2 vols. Vol 2. Mumbai: Hindustan Book Trust, n.d.

Amin, Shahid. 'Gandhi as Mahatma: Gorakhpur District, Eastern UP, 1921–22' *Subaltern Studies* III, Delhi: OUP, 1984. 1–55.

Anand. *Goverdhan's Travels.* Originally written in Malayalam, 1995. Translated by Gita Krishnakutty. New Delhi: Penguin, 2006.

Ananthamurthy, U.R. 'The Search for Identity: A Kannada Writer's View' *in Creating Theory: Writers on Writing.* Ed. Jasbir Jain. Delhi: Pencraft International, 2000. 145–158.

——. 'What Does Translation Mean in India?' in *The Writer as Critic*. Ed. Jasbir Jain, Jaipur: Rawat Publications, 275–282.

Anand, Mulk Raj. *Apology for Heroism* (1946). New Delhi: Arnold Heinemann, 1975.

Anzaldua, Gloria. *Borderlands La Frontera*. San Francisco: Aunt Lute Books, 1987.

Apte, Hari Narayan. *Mein* (1893), Punjabi translation Swaran Singh. New Delhi: National Book Trust, 1972.

——. *Pan Lakshant Kon Gheto.* Translated into Hindi as *Kaun Dhyan Deta Hai* by Srinivas Kochkar. Delhi: Sahitya Akademi, 1961.

Ashcroft, Bill. *Post-Colonial Transformations.* London and New York: Routledge, 2001.

Ashcroft, Bill, Gareth Griffiths and Helen Tiffin. eds. *The Post-Colonial Studies Reader*. London and New York: Routledge (1995), 1997.

Badami, Anita Rau. *Can You Hear The Nightbird Call?* New Delhi: Penguin/Viking, 2006.

Bair, Deirdre. *Samuel Beckett: A Biography* (1978), London: Picador, 1980.

Bakhtin, M.M. 'Discourse in the Novel' in *The Dialogic Imagination: Four Essays.* Ed. Michael Holquist. Translated by Caryl Emerson and Michael Holquist. Austin: University of Texas Press (1981), 1987.

——. *The Dialogic Imagination: Four Essays.* (Russian edition, 1975). Ed. Michael Holquist, translated by Caryl Emerson and Michael Holquist. Austin: University of Texas Press (1981), 1987.

Barnes, Julian: *A History of the World in 10½ Chapters* (1989). London: Picador in association with Jonathan Cape, 1990.

Bassnett, Susan. 'Reflections on Comparative Literature in the Twenty-First Century' *Comparative Critical Studies* 3. 1–2 (2006) 3–11.

Beckett, Samuel. *Waiting for Godot.* London: Faber and Faber (1956), 1977.

Benjamin, Walter. 'The Work of Art in the Age of Mechanical Production' (1935) in *Illuminations: Essays and Reflections.* Ed. Hannah Arendt (1968). Harcourt Brace, 2007. 217–252.

Berhneimer, Charles. ed. *Comparative Literature in the Age of Multiculturalism*. Baltimore: The John Hopkins University Press, 1995.

Bettleheim, Bruno. *The Uses of Enchantment: The Meaning and Importance of Fairy Tales*. London Peregrine, 1980.

Bhabha, Homi K. 'The Postcolonial and the Postmodern', *The Location of Culture.* London and New York: Routledge, 1994. 171–197.

——. *The Location of Culture*. London: Routledge, 1994.

——. 'Foreword: Remembering Fanon', *Black Skin White Masks* by Frantz Fanon (1952), Translated by Charles Lam Markman. London: Pluto Press (1986) 1993.

Bhutto, Benazir. *Daughter of the East: An Autobiography*. London: Simon and Schuster, (2007) 2008.

Bhutto, Fatima. *Songs of Blood and Sword: A Daughter's Memoir*. New Delhi: Penguin/Viking 2010.

Blackburn, Stuart and Dalmia, Vasudha, eds. *India's Literary History: Essays on the Nineteenth Century*. New Delhi: Permanent Black, 2004.

Blaise, Clark and Bharati Mukherjee. *The Sorrow and the Terror*. London: Penguin Books, 1987.

Bond, Ruskin. *A Flight of Pigeons*, New Delhi: Penguin, (1980) 2003.

Bonheffer, Dietrich. 'Two Conversations from the Attempt at a Novel (1943–4)', *True Patriotism: Letters, Lectures and Notes 1939–45. From the Collected Works of Dietrich Bonhoeffer*. Vol. III, Ed. Edwin H. Robertson. Translated by Edwin H. Robertson and John Bowden. London: Collins, 1973. 220–235.

——. 'Passages from a Drama Fragment (1943)', *True Patriotism*. Ed. Edwin H. Robertson. London: Collins. 197–215.

Byatt, A.S. 'A New Body of Writing: Darwin and Recent British Fiction,' *New Writing* 4. Eds. A.S. Byatt and Alan Hollinghurst. London: Vintage in association with the British Council, 1995. 439–448.

Carter, Paul, 'Spatial History' in *The Post-Colonial Studies Reader*. Eds Bill Ashcroft, Gareth Griffiths and Helen Tiffin. London: Routledge (1995), 1997, 375–377

Chandra, Sudhir. *The Oppressive Present: Literature and Social Consciousness in Colonial India*. (1990). New Delhi: OUP, 1994.

Chang, Jung. *Wild Swans: Three Daughters of China* (1991). New York: Touchstone (Simon and Schuster), 2003.

Chatterjee, Bankim Chandra. 'Bengali Literature' *Bankim Rachnavali* (3 vols) Vol. 3. Ed. J.C. Bagal. Calcutta Sahitya Samsad, 1969.

——. *Anand Math* (1882) Hindi translation from the original Bengali. Delhi: Hind Pocket Books, 1992.

——. *Kapala Kundala* (1865), Hindi translation. New Delhi: Hind Pocket Books, 1990.

——. *Mrinalini* (1869). Hindi translation, Delhi: Sanmarg Prakashan, 1989.

——. *Rajmohan's Wife*. Eds Brajendra Nath Banerji and Sajani Kanta Das. Calcutta: Bangiya Sahitya Parishad, 1940.

Chomsky, Noam. 'An Exchange on Manufacturing Consent: Noam Chomsky interviewed by various activists' (Excerpted from *Understanding Power*, The New Press, 2002) www.comsky.info

——. *Powers and Prospects: Reflections on Human Nature and the Social Order*. New Delhi: Viva Books Private Limited. 2007.

Currie, Mark. *Difference*. London: Routledge, 2004.

Daruwalla, Keki. *For Pepper and Christ*. New Delhi: Viking, 2009.

Das, Sisir Kumar. *A History of Indian Literature 1800–1910: Western Impact: Indian Response*. Vol. VIII. New Delhi: Sahitya Akademi (1991), 2000.

——. *A History of Indian Literature. Struggle For Freedom: Triumph and Tragedy*. New Delhi: Sahitya Akademi, 1995.

Das, Veena. 'Subaltern as Perspective', *Subaltern Studies VI*. Ed. Ranajit Guha Delhi: OUP, 1994. 310–324.

Derrida, Jacques. *Of Grammatology*. Trans. Gayatri Spivak. Baltimore: Johns Hopkins University, 1976.

Desai, Anita. *Baumgartener's Bombay* (1988). London: Penguin Bks, 1989.

——. *Clear Light of Day*. New Delhi: Allied Publishers, 1980.

——. *Cry, the Peacock*. (Peter Owen Ltd., 1963) Orient Paperbacks,1980.

——. *Fasting, Feasting*. London: Chatto and Windus, 1999.

——. *Fire on the Mountain*. (1977). New Delhi: Penguin, 1983.

——. *In Custody*. London: William Heinemann Ltd, 1984.

——. *Journey to Ithaca*. New Delhi: Ravi Dayal Publishers, 1996.

——. *The Zigzag Way*. London: Chatto and Windus, 2004.

——. *Voices in the City (1965)*. Orient Paperbacks, 1985.

——. *Where Shall We Go This Summer?* (1975). Orient Paperbacks, 1982.

Dev, Amiya. 'Comparative Literature in India'. *Comparative Literature and Culture*. CLC Web. Vol. 2 No. 4. December, 2000. http://docs. Lib. purdue.edu/clcweb/vol2/iss4/10

Devi, Ashapurna. *Suvarnlata*. Translated from the original Bengali into Hindi by Hanskumar Tiwari. New Delhi: Bhartiya Jnanpith Prakashan (1979), 1989.

Devi, Ganesh. *Of Many Heroes: An Indian Essay in Literary Historiography*. Mumbai: Orient Longman Ltd, 1998.

Devi, Mahasweta. 'Draupadi.' 1987. *Breast Stories*. Trans. Gayatri Spivak. Calcutta: Seagull, 1997.

——. *Operation? Bashai Tudu.* 1978. Trans. Samik Bandhopadhya. Calcutta: Thema, 1990.

——. *Pterodactyl, Puran Sahay and Pritha* in *Imaginary Maps.* Trans. Gayatri Spivak. Calcutta: Thema, 1993.

——. *Titu Mir.* Translated from the Bengali original by Rimi B. Chatterjee (2000). Calcutta: Seagull Books, 2003.

Dimock Jr, Edward C. et al. *The Literatures of India.* Chicago: Chicago UP, 1974.

Dirlik, Arif. 'The Postcolonial Aura: Third World Criticism in the Age of Global Capitalism', *Critical Inquiry.* Vol. 20 Nos. 1–3, 1993–1994. 328–356.

Dutt, Toru. *Bianca* or *The Young Spanish Maiden.* Ed. Subhendu Mund. New Delhi: Prachi Prakashan, 2001.

Edwards, William. *Personal Adventures during the Indian Rebellion in Rohitcund, Futtehgarh, and Oude* (1858). Allahabad: Legend Publications, 1874.

Ehtesham, Manzoor. *Sookha Bargad.* 1986. (Hindi). Delhi: Rajkamal, 2003.

Espinet, Ramabai. *The Swinging Bridge.* New Delhi: Penguin, 2003.

Fanon, Frantz. *Black Skin, White Masks.* 1952. Trans. Charles Lam Markmann. London: Pluto, 1986.

——. *The Wretched of the Earth.* (published in French in 1961). Translated by Constance Farrington. New York: Grove, 1963.

Feldman, Keith. P. 'fuga': Review of Edward W. Said's On *Late Style: Music and Literature Against The Grain.* New York: Pantheon 2006. http://pmc.iath.virginia.edu/current. issue/18.3Feldman. html. checked 14 June, 2010.

Foucault, Michel. 'Structuralism and Post-structuralism', *Aesthetics: Essential Works of Michel Foucault 1954–1984.* Vol. 2, Ed. James D. Faubion, London: Penguin Books (1994), 1998. 433–458.

——. 'The Thought of the Outside'. *Aesthetics: Essential Works of Michel Foucault 1954–1984.* Vol. 2, Ed. James D. Faubion, London: Penguin Books (1994), 1998. 147–170.

——. 'Two Lectures: Lecture One. 7 January, 1976' in *Power/Knowledge: Selected Interviews and Other Writings 1972–1977.* Translated by Colin Gordon, Leo Marshall, Joun Mepham, Kate Soper, New York: Pantheon Books, 1980, 78–92.

——. 'What is an Author'. *Aesthetics: Essential Works of Michel Foucault 1954–1984.* Vol. 2, Ed. James D. Faubion, London: Penguin Books (1994), 1998. 205–222.

——. *Power/Knowledge: Selected Interviews and Other Writings 1972–1977*. Edited by Colin Gordon. Translated by Colin Gordon, Leo Marshall, John Mephans and Kate Soper. New York: Pantheon Books, 1980.

Freud, Sigmund. *Civilization and Its Discontents* (1929). London: W.W. Norton & Co., 1989.

Gandhi, Leela. *Postcolonial Theory: A Critical Introduction*. Edinburgh: Edinburgh University Press, 1998.

Gandhi, M.K. 'Quit India Speech.' 1942. *Hind Swaraj and Other Writings*. Ed. Anthony J. Parel. New Delhi: Foundation Books, 2004 (1997). 184–85.

——. 'The Great Sentinel'. (originally published in *Young India*. October 21, 1921) *The Moral and Political Writings of Mahatma Gandhi*. Vol. I. Ed. Raghavan Iyer. Oxford: Clarendon Press, 1986. 217–221.

——. 'The Poet's Anxiety', (originally published in *Young India*, October 13, 1921) *The Moral and Political Writings of Mahatma Gandhi*. Vol. I. Ed. Raghavan Iyer. Oxford: Clarendon Press, 1986. 217–221.

——. *Hind Swaraj* in *Hind Swaraj and Other Writings*. Ed. Anthony J. Parel (Cambridge: CUP, 1997), New Delhi: Foundation Books 2005.

——. *Hind Swaraj or Indian Home Rule* (1909) Ahmedabad: Navajivan Publication House, (1938) 1996.

——. *My Experiments with Truth*. 1927. Ahmedabad: Navajivan, 1996 (1938).

Gasset, Ortega Y. *The Dehumanization of Art and Other Writings on Art and Culture* (Spanish original 1925) (1948). New York: Doubleday, 1985.

Gautam, M.R. *Musical Heritage of India*. New Delhi: Munshilal Manohar Lal Pvt. Ltd., 2001.

Ghosh, Amitav. 'The Ghosts of Mrs Gandhi' in *Imam and the India: Prose Pieces*. Delhi: Ravi Dayal and Permanent Black, 2002. 46–62.

——. *The Circle of Reason* (1986). New Delhi: Ravi Dayal and Permanent Black, 2003.

Giriraj, Kishore. *Pahla Girmitya*. New Delhi: Bharatiya Jnanpith, 1999.

Goode, Luke. *Jurgen Habermas: Democracy and Public Sphere*. London: Pinto Press, 2005.

Govindji. ed. *Itihaaskik Upanayas* (A Collection of Essays), Meerut. n.d.

Grewal, Manraj. *Dreams after Darkness: A Search for a Life Ordinary Under the Shadow of 1984*. New Delhi: Rupa & Co. 2004.

Grewal. J.S. *Guru Nanak and Patriarchy*. Shimla: Indian Institute of Advanced Study, 1993.

Guha, Ranajit. 'The Prose of Counter-Insurgency', *Subaltern Studies* II. Delhi: Oxford University Press, 1983.

Gulzar. *Two Tales of My Times: New Delhi Times* and *Maachis*. Translated by Devina Dutt. New Delhi: Rupa & Co. 2008.

——. *Maachis* in *Two Tales of My Times*. Trans. Devina Dutt. New Delhi: Rupa & Co. 2008.

Habermas, Jürgen. *The Structural Transformation of the Public Sphere: An Inquiry into a Category of Bourgeois Society* (1963). Translated by Thomas Burger with the assistance of Frederick Lawrence. (1989). Massachusetts: MIT Press, 1991. http://www.amazon.com/StructuretTransformation–Public_sphere_contemporary/dp/02625 81086 reader_026251086

Habib, Irfan. 'There are fundamental matters for the SC to consider on Ayodha', an interview with Akshaya Mukul. *The Times of India*. Jaipur. November 3, 2010, 10.

Harishchandra, Bhartendu. *Andher Nagari Chaupat Raja* in *Bhartendu Samgera: Collected Works of Bhartendu Harishchandra*. Ed. Hemant Sharma. Varanasi: Hindi Pracharak Sangh, 1987.

Holloway, John. 'The Literary Scene', *The Present, The New Pelican Guide to English Literature* Vol. 8. Harmondsworth, England: Penguin 1983. 65–125.

Holquist, Michael. Introduction. *The Dialogic Imagination*. Austin: University of Texas Press, 1987. xv-xxxiv.

Hosain. Attia. *Sunlight on a Broken Column* (1961). New Delhi: Arnold Heinemann, 1979.

Hosain, Rokeya Shakawat. 'Sultana's Dream.' (1905). *Women Writing in India 600 B.C. to the Early Twentieth Century*. 2 Vols. I. Ed. Susie Tharu and K. Lalita. Delhi: Oxford UP, 1991. 342–352.

Hosseini, Khaled. *The Kite Runner*. London: Bloomsbury Publishing (2003) 2004.

Human Rights Watch/Asia. *Dead Silence: The Legacy of Human Rights Abuse in Punjab*, USA, 1994.

Indira, M.K. *Phaniyamma* (1976). Translated from Kannada by Tejaswani Niranjana. New Delhi: Kali for Women, 1989.

Interview with Chimamanda Ngozi Adichie: *Half of a Yellow Sun*. internet source http://www.halfofayellowsun.com/content. php? page=tsbtbsn= 5&f=2. checked 3 June, 2010.

Ishiguro, Kazuo. 'Crooners' in *Nocturnes: Five Stories of Music and Nightfall*. London: Faber and Faber, 2009. 1–33.

——. 'Nocturnes' in *Nocturnes: Five Stories of Music and Nightfall*. London: Faber and Faber, 2009. 125–185.

Iyengar, Srinivasa K.R. *Indian Writing in English*. Revised and updated edition New Delhi: Sterling Publishers Pvt. Ltd., 1983.

Jain, Jasbir and Veena Singh. eds. *Contesting Postcolonialisms*. Jaipur: Rawat Publications (2000), 2nd edition. 2004.

Jain, Jasbir. 'Destabilising Meaning: *In Theory* and *Orientalism*', *Contesting Postcolonialisms*, 2004. 99–111.

——. 'Evolving Traditions, Retreating Modernities: Women and Gendered Social Reality'. *Feminism, Tradition and Modernity*. Ed. Chandrakala Padia. Shimla; Indian Institute of Advanced Study, 2002. 289–302.

——. 'From the *Water Babies to the Waterland*: Swift's Fairy Tale/History,' *Occasional Papers*; Research Journal Punjab University, 1996.

——. 'A Phoenix Called Resistance', *Journal of Postcolonial Writing*. Vol. 43 No. 2. August 2007. 172–182.

——. *Adhuniktavad de Sandarbh: Bhartiya Novel: 1880–1950* (Panjabi). Panjabi Sahitya Akademi, Chandigarh and Ludhiana; Chetna Prakashan, 2001.

——. *Beyond Postcolonialism: Dreams and Realities of a Nation*. (The Novel in India 1950 to the Present). Jaipur and New Delhi: Rawat Publications, 2006.

——. *Feminizing Political Discourse: Women and the Rise of the Novel in India*. Jaipur and New Delhi: Rawat Publications, 1997.

——. ed. *Reading Partition/Living Partition*. Jaipur: Rawat Publications, 2006.

Jay, Martin. 'Taking on the Stigma of Inauthenticity: Adorno's Critique of Genuineness'. 12–24. Keynote Address, *Forum for Contemporary Theory Conference*, Mangalore, 2005.

Jones, Rebecca. 'The Aesthetics of Protest'. *The Aesthetics of Protest: Using Image to Change Discourse. Enculturation* 6.2 (2009): http://enculturation. gmu.edn/6.2/jones

Joshi, Umashankar. *Sarasvati Chandra*: A Modern Gujarati Classic, *Indian Literature: Personal Encounters*. Calcutta: Papyrus, 1988.

Kafka, Franz. 'Metamorphosis' in *Metamorphosis and Other Stories.* Translated by Willa and Edwin Muir (1933). Harmondsworth: Penguin, 1977, 7–63.

Kakar, Sudhir. *The Inner World: A Psycho-analytic Study of Childhood and Society in India* (1978). Delhi: OUP, 1988.

Kamban. *Kamba Ramayana*. Translated from the Tamil original by P.S. Sundaram. New Delhi: Penguin Books, 2002.

Kamble, Baby. *Jeevan Hamara*. Translated into Hindi from the original Marathi by Lalita Asthana. New Delhi: Kitab Ghar, 1995. (Also available in an English translation by Maya Pandit, as *Prisons We Make*. Orient Longmans, 2008.

Kar, Prafulla C. *Critical Theory: Western and Indian,* Delhi: Pencraft International, 1997.

Karlekar, Malavika. *Voices from Within: Early Personal Narratives of Bengali Women*. Delhi: OUP, 1991.

Karnad, Girish. 'Preface', *Talé-Danda*. Delhi: Ravi Dayal, 1993.

——. *Talé-Danda*. Trans. Girish Karnad. Delhi: Ravi Dayal, 1993.

——. *The Fire and the Rain*. Translated by the author. New Delhi: OUP, 1998.

Kesavan, Mukul. *Looking Through Glass*. Delhi: Ravi Dayal, 1995.

Khan, Mukhtar A. 'India's Sikh Militants Forming Ties with Lashkar-e-Taiba and Pakistani Intelligence'. Publication: Terrorism Monitor Volume: 7 issue: 1 dated January 9, 2090. internet reference: http://ww.jamestown.org/single/? no_cache = 1 & tx _ ttnews%5B/T_news%5D=34319. Referred 25.01.09.

Khatri, Devaki Nandan. *Kajar Ki Kothri* (Hindi, 1902). New Delhi: Raj Kamal Paperbacks, 1988.

Kishore, Giriraj. *Pahla Girmitya*, New Delhi: Bhartiya Jnanpith, 1999.

Krishnamurti, J. *The Nature of the New Mind.* Chennai: Krishnamurti Foundation India. 2001.

Kureishi, Hanif. 'My Son the Fanatic.' *New Writing 4*. Ed. A.S. Byatt and Alan Holling-hurst. London: Vintage and the British Council, 1995. 100-111.

Kuruvachira, J. *Politicisation of Hindu Religion in Postmodern India*. Jaipur: Rawat Publications, 2008.

Larsson, Stieg. *The Expo Files. Articles by the Crusading Journalist Stieg Larrson*. Ed. Daniel Poohl and translated by Laurie Thompson. London: MacLehose Press, 2012.

——. 'Terror Killings Can Happen in Stockholm'. *The Expo Files. Articles by the Crusading journalist Stieg Larrson.* Ed. Daniel Poohl and translated by Laurie Thompson. London: MacLehose Press, 2012 , 21–29.

Lee, Hermoine. 'Shutter and Lens', *The Observer*, March 13, 1988.

Loomba, Ania. *Colonialism/Postcolonialism.* London: Routledge, 1998

Malleson, G.B. *The Indian Mutiny of 1857.* London: Seeley and Co. Ld. 1896.

Mander, Harsh. 'Conscience, Not Obedience', A Symposium on Effective Government. *Seminar* 594. February, 2009. 53–57.

Mantel, Hilary, *Wolf Hall.* London: Fourth Estate, 2009.

Markovits, Claude. *The Un-Gandhian Gandhi: The Life and Afterlife of the Mahatma.* Translated from French by the Author. Delhi: Permanent Black (2004) 2007.

Marx, Karl and Frederick Engels. *The First Indian War of Independence 1857–1859.* Moscow: Progress Publishers 1959.

Masood, Iqbal. 'The Lean Legend', *The Indian Express.* 5 May 1991.

Mehta, Rama. *Inside the Haveli* (1977). New Delhi: Penguin, 1996.

Menon, Chandu O. *Indulekha* (Malayalam) translated into English by W. Dumergue (1890). Ed. used Ernakulam: Mathrubhumi Press, 1965.

Metcalf, Barbara Daly. Introduction, *Perfecting Women,* a partial translation of Maulana Ali Thanawi's *Bihisti Zewar.* Delhi: OUP, 1992.

Mills, Sara, *Discourse:* The New Critical Idiom Series. London: Routledge, 1997.

Minturn, Leigh. *Sita's Daughters: Coming Out of Purdah.* New York: Oxford University Press, 1993.

Mishra, Vijay. 'Diaspora and the Art of Impossible Mourning' in *In Diaspora: Theories, Histories, Texts.* Ed. Makarand Paranjape. New Delhi: Indialog Publishers, 2001, 24–61.

Mistry, Rohinton. *Such a Long Journey.* Toronto: Mc Clelland and Stewart Inc. 1991.

Mohanty, Chandra Talpade. *Feminism Without Borders.* North Carolina: Duke University, 2003.

Mohanty, Satya P. *Literary Theory and Claims of History: Postmodernism Objectivity, Multicultural Politics.* Delhi: OUP, 1998.

Moore-Gilbert, Bart. *Postcolonial Theory: Context, Practices and Policies.* London: Verso, 1997.

Morrison, Toni. *Playing in the Dark: Whiteness and Literary Imagination.* London: Picador, 1992.

Mukherjee, Arun Prabha. 'Introduction' *Her Mother's Ashes.* Ed. Nurjehan Aziz. Toronto: Tsar, 1994.

——. 'On Reading Renu: Text/Language/Culture Translation *Oppositional Aesthetics: Readings from a Hyphenated Space.* Toronto: Tsar, 1994.

——. 'The Poetry of Rienzi Crusz', *Oppositional Aesthetics.* Toronto: Tsar, 1994. 133–143.

——. *Oppositional Aesthetics: Readings from a Hyphenated Space.* Toronto: Isar, 1994.

Mukherjee, Sujit. 'Indo-English Literature: An Essay in Definition', *Critical Essays on Indian Writing: Presented to Armando Menezes.* Eds. M.K. Naik et al. Dharwar: 1968.

——. *Some Positions on a Literary History of India.* Mysore: Central Institute of Indian Languages, 1981.

——. ed. '*The Idea of Indian Literature.* Mysore: Central Institute of Indian Languages, 1981.

Nagar, Amritlal. *Gadar Ke Phool: Ek Diary.* (People's Memories of Awadh Region, 1857–1858), Information Centre: Lucknow, 1957.

Nagpal, Sahil. 'US backs Benazir Bhutto's call for mass protest against the emergency rule'. TopNews.in MHT submitted by Sahil Nagpal on Thu, 11/08/2007 14.42.

Naik, M.K. *A History of Indian English Literature.* New Delhi: Sahitya Akademi (1982), 1989.

Naik, M.K., Amur G.S. and Desai, S.K. eds. *Critical Essays on Indian Writing in English: Presented to Armando Menezes.* Dharwar: Karnataka University Press, 1968.

Nandy, Ashis. *The Illegitimacy of Nationalism.* Delhi: OUP. 1994.

——. *The Intimate Enemy.* Delhi: OUP (1983), 1989.

Narayan, Shyamala. 'The Nation and the Anglo-Indian: A Study of *The Trotter-Nama*' in *Narrating India: The Novel in Search of the Nation.* Ed. E.V. Ramakrishnan. New Delhi: Sahitya Akademi, 2005, 379–392.

Nayak, Nihar Ranjan. 'Drug Trafficking in Punjab: An ISI Game Plan to Revive Militancy', Article No.1066. Institute of Peace and Conflict Studies internet reference http://www.ipcs.org/ Terrorism_ Kashmir Level 2. jsp?action= show View & K Value = 1075 dated 24 June 2003. Referred 25.01.2009.

Okri, Ben. *The Famished Road.* London: Vintage, 1992.

Ondaatje, Michael. *Anil's Ghost.* New York: Vintage, 2000.

——. *The English Patient.* 1992, Vintage Books, 1993.

Pal, Deepangani. 'The brush speaks, louder ...', http://www.livement.com/2010/08/13205030/The_brus_speaks_louder_tran.html. checked 16 February, 2011.

Pal, Ila. *Beyond the Canvas: An Unfinished Portrait of M.F. Husain*. New Delhi: Indus, Imprint of Harper Collins, 1994.

Pamuk, Orhan. *Other Colours: Writings of Life, Art, Books and Cities* Translated from the Turkish by Maureen Freely. London: Faber and Faber 2007.

——. *Snow.* Translated by Maureen Freely. London: Faber and Faber 2004.

Paranjape, Makarand, ed. *Nativism: Essays in Criticism.* New Delhi: Sahitya Akademi, 1997.

Perushek, Darshan. 'Postcolonial Realities, Poststructuratist Diversions: An Unamused Exchange', *Economic and Political Weekly.* Vol XXIX. No 5, January 29, 1994. 243–247.

Phillips, Caryl. *Crossing the River.* London: Picador, 1993.

——. *The Nature of Blood.* London: Faber and Faber, 1997.

Prasanna. 'A Critique of Nativism in Contemporary Indian Theatre', *Nativism: Essays in Criticism.* Ed. Makarand Paranjape, 1997, 95–101.

Prichard, Iltudus Thomas. *The Mutinies in Rajpootana: Being a Personal Narrative of the Mutiny at Nuseerabad.* London: John W. Parker and Son, 1860.

Rao, P.V. Narasimha Rao. *Ayodha: 6 December 1992*. New Delhi: Penguin/Viking, 2006.

Rao, Raja. *Kanthapura* (1935). New Delhi: Orient Paperbacks.1970.

——. *Kanthapura* (1938). Delhi: Orient Paperbacks, 1971.

Ray, Rajat Kanta. *Exploring Emotional History: Gender, Mentality and Literature in the Indian Awakening.* New Delhi: OUP, 2001.

Ricoeur, Paul. 'Human Sciences and Hermeneutical Method: Meaningful Action Considered as Text', *Explorations in Phenomenology.* Eds. David Carr and Edward S. Casey. Hague, Netherlands: Martin Nijoff, 1973. 13–46.

——. 'Human Sciences and the Hermeneutical Method: Meaningful Action Considered as Text', in *Hermeneutics and the Human Sciences*. Ed. John B. Tomson. Cambridge: CUP, 1981. 146–167.

Roberts, Gregory David. *Shantaram* 2003. London: Abacus, (2004) 2006.

Roy, Arundhati. 'Listening to Grasshoppers: Genocide, Denial and Celebration', *Outlook*, February 4, 2008.

Rushdie, Salman. 'Imaginary Homelands', *Imaginary Homelands* (London: Granta, 1991) included in *Creating Theory: Writers on Writing*. Ed. Jasbir Jain. Delhi: Pencraft International, 2000. 213–224.

Ruswa, Mirza Hadi. *Umrao Jan Ada* (1899). Translated into Hindi by Prakash Pandit. Delhi: Hind Pocket Books, 1987.

Sahgal, Nayantara. 'The Schizophrenic Imagination', *Creating Theory: Writers on Writing*. Ed. Jasbir Jain. Delhi: Pencraft International, 2000. 104–111.

——. *Lesser Breeds*. New Delhi: Harper-Collins Publishers, 2003.

——. *Mistaken Identity*. London: Heinemann Ltd., 1989.

——. *Rich Like Us*. London: Heinemann Ltd. 1985.

Sahgal, Priya. '1990 – L.K. Advani's rath yatra: Chariot of fire' Cover story by Priya Sahgal December 24 2009. http://indiatoday.intoday. in/site/story/76389/Cover%20Story/1990_L.K.+Advani+rath+yatra+chariot+of+fire+html. India Today, October 15, 1990.

Said, E. 'Introduction: Secular Criticism.' *The World. The Text and the Critic*. London: Faber, 1984, 1–30.

Said, Edward. 'Travelling Theories' in *The World, The Text and the Critic* (Cambridge: Mass. Cambridge University Press, 1984), 226–247.

'Salt of Freedom' http://www.utexas/edu/cola/insts/southasia/_files/pd.

Sartre, Jean Paul. Preface. *The Wretched of the Earth* by Frantz Fanon. New York: Grove, 1963.

Satthianadhan, Krupabai. *Kamala: The Story of a Hindu Life* (1894) Ed. Chandani Lokuge. Delhi: OUP, 1998.

——. *Saguna: A Story of Native Christian Life* (serialised 1887–8, first published, 1895). Ed. used *Saguna: The First Autobiographical Novel in English by an Indian Woman*. Ed. Chandani Lokuge. Delhi: OUP, 1998.

Savarkar, Vinayak Damodar. *Hindu Sanghathan: Its Ideology and Immediate Programme*. Bombay: Hindu Mahasabha Presidential Office. 1940.

——. *The Indian War of Independence 1857*. New Delhi: Rajdhani Granthagar. (1909), 1970.

Scott, Paul. *A Division of Spoils*. London: Pan Books, 1975.

——. *The Day of the Scorpion*. London: Pan Books, 1968.

——. *The Jewel in the Crown*. London: Pan Books in association with Heinemann, 1966.

——. *The Towers of Silence*. London: Pan Books, 1973.

Sealy, I Allan. *The Trotter-Nama: A Chronicle*. New York: Alfred A. Knopf. 1988.

Sharpe, Jenny. 'Figures of Colonial Resistance.' *Modern Fiction Studies* 35. 1. Spring 1989, 137–55.

——. 'Figures of Colonial Resistance', *The Postcolonial Studies Reader*. Eds. Bill Ashcroft, Gareth Griffiths and Helen Tiffin. London: Routledge, 1995. 99–103.

Shukla, Ram Charan Acharya. *Hindi Sahitya Ka Itihaas*. Varanasi: Nagaripracharan Sabha (1976) 1997.

Singh, Arvindpal. 'Writing Otherwise than Identity: Translation and Cultural Hegemony'. *Punjabi Identity in a Global Context*. Eds. Pritam Singh and Shinder Singh Thandi. New Delhi: OUP, 1999. 111–137.

Singh, Gurbhagat. 'The Betrayal of Polyphony: Blocked Possibilities of Criticism in India' *Nativism: Essays in Criticism*. Ed. Makarand Paranjape, New Delhi: Sahitya Akademi, 1997, 84–94.

'Singhal'. http://www.zeenews.com/news562033.html.accessed11 November, 2010.

Slemon, Stephen. 'Unsettling the Empire: Resistance Theory for the Second World.' *The Postcolonial Studies Reader*. Ed. Bill Ashcroft, Gareth Griffiths, and Helen Tiffin. London: Routledge, 1995, 104–10.

Sobti, Krishna and K.B. Vaid. *Sobti-Vaid Samvaad*: *Lekhan aur Lekhak* (Hindi). New Delhi: Rajkamal Prakashan, 2007.

Sobti, Krishna. *Zindaginama* (1979) Hindi. New Delhi: Rajkamal Prakashan, 1994.

——. 'Anamika ki Baat-cheet' in Krishna Sobti's *Shabdon ke Aalok Mein* (Hindi). New Delhi: Rajkamal Prakashan, 2005, 172–197.

Sobti, Krishna. 'Jaidev' in Krishna Sobti's *Shabdon ke Aalok Mein* (Hindi). New Delhi: Rajkamal Prakashan, 2005.198–228.

——. 'Niranjan Dev Sharma se Baat-cheet' in Krishna Sobti's *Shabdon ke Aalok Mein* (Hindi). New Delhi: Rajkamal Prakashan, 2005. 305–322.

——. *Dilo-danish* (Hindi). New Delhi: Rajkamal Prakashan, (1993), 1999.

——. Extracts from *Zindaginama*. Translated by Tripti Jain, *Reading Partition/Living Partition*. Jaipur: Rawat Publications, 2006. 10–21

——. *Mitro Marjani* (Hindi). New Delhi: Rajkamal, 1967.

——. *Shabdon ke Aalok Mein* (Hindi). New Delhi: Rajkamal Prakashan, 2005.

——. 'Uttaradh', in Krishna Sobti's *Shabdon ke Aalok Mein* (Hindi). New Delhi: Rajkamal Prakashan, 2005. 238–274.

Soja, Edward. *Postmodern Geographies: The Reassertion of Space in Critical Social Theory*. Jaipur: Rawat, 1997.

Solanki, Ram Singh. *Vinayak Damodar Savarakar: Social Political Thought and the Concept of Hindutva*. New Delhi: Aashish Publishing House, n.d.

Soyinka, Wole. *The Open Sore of a Continent: A Personal Narrative of the Nigerian Crisis*. New York: OUP, 1996.

Spivak, Gayatri. 'The Author in Conversation'. in *Imaginary Maps,* Stories by Mahasweta Devi, Trans. by Spivak. Calcutta: Thema, 1993, i–xvi.

——. Translator's Preface in *Imaginary Maps,* Calcutta: Thema, 1993. xvii–xxvii.

——. Appendix in *Imaginary Maps,* Calcutta: Thema, 1993. 199–210.

——. *Death of a Discipline*. New York: Columbia University Press, 2003.

Srinivasan, K.S. *The Ethos of Indian Literature: A Study of Its Romantic Tradition*. Delhi: Chanakya Publishers, 1985.

Suleri, Sara. 'The Rhetoric of English India', *The Postcolonial Studies Reader*. Eds Bill Ashcroft, Gareth Griffiths and Helen Tiffin. London: Routledge, 1995.111–113.

Sundar Rajan, Rajeshwari. 'The Scene of Theory in India at the Present Moment: An Emblematic Encounter,' *Critical Theory*. Ed. Prafulla C. Kar, 1997. 79–93.

Swift, Graham. *Ever After*. London: Picador, 1992.

——. *Out of the World*. London: Picador, 1988.

——. *Waterland*. London: Picador in association with William Heinemann Ltd. (1984), 1992.

Tagore, Rabindranath. 'The Call of Truth' (originally published in the *Modern Review*, October, 1921). *Excerpt in The Moral and Political Writings of Mahatma Gandhi*. Vol. I. Ed. Raghavan Iyer. Oxford: Clarendon Press, 1986. 222–227.

——. *The Home and the World.* English translation of *Ghare Baire* by Surendranath Tagore. Madras: Macmillan, 1916.

Tharu, Susie and K. Lalitha, eds. *Women Writing in India: 600 B.C. to the Present.* 2. Vols. New Delhi: OUP. 1991. Vol. 1.

——. *Women Writing in India: 600 BC to the Present.* 2 vols. New Delhi: Oxford University Press, 1995, Vol. 2.

Thiong'O, Ngugi Wa, *Decolonising the Mind: The Politics of Language in African Literature.* Oxford: James Currey Ltd. F.P. 1986. (essays written between 1981 and 1986).

Tolkein, J.R.R. 'On Fairy Tales', *The Tolkien Reader.* New York: Ballantine Books, 1966. (The essay was written in 1938–39).

Trilling, Lionel. *Sincerity and Authenticity.* Cambridge: Massachusetts: Harvard University Press, 1972.

Tripathi, Goverdhamram. *Scrap Book 1888–1894.* (4 volumes) Vol.1 edited by Kantilal C. Pandya, Pamprasad P. Bakshi and Sanmukh Lal J. Pandya. Bombay: N.M. Tripathi Pvt. Ltd. 1959.

Tulsidas. *Ramcharit Manas.* Commentary by Vidyaratan Pandit Jwala Prasadji Parashar. Mumbai: Ramayana Press, 1986.

——. *Shri Ramcharit Manas.* Gorakhpur: Gita Press, Samvat 2959 C.E. 2002.

Valmiki. *The Ramayana.* Abridged and Translated by Arshia Sattar, (1996). New Delhi: Penguin, 2000.

Vassaikar, Vishnubhatt Godse. *Ankhon Dekha Gadar,* Hindi translation of the original Marathi text *Majha Pravas.* Trans. Amritlal Nagar Lucknow: Sahitya Kutir, 1949.

Vatsayan, S.H. (Agyeya). *Smritichhanda* (Hindi). New Delhi: National Publishing House, 1989.

——. 'Memory and Country', Trans. Tripti Jain *The Writer as Critic.* Ed. Jasbir Jain. Jaipur: Rawat Publications, 2011. 206–220.

——. 'Memory and Time', Trans. Tripti Jain *The Writer as Critic.* Ed. Jasbir Jain. Jaipur: Rawat Publications, 2011. 191–205.

Vivekananda, Swami. 'Addresses to the Parliament of Religions', *Swami Vivekananda: An Anthology.* Ed. Bimal Prasad. New Delhi: Vikas Publishing House Pvt. (1994), 1996.

Walcott, Derek. 'The Muse of History' in *The Post-Colonial Studies Reader.* Eds. Bill Ashcroft, Gareth Griffiths and Helen Tiffin. London: Routledge (1995), 1997, 370–374.

Walsh, William. *Indian Literature in English.* London and New York: Longman 1990.

Ward, G.E. Preface *The Bride's Mirror*. English translation of Nazir Ahmad's *Mirat-ul-Arus* (1903). New Delhi: Permanent Black, 2001.

White, Hadyen. *Tropics of Discourse: Essays in Cultural Criticism*. Baltimore and London: The Johns Hopkins University Press, 1978.

——. *Metahistory: The Historical Imagination in Nineteenth Century Europe*. Baltimore and London: The Johns Hopkins University Press (1973), 1974.

Yun, Ch'oe. 'The Aesthetic Dilemma of Writing Reality'. Translation by Kim Ji-woon and Mark Morris. Internet source http://www.japanfocus.org/-ch_oe-Yun/3297. checked 9 June, 2010.

Filmography

Albert Pinto Ko Gussa Kyun Aata Hai. Director and Producer: Saeed Akhtar Mirza. Story: Saeed Akhtar Mirza. Perf. Naseeruddin Shah, Shabana Azmi, Smita Patil and Om Puri, 1980.

Amu. Director and Writer: Shonali Bose, Performers: Konkana Sen Sharma, Ankur Khanna, Brinda Karat. 2006.

Bombay. Director: Mani Ratnam. Production. Amitabh Bachchan Corporation Limited, Madras Talkies. Performer: Arvind Swamy, Manisha Koirala, Sonali Bendre. Tinnu Anand. 1995.

Father, Son and Holy War. Production. Amitabh Bachchan Corporation Limited, Madras Talkies. Camera Editing: Anand Patwardhan. Sound: Simantini Dhuru, Narinder Singh, Sanjiv Shah. Music Navnirman, Vinay Mahajan, Production Assistance: Simantini Dhuru, Paromita Vohra, 1995.

Fire. Director: Deepa Mehta. Perf. Shabana Azmi, Kulbhushan Kharbanda, Nandita Das, Javed Jaffrey, 1996.

Fishing: In the Sea of Greed. Anand Patwardhan, 1998.

Gandhi. Director: Richard Attenborough. Production Co. Columbia Pictures, Goldcrest Films International et al., Performers. Ben Kingsley, Candice Bergen, John Geilgud, Rohini Hattangadi, Saeed Jaffrey, Amrish Puri, Alyque Padamsee, Roshan Seth, Athol Fugard 1982.

Jung Aur Aman / War and Peace. Camera and Editing: Anand Patwardhan. Production: Monica Wahi and Sanjiv Shah, 2002.

Lawrence of Arabia. Director: David Lean, Producer: Sam Spiegal/Horizon Pictures, Screenplay: Robert Bolt, Perf. Peter O'Toole, Alec Guiness, Anthony Quinn, Omar Sharif, 1962.

Maachis. Director and Writer: Gulzar; Performers: Om Puri, Tabu, Chandrachur Singh, Kulbhushan Kharbanda, Jimmy Shergill, Navninder Behl and Kanwaljit Singh. 1996.

Mahabharata. Producer B.R. Chopra, Director Ravi Chopra, Performers: Raj Babbar, Asha Lata, Ram Mohan, Prem Sagar, Kiran Juneja, Rafique Mukadan, 1988–1990. 94 episodes. www.rajshri.com/tvshow/mahabarat.

Meenaxi: A Tale of Three Cities. Director M.F. Husain, Producer Reina Husain, Perf. Tabu, Raghubir Yadav, Kunal Kapoor, Nadira Babbar, 2004.

Mr and Mrs Iyer. Director. Aparna Sen. Production Company Triplecom Media Production. Perf. Rahul Bose, Konkana Sen Sharma, Bhisham Sahni. 2002.

Ram Ke Naam (In The Name of God). documentary. Camera and Editing Anand Patwardhan Production and Editing Assistance: Paromita Vohra, Pervez Merwanji, Narinder Singh, Simantini Dhuru, Jabeen Merchant, Shashi Mehta. 1991.

Ramayana. Producer and Director: Ramanand Sagar. Perf. Arun Govil, Deepika, Sunil Lahri, Sanjay Jog, Arvind Trivedi Dara Singh and others. January 25 1987 to July 31st, 1988 (78 episodes).

Saleem Langde Pe Mat Ro. Director: Saeed Akhtar Mirza. Produced by NDFC. Story: Saeed Akhtar Mirza. Perf. Pavan Malhotra, Markand Deshpande, Ashutosh Gowarikar, 1989.

Waiting for Godot. Director: Michael Lindsay-Hogg. Producer Michael Colgan, Perf. Barry McGovern, John Murphy, Alan Stanfor Stephen Brennan, Sam McGovern, 2001.

Index